How to Read
SIGNS
and
OMENS
in Everyday Life

How to Read
SIGNS
and
OMENS
in Everyday Life

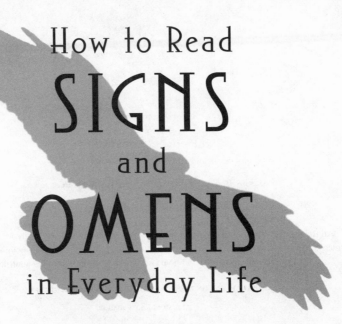

Sarvananda Bluestone, Ph.D.

Destiny Books
Rochester, Vermont

Destiny Books
One Park Street
Rochester, Vermont 05767
www.InnerTraditions.com

Destiny Books is a division of Inner Traditions International

LIBRARY OF CONGRESS CATALOGING-IN-PUBLICATION DATA

Bluestone, Sarvananda.
[Signs of the times]
How to read signs and omens in everyday life / Sarvananda Bluestone.
p. cm.
Originally published: Signs of the times. New York : Berkeley Pub. Group, 1997.
Includes bibliographical references.
ISBN 0-89281-901-4
1. Omens. I. Title.
BF1777 .B54 2001
133.3'34—dc212001037181

Printed and bound in Canada

10 9 8 7 6 5 4 3 2 1

This book was typeset in Times with Gill Sans, Lithos, Xavier Sans, and Kingsbury as the display typefaces.

To
Ma Satyam Divya
(Ana Luisa Paredes Bascuñan)
"Tontisima Bellisima Mia"

When it is evening, ye say, It will be fair weather: for the sky is red. And in the morning, It will be foul weather today: for the sky is red and lowering. O ye hypocrites, ye can discern the face of the sky; but can ye not discern the signs of the times?

—*Jesus to the Pharisees,* Matthew *xvi, 3*

Contents

Thank You

Fɪʀsᴛ, thanks must go to the countless diviners, seers, witches, and medicine men and women who have trusted their own sight often at the risk of their lives. They have kept alive a light through many centuries of darkness.

So many people have, along the way, helped in the creation of this book. My old and dear friend Devabodhi supported me when this project was only a pompous and ponderous introduction. My mother, Ruth Dale Levin, provided support and help all along the way before her death, and she continues to do so after her death. Her husband Ed Levin has always provided excellent critical support. Thanks to my stepfather, Ralph Dale, who has always been a continual source of support and a cornucopia of suggestions.

My dear friend and fellow reader, Prartho (Gwen Sereno) has been in tune with this book from its inception. Her support has been there from the start, and one of her illustrations graces the book. Thanks also to my dear friends Laila Frank and Maureen Brennan, who have been there in substance. Thank you, Helen Weaver and Hariet Hunter, for long talks and stimulation. Thank you, John Palm and Belinda Gold, for helping me take the first step way back when. Thank you, Premrup, for getting the ball rolling in so many ways. Thank you, Arnie, for everything.

Many of the illustrations in this book are the original work of Raphael Abrams. A brilliant young artist, Raphael took on the challenge of this book with very little warning and has been a delight to work with. Thanks, Raph.

Many kids (now no longer kids) have helped me try out the games. Thank you, Premda, for ideas and some games. Thank you, Jenny Epstein, Lisa Aurigemma, Samantha Lesiger, Amy Hendricks, Nicole Press, Tracee Beroza, Sara Slochotka, Nella Bloom, Phoebe Zinman, Riva Pearson, Sarah Rosenblum, Samantha Johnson, Erika Katz, Frances Mills, Lisa Tan, Robin Arrington, Jon Novick, Katy Groskin, Greg Parker, Katy Harper, Emily Mahlman, Jennifer Hassenberg, Sonnyte Gheneen, Ian Alteveer, Sheila Azzad, Jordan Lee, Sam Haar, David Gokhin, Leah Hamburg, Rebeca Jo Loeb, Sharon Zetter, Adam Green, Meggie Stoltzman, Sara Radbill, Jamie Rubin, and Rachel Kolster. Thank you, Hank Hijink and Melanie Wesley. Thank you, Mark Packer and Rena Levitt, for letting it happen at Appel Farm.

My daughter, soulmate, and intellectual foil, Hira Bluestone, spent many years, as a child, driving around with me in the car helping me to make up games to wile away the time. Thanks for the patience, Hira.

Many gave me a chance to practice my skills. Among these are some of the folks who run the legendary "Borscht Belt" in the Catskills. Thank you, Michael Hopson and Henry Zabatta of the former Granit and Mannie Halbert and the late George Gilbert of the Raleigh. Thank you, Tim Dreher, Alberto Garcia. It was the late Johnny Greco of the now-defunct Pines Hotel, who first suggested that I give a talk to the guests if I wanted to do any readings. It was out of these talks that the idea for this book emerged.

Thank you, Gena Caliendo and Nina Smiley, for giving me a chance to try out the games with a mixed group of adults and kids at the Mohonk Mountain House. Thank you, Ann, Jeff, and Audrey, for letting me use the wonderful resources of Mirabai to collect my thoughts and research at my leisure while waiting for readings. Thank you, Mr. Pankaj Baliga of the Taj Group in India, for giving me a chance. Thank you, Betsy Stang, for sharing your time and insight on Native American cultures.

As every researcher knows, reference librarians are our secret weapons. Thanks to the reference librarians at the University of Pennsylvania Museum Library and SUNY Albany library. You made my task so much easier. Thank you, Tara and Shirin, for putting up with my monomania during the last phases of this book. Thank you for your love and support. Thank you, Suzanne Bober, for always being helpful, thorough, and available. You are a dream of an editor.

Thanks to Janis Vallely. As an editor she nurtured the book when it was only a crazy quilt of ideas. As an agent she nurtured the author.

Introduction: The First Sense

The most beautiful thing we can experience is the mysterious. It is the source of all true art and all science. He to whom this emotion is a stranger, who can no longer pause to wonder and stand rapt in awe, is as good as dead: his eyes are closed.

—Albert Einstein

WHEN my daughter, Hira, was seven months old, my wife and I rented a house in Arlington, Vermont, for the summer. I was still on my first sabbatical leave from teaching. It had begun three weeks after Hira was born. It was a period that consisted largely of the care and nurturing of an infant, something with which few fathers are blessed.

The day after our arrival in Arlington we went to see an old friend of mine, his wife, and two apple-cheeked children. They lived in a house with a white picket fence and the whole scene seemed to have been plucked from a Norman Rockwell painting. Everything was wholesome. The family smiled to greet us. We were all set for a peaceful and relaxing day with friends. But it was not to be so.

I carried Hira through the front door. As soon as we entered the house, she began to scream. Her mom and I were quite surprised. She was a good-tempered baby and rarely screamed. And this time she would not stop. Rocking, cooing, coaxing—no method was effective. Finally, in desperation, I fled outside with Hira.

As soon as we stepped out of the house, Hira stopped crying. I then turned around and went back in with her. Once again, she began to scream. I took her outside again. She stopped crying. I did this four or five times until it became quite clear that we would have to leave. We did.

The next day I phoned my friend to check in. After all, I had only had about three minutes of conversation with him the day before. It was during that phone call that the reason for Hira's screaming became apparent. On the day of our visit my friend and his wife had decided to get a divorce. Their marriage was on the rocks. Rather than postpone our social visit, my friend and his wife had decided to put on a happy face and entertain us. This fooled me. This fooled my wife. But it did not fool Hira. There was pain in that house. There was agony. It filled up the house, it overflowed from the bedroom. It crawled along the floor. It shivered along the windowpanes. And only Hira felt it.

All seven-month-old babies feel. All seven-month-old babies are endowed with the ability to communicate their pain. It's very simple: When something hurts, they cry. When it stops hurting, they stop crying. There was enough pain in that household in Arlington, Vermont, to make my baby daughter scream. She knew nothing of marriage or divorce, of body language or innuendo, of hypocrisy. She only knew that it hurt in there. She was in tune with her surroundings.

Babies see things that we no longer allow ourselves to see. Babies feel things that we don't allow ourselves to feel. Clearly we can not always stay in the level of sensitivity of a seven-month-old baby. If we did, the pain of the world would soon overwhelm us. So we learn to protect ourselves. We learn to insulate ourselves. This is natural, even necessary.

However, we do more than just protect ourselves. There is so much of the world of children that is lost as they get older. We learn to look at the world in certain prescribed ways. That is, after all, one of the goals of education. But the longing for our childhood sight still haunts us. The word *nostalgia* means "a longing for the past," but the word is the literal Greek term for "homesickness." Part of our nostalgia is a longing, for homesickness, for that quality we had as children. It is a quality of exploration and the innocence of wonder.

In many cultures the wisdom of the child is respected. In the African country of Togo, children are said to be born with the power to see clearly, and the intuitive clarity of children is recognized as fact. On the other side of the globe, Chippewa Indians of the Great Plains encourage their children to fast and to dream. A child will then be visited by guardian spirits. The adults among the Ute people listen carefully to the dreams of their children.

In Western culture the wisdom and the innocence of the child are spoken from the mouth of Christ. Unless you become "as little children, ye shall not enter into the kingdom of heaven."

The children may remain in innocence, but the adult still needs to make sense out of his world. Throughout our history we humans have been trying to understand our world and ourselves. We are a self-centered race. We have always seen the world as a mirror for ourselves.

Looking across time and cultures, we find that what is called "psychic" or "intuitive" is one of the cornerstones of human experience. It does not matter whether one is looking at Babylonia in the third millennium before Christ or the

Naskapi Indians of Labrador in the 1930s. All peoples have utilize their sixth sense to interpret their world.

Perhaps we owe our survival as a species to the existence of this sixth sense. When it comes to sight, the hawk is much better equipped than a human. The bat hears infinitely more acutely. The common grub has a more developed sense of touch. The dog has a better sense of smell. The cheetah is faster, the elephant stronger, and the cockroach more physically adaptable. And any number of animals have a more acute sense of taste.

On the whole, the human race would be a very vulnerable one if it had to rely solely on physical attributes. It was the development of the intellect that allowed humans to see beyond the present moment. Intellect gave us human creatures something that no other animals had: a plan. We are the only species that plans ahead—and intuition gave us insight into the moment.

The *Oxford English Dictionary* defines *intuition* as "knowledge or natural perception that consists in immediate apprehension, without the intervention of any reasoning process." The word comes from the Latin term that means "to look upon." And looking upon the world in an intuitive sense was essential to the survival of our ancestors. They needed to know when the weather was going to change and how to read the whisper of the wind in the leaves. Our forbears needed to know that the unexpected fluttering of birds in the forest and a sudden silence meant danger. After all, it was better to be aware of a saber-toothed tiger before the tiger became aware of you. Other animals would rely entirely on their five senses. The human animal would need to rely on the sixth.

This sixth sense is our birthright. Today we have come a long distance from standing in the jungle and tuning in to the presence of a saber-toothed tiger. Yet even in our modern, technological world, we still tune in to our surroundings. Our psychic ability is as much a part of us as our intellect.

There are countless instances of mysterious spontaneous insight that we can experience in our daily lives. For example, just about everybody has had the experience of thinking of someone just as she telephoned. Or we'll dream of somebody and then receive a letter from her the next day. How do such events occur? How can I be thinking of someone on the other side of the country a split second before she phones? There really is no explanation for such concurrence. There is no explanation, but the reality persists.

We are all psychic. And even if we have suppressed that quality in our conscious lives, it emerges night after night in our dreams. For our dreams appear despite us. They are our nightly window into our own psychic awareness. As we shall see in the course of this book, we can peer through this window while we are awake and interpret our visions.

There is widespread distrust and fear of our intuitive powers. For one thing,

we are taught to be wary of our "fortune-tellers." However, true psychic or intuitive sensitivity is the exact opposite of "fortune-telling." It is our intellect, not
our intuitive ability, that looks toward the future. It is the intellect that is directed
toward the plan, the goal, and the ultimate end. Our intuitive sense, on the other
hand, is most profoundly directed into the moment—into the *here* and *now.*

Fortune-telling is a misnomer. Anybody who claims to consistently predict
the future is either a fool or a liar. The fact is that psychics aren't so good in the
predictive area. Meteorologists are better at prediction. After all, there has never
been a professional psychic who has ever won the grand prize in any lottery. And
that should tell us something.

Another work for the use of intuitive is *divination.* It's an interesting word
that simply means allowing the divine to become manifest. Some cultures may
see this as the literal intervention of the deity or deities. But *divination* is just
another word for going beyond our ordinary awareness into the realms of the
divine. Divination has existed since the beginning of recorded history. Fortune-
telling is a relatively recent perversion of divination. Fortune-telling panders to
our need for certainty in an uncertain world.

Divination is as natural as breath and breathing. The Greek goddess Psyche
was, among other things, the goddess of breath and the soul. One meaning of the
Greek word *psyche* is literally "breath." The soul and breath were intertwined
and are regarded so in many cultures.

We do not struggle to breathe. Similarly, use of the psychic ability is something that happens with ease. One does not work to achieve a Ph.D. in psychic
awareness any more than one studies to breathe. It comes naturally and with
ease. And the younger we are, the more naturally we breathe. All we need to do
is watch an infant sleep, watch the deep and relaxed breaths, to see how natural
it is.

This naturalness does not last. From the time we enter school we are taught
to deny a basic part of ourselves. While science now recognizes that there are
two sides of the brain, we are taught to accept only one. We are essentially taught
to deny half of our intelligence. We learn to distrust our own sight and hearing
at a very early age. Imagination is the intellectual tool of the child, yet it has little place in the educational system and becomes more and more of a liability to
the student as he or she progresses through the system.

It is imagination that is the mainstay of the psychic. Joan of Arc claimed to
have heard the voice of God speaking to her. During her trial as a witch her
accusers stated that she didn't hear God, she just had a very active imagination.
Her response was simple: "God speaks with us through our imagination."

The right side of the brain governs imagination, emotions, and intuition.
Physiologically, it crosses over and controls the left side of the body. On the

other hand, the left side of the brain, controlling the right side of the body, is the practical and problem-solving side. Clearly we need both sides to be whole. However, it is the problem-solving, logical, and rational side that has been encouraged in people. But right-brain (left-handed) folks have suffered through the centuries from a fear of the physiology of intuition. Even the derivation of the word *left* reflects this. The Latin term for left is *sinsitra,* from which we get the word "sinister." Thus, the intuitive and creative side is considered dangerous and evil in the lexicon of our mother tongue.

The fear of the intuitive has been a recurrent theme throughout history. Until only three hundred years ago, from the thirteenth to the seventeenth centuries, over 9 million people throughout Europe were accused as witches and burned and tortured. The leading theological text of the time dictated that "thou shall not suffer a witch to live." This justified the genocide of millions of people, most of them women. These were not Walt Disney creations flying around on broomsticks, but women, mainly midwives, herbalists, and healers, who still utilized a connection to the earth, sky, and living creatures. These were women who were in tune with the earth, with the processes of life and death, and with each other. It was believed that the mysterious, psychic power of witches brought about the plague, rendered husbands impotent, and caused famine.

Intuition is natural. It is human. How can it be scary? People have come up to me time and again with stories of their own psychic experiences. Almost without exception these stories are terrifying. One person dreamed that his grandmother was deathly ill. And she was. Somebody else had an eerie feeling that her son was in a car crash. And he was. Another person looked at a man she was meeting for the first time and knew that he had some dreaded disease. And he did.

I could never understand these stories. This was not my experience of the psychic world. Yet I couldn't deny that people were telling the truth. Finally it hit me. Imagine that we grew up fearing our sense of hearing. Imagine that we were convinced that if we listened and heard, we would hear things that we didn't want to hear. So we walked around with our fingers in our ears so we wouldn't hear scary things: explosions, screams of terror and agony. However, the life of hearing includes other, softer sounds: the gurgle and chirp of a happy baby, the whispers of lovers in each other's arms, the rustle of the wind through the leaves of autumn. Such sounds are lost to us when we have our fingers in our ears. Because of our fears, we risk losing the sounds of softness.

So it is with our psychic sense. We are told how frightening it is. We do not use it. We deny its existence and hope it disappears. But the more we use our intuitive sense, the less scary it becomes.

This is not to deny that there are things in life that are scary. However, we mortals constantly face two choices: security or adventure. To opt for security means going for the sure thing. Adventure means pressing through boundaries and opening up to the possibilities beyond our frontiers. The Chinese word for crisis is *wei-chi. Wei* means "danger." *Chi* means "opportunity." Opportunities lie even within the fearsome dangers and crises.

The intuitive sense allows us to go beyond the normal mind. It is both the child *and* mother of imagination. It provides us with vision beyond our ordinary sight—beyond that which we already know. And it is such vision that has propelled us from four-legged creatures with our face to the ground into two-legged beings with our eyes to the stars.

It is the intuitive sense that allows us to see the world with new eyes. We would be in limbo without it. After all, our ancestors had seen and feared fire for thousands of years until one person had the vision to transform it from an enemy into an ally. This person had seen the flames in a new way. The divine had spoken through fire much as it did to Moses many thousands of years later. Likewise, our followers had lived with trees and round stones for millennia until one saw a wheel hiding in the form of the rock or the log and changed the world forever.

The intuitive is our heritage. It is our doorway to new sight—to new vision. It, as much as the intellect, defines us as human. Within each of us there is the visionary. Within each of us there is the seer who can leap beyond our normal sight. Each of us has the power, privilege, and right to see the divine in a candle or burning bush.

The intuitive has nothing to do with belief, which is the acceptance of someone else's experience. It has to do with one's own experience. This book is not about belief. It about *knowing.* People often ask, "Do you believe in this stuff?" I tell them that I try not to believe in anything. I do not believe in the reality of the world of divination. I know it. There is a vast difference.

This book is the result of the convergence of many paths.

As a child in the 1940s I spent a lot of time traveling with my mother in the car. Her right arm was my safety belt, and much of my early education took place in the front seat of a series of old Pontiacs, the ones with Chief Pontiac on the hood.

Reality flows swiftly past the window of a moving car. A person standing on a street corner is an instant memory. An old lady crossing a street—she's there and then she's gone. Sometimes my mother would say strange things. We would pass a young man waiting for the light to change. My mother would say something like, "He's broken up with his girlfriend and it looks like the world is going to end." Or we would pass another car and my mother would glance at the driver and exclaim, "It's about time that things went well for her. It's been a real good day."

Of course, we never had a chance to verify my mother's lightning observations, but somehow I knew she was right. And it was a wonderful game. Sometimes I would even join in. My fascination with looking into other people grew with time.

Another path took me to Madison, Wisconsin, in 1973, where after seven years of procrastinating, teaching, and settling into married life, I finally finished my doctoral dissertation in history. It was a turning point in my life. The very same day I received my doctorate, I had my first tarot card reading at the house of friends in Chicago. The newly minted Dr. Bluestone was ushered into the world of divination.

My friends were not skilled readers, rather they were enthusiastic novices. As I remember it, the reading took about an hour. There was much explanation as I was guided along. There was a new influence coming into my life that was represented by the heart. There was an old influence that was leaving that was represented by material security. The card that represents both hopes and fears indicated that I was moving into new areas and exploring. The reading was so powerful that I did something that I never remember doing before. I simply conked out. When I awoke four hours later on the living room floor, the dawn was breaking.

My first tarot reading taught me several things. First, any reading involves the participation of the reader and the person who is being read. Half of every reading is the resonance in the "readee." Second, as I looked back on this reading, I realized that there was nothing that I had heard that I didn't on some level, already know. It showed me that a reading is more of an affirmation than a discovery. It seems to me that the greatest truths are those that we already know. And how can that be scary?

That warm spring evening in Chicago in 1973 marked a new beginning for me. I continued to teach, but a seed had been planted. The academic life of the mind had its limitations for me. I was moving away from academia and beginning to embrace a different way of looking at the world.

In 1981 I left the groves of academe and took my six-year-old daughter, Hira, to India, where we stayed near the ashram of Bhagwan Shree Rajneesh. When we returned to America, I set up a school at a spiritual commune in Oregon. The study of history was about as far from my mind as it had ever been. Four years later I left the commune and began my career as a professional psychic.

This book is thus the result of the journey that began in the front seat of a Pontiac in 1941. It wound through several history departments, an ashram in

India, a commune in Oregon, several resort hotels in the Catskill Mountains of New York, and has ended up here.

This book provides only a small sampling of the divinatory practices across cultures and through time. Divination is as old and universal as the human race—it is amazing how so many practices cross continents, language groups, and time itself. The reading of bones, for example, one of the most common divinatory practices, is found on every inhabited continent in the world.

The stories that fill these pages offer a glimpse of different times and cultures. They speak to us from the folk wisdom of people as they faced the mysteries of everyday life. Each chapter provides a survey of a group of divinatory practices. And each chapter provides games so that people may find, for themselves, their higher powers of perception—their ability to divine.

Most of the games and practices in this book are derived from other cultures and other spiritual traditions. I pay the deepest honor to the shamans of Puerto Rico and Siberia, the Han geomancers, and all of the millions of seers throughout history who have sought to look beyond the mundane. I hope that they will approve of my effort at lightness as a sign of my greatest respect. Other games I have created out of my own fabric.

This book is not meant to be read from beginning to end. In fact, each chapter does not need to be read in its entirety. If some readers wish to read the historical descriptions and skip the games, that's fine, too. Games, however, are meant to be played. These are noncompetitive exercises. They are all geared to help us look at the world through different eyes. At first this might seem difficult. And some games may seem more interesting to you than others. But with all of the games, we need to be light and playful. The lighter we become, the more we see. And the more fun it is.

Now, having fun isn't easy as it used to be. For most of us it has been a long time since we were asked to use our imagination. Most of us find it easier to work than to play. I do not mean to make light of this. Enjoying ourselves has become a very serious business indeed. Indeed, play has become a major industry. This book is not meant to be work. It is meant to be play. It is meant to be enjoyed. There are no tests. There are no right answers and no wrong answers. Strange as it may seem, the more we play the easier it gets.

We have regulated our intuition to the closet for too long. There, in the darkness, it has had to keep company with ghosts and goblins and things that go bump in the night. A word about fear: We have all been told and taught to fear our intuitive sense. That's like being taught to fear ourselves. Why should we fear that which is part of us?

Once upon a time this lesson of fear was taught with the rack, flaming stakes, and other forms of torture. That's passé. Today, the fear of being crazy is the fear that keeps us from our psychic sense.

In this book I ask people to see things. I ask folks to see images in clouds and to hear the voice of the wind. Is that crazy? Hundreds of cultures have been doing things like that for thousands of years. In this book I ask people to see things, hear things, and even smell things that are not ordinarily visible, audible, or smellable. Is that crazy?

What's normal? Well once again we are back to the normal mind. That's normal. And, if we had to rely entirely on that, we would still be afraid of fire. Maybe one way to get over the worry about being crazy is for each of us to admit that we are all a little bit wacky. Who isn't? It is that wackiness that contains our vision. And, if this be crazy, to paraphrase Patrick Henry, let us make the most of it. It is time to reclaim or psychic heritage. We all have it as our birthright. And when we look around us with new eyes, a new world opens.

Most important. I urge you to enjoy the process. If this book helps you to enjoy you own awareness, if it helps you to play and see things in a new light, it has succeeded. So, in the words of Maurice Sendak, "Let the rumpus begin!"

CHAPTER 1

Ides and Tides or a Wind That Comes: Non-Ominous Omens

maggie and milly and molly and may
went down to the beach (to play one day)

and maggie discovered a shell that sang
so sweetly she couldn't remember her troubles, and

milly befriended a stranded star
whose rays five languid fingers were;

and molly was chased by a horrible thing
which raced sideways while blowing bubbles: and

may came home with a smooth round stone
as small as a world and as large as alone.

for whatever we lose (like a you or a me)
it's always ourselves we find in the sea.
                                    —e. e. cummings

One, two, three, four, five, I wish the truth of the word be shown me
            The truth of the word
            Or a wind that comes.
                        —Yucatán Maya diviner's prayer[1]

Ask anybody. Omens are scary. Even the sound of the word is scary: *OH-min.* Our lips form big *O*'s to say it, the same way we say "No" or "Don't." Omens are connected with superstitions. A black cat crossing in front of us is an omen. A broken mirror is an omen.

Omens are associated with death. The ancient soothsayer was said to have told Julius Caesar to "beware the Ides of March." That was an omen. And on March 15, the Ides of March, Julius Caesar was assassinated.

Omens are associated with fear. After all, "omen" forms the root of the word "ominous." Something that is ominous is something that is fearful. There is nothing "ominous" in writing a friend you haven't heard from in years and having a letter from that friend cross in the mail with yours. It is very different, though, if we dream that the same friend is deathly ill. Fear, death, and superstition. Little wonder that people regard omens in a guarded way. But has it always been so? Have omens always been scary? Not in the beginning.

Omens are rooted very much in the human condition. People have always wanted some security in the face of the unknown. We have always wanted certainty and a measure of control over that which was coming to be. To a cave dweller ten thousand years ago, the world must have seemed a scary place. For one thing, this cave dweller did not know whether he would have enough food to last the winter. If the right animal did not come his way or if he and his fellow hunters did not locate enough food before the snows came, he would die, along with his family and community.

Human beings are the only species on this planet with a consciousness of mortality. And there is no doubt that omens are a response to our ancient fear of death. It is the knowledge of our mortality that gives us a notion of time passing and time coming to be.

We look for signs to guide us into the unknown. We are the only species that consciously plans and tries to live beyond the here and now. We are the only species that wants to know what will happen. And how. And when. And where. And we are undoubtedly the only species that asks "why?"

The Most Natural Thing in the World: Omens in Nature

Originally omens were quite natural. Human beings have always used omens to figure out the world around them. When would the rains come? When would winter's ice and snow cover the land? Where were the animals necessary for food? It was only through generations of observation and perception that people came to know the world around them and the signs that helped them to decipher it.

On land or at sea, all activities of people have always been affected by nature. On land, people sought signs to find the best time to raise the seasonal crops. At sea, they sought the signs that could take them home to firm land. *Red sky at night, sailor's delight. Red sky in the morning, sailors take warning.* Now a children's chant, this was once part of a sailor's oral guide to the sea. The sea is awesome. To be surrounded by, and suspended upon, water is one of the most humbling experiences known to man. Yet people have gone down to the sea in ships for as long as there is memory.

Our seafaring ancestors needed all the help they could get. They deciphered every sign to find meaning and the way home. Birds were probably among the first omens, the first signs. For the people who navigated the sea, the appearance of birds indicated the proximity of a landmass. For the people of the land, birds were often the harbingers of the impending rains.[2]

We learn to pick up signs when we are very young. When we are babies, our mothers communicate to us with a host of signs. There is the smell of tension or love or fear. There is the quality of touch. There is the taste of mother, of home and the milk of life. The Earth Mother gives us signs all the time. Nowhere was this more evident than among the people of the New World. For the Native Americans the Earth Mother and nature have been the guiding forces in all divination. From the dawn of the rich oral tradition to the present, Native American people have looked to nature for signs, omens, and guidance. This has always been a way of life rather than a philosophy or religion. It has been born out of the experience of the natural world.[3]

This tradition of heeding natural omens continues to this day. The people of the Yucatán Peninsula in Mexico, who trace their ancestry back to the ancient civilizations of the Mayas, have some very ancient interpretations of weather signs. Experience has told these people that if it is very cold at night, the next day will be very hot. If the wind blows hard for several days, they say that the sky is full and that it will rain hard for many days. It is then that the men go to plant. Or when the Pleiades appear to be "half lying down," it is a sign of rain. When the ceibas, plums, and other fruit trees bear much fruit, then they know that the maize harvest will be good. If turkeys take baths in the dust or if the soot drops from the ceiling, rain is coming. When the leaf-cutting ants are seen to be carrying many bits of leaf into their houses, then the season will be rainy.

Some of these signs sound weird, but all of them have proved to be accurate over the millennia of watching and living. All of these signs are natural omens.[4]

The search for signs in nature is universal. In Bulgaria people look for rain if the sun is surrounded by a circle. And the surest sign of bad weather is the sight of pigs carrying straw to the sty at sunset.[5]

In China there is an ancient connection between natural occurrences and omens. The Chinese saw the wind as the breath of the universe. To see the course and quality of the wind was to see the nature of both crops and famine as well as human passions and migrations. During the Chou dynasty, three thousand years ago, Chinese imperial court astrologers were responsible for observing clouds, rain, and wind and harmonizing the realms of Heaven and Earth.[6]

The Papago Indians of the American Southwest feel deeply connected to the sea. They believe that the sea holds gifts that come from beyond. The Papagos feel that any object a man sees in the sea is a gift that has bearing on his life, whether it be a strand of seaweed, a shell, or a pebble. And when a Papago man runs along the sea or through the woods, anything that comes to him is a sign for his run through life—his career. Any living creature—animal, bird, insect, or fish—that crosses his path is subject to interpretation. These signs do not have fixed meanings but are interpreted by the man as he will.[7]

From Greece to China, from Bulgaria to Dahomey, from the Yucatán Mayas to the Mescalero Apaches, people have sought to see the signs in nature. These are the first omens.

Winter in Summer and the Fall of Spring

We know that a season is more than a date on the calendar. But we sometimes forget. In the northern and southern temperate zones there are four seasons: spring, summer, fall, and winter. Every part of the earth has its own particular seasons. And all of us have our own particular connections to them.

Our calendar reflects the changing seasons. For example, December 21 is the winter solstice and the first official day of winter. It marks the shortest day and the longest night of the year. It is thus the finish line of a race that began on June 21, the summer solstice. Let's look at it another way. After the shortest day of the year, which is the first day of winter, the days start getting longer and longer until June 21, the longest day and the first official day of summer. So the beginning of winter is actually the birth of summer. Summer is the child of winter.

Our ancestors paid careful attention to the earth, sea, skies, and seasons. In our modern technological world we sometimes forget our connection to the ebbs and flows of earth. Sometimes Mother Earth reminds us. She will drop three feet of snow on the most powerful city in the world and bring it to a screeching halt. Or she will shake the very foundations of the earth itself. At times like these we remember our connection to the earth and to the seasons.

We don't need earthquakes, blizzards, and tornadoes to help us remember our connection to the seasons. For deep down, we have the memory of all our ancestors to help us remember.

Our ancestors connected with the rhythms of their time. They were also able to interpret the signs of the times. We, too, can connect with our world. And, as we open ourselves to recognize the signs around us in the cycle of the seasons, so we begin reclaiming our ability to see the omens, the signs, of our times.

The first game in this book helps create an awareness of the seasons in which we live. It can be the first step toward reconnecting with the rhythms of the natural world.

To Everything There Is a Season

> *To every thing there is a season, and a time to*
> *every purpose under the heaven: A time to be*
> *born, and a time to die; a time to plant, and*
> *a time to pluck up that which is planted.*
> —*Ecclesiastes 3:1–2*

I. No matter what season it is, go outside.
II. Take in and note all the characteristics of the present season—weather, foliage, birds and animals, temperature, and so forth.
III. What is the most important representation of this season? Pick one or two aspects that are the most characteristic of this season for you.
IV. Look around for signs of the season past.
V. What indications are there that the present season has emerged from another?
VI. Look around for signs of the coming season. What are they?

This is a game that can be played at the same spot over an extended period of time. Then you can watch a specific area, see how the seasons change, and recognize what signs indicate the changes to come. Don't overthink this; after all, it's a game. And all the games in this book are meant to be enjoyed.

> *A ring around the moon is a sign of bad weather. The old*
> *woman who dwells there is pulling a hood over her head, a white*
> *hood for frost or snow and a black one for rain or a sudden*
> *thaw.*
> —*Ojibwa omen*[8]

The wind and the rain, the ice and snow, the sun and clouds are the most ancient and intimate associates of human beings. To this day we still try to interpret weather signs. Overall, our weather-predicting skills may not be much greater than they were ten thousand years ago.

Omens and weather signs have always been closely connected. For the Shoshones of the American West the appearance of a rainbow indicated that the rain would stop. This was an auspicious sign, and thus a rainbow became a good omen as well as a weather sign.[9]

The rainbow, in fact, has almost become a universal symbol of good luck. It is the sun shining through the rain and represents the hope of a clearing, a shining, a softer time. Again, the roots of this interpretation are in the meteorological observation by peoples who must rely on the weather. For the inhabitants of the Marshall Islands, closely connected to the sea and the changes of the weather, understanding proper times for sailing are a matter of life and death. For the Marshall Islanders, if there is a rainbow somewhere, one may sail off without anxiety because the weather will hold even if the sky is black.[10]

Through observation comes a familiarity with the signs. So the Iroquois Indians note that lots of husk on an ear of corn means a cold winter, while less husk indicates a mild winter. Cirrus clouds, according to the Iroquois, mean a short rainy spell, while a sure sign of rain is a series of small explosions or puffs during the burning of hardwood fuel. If the feet of a skunk or coon are well furred, according to Iroquois lore, there will be a cold winter. And mice coming out and running about on snow is a sign of thaw.[11]

Check Out the Clouds

The clouds are a constant mystery. At one moment in time the sky is blue and endless. Minutes later there is nothing but a gray shroud overhead. There are cloud puffs and fog clouds, long rain clouds shaped like fish, and wisps of gray. Clouds have always been excellent signs of the condition of nature. For a long time people have been seeing themselves in the clouds.[12] The clouds are a kind of mirror in which we can see ourselves and our thoughts.

Most parts of the world have clouds. It's one of the ways that we appreciate the sun. In the temperate zones the billowing, changing clouds of a summer day are the cumulonimbus that we associate with summertime.

As children we look at the clouds and see within their shapes animals, people, creatures of all kinds. As adults we can, once again, play as children. But as adults we can see more deeply into the clouds.

I. The first thing to do is to get relaxed. This is a game, not a test. So find a place where you can watch the clouds. It's best to do this outdoors while lying on your back.

II. Find a cloud. Look at it carefully. Now you are a cloud watcher.

III. Take it all in. Look at the shape of the cloud—its details, little ridges, and roundnesses.

IV. Now close your eyes and take a few deep breaths. With your eyes closed try to remember all you can about the cloud.

V. Open your eyes and look at the cloud again. Is it still there? If so, does it look the same?

VI. Pay attention to the shape of the cloud and see what kind of images you can create from it. You can do it. You just have to let your imagination go.

VII. Take a few of those images and ask yourself how they relate to you. For example, if you see images of an angry dog, it could mean one kind of thing in your life. If you see an image of an ocean with gentle waves, it would mean something quite different.

VIII. Create a story from the images of the clouds.

Don't worry if you don't actually "see" a shape. Just stare at the cloud for a few minutes and let your thoughts wander freely.

How Cloudy Are You Today?

Weather doesn't just happen outside of us. It happens inside, too. In this game we try to see just what the weather is like inside. This game involves four or more people and can be played in combination with other games.

I. Everybody sits in a circle facing toward the center.

II. Close eyes and take some deep breaths.

III. The person in charge of this game starts out asking, "What is the weather today?"

IV. Each person describes what the "weather" is like for them. For example, if you were feeling a bit depressed but saw the light at the end of the tunnel, you might say, "It's cloudy, but I feel a warm front moving in." Another person might say, "I am raining hard and very cold." There are an infinite number of weather variations.

V. Go once around the circle and then find out if anybody's weather has changed.

It would be a good idea to come back to this game after playing other games to find out if and how the weather has changed for people in your group.

How Very Unnatural: Omens with a Difference

As long as they were purely natural, as long as they related specifically to nature, omens were precise. However, at some point signs became more than natural. They became "supernatural." It was not long before the readers of omens became more than weather forecasters.

Sometimes the signs just didn't seem natural. In the middle of the day, while the sun was shining brightly in a cloudless sky, a shadow would fall and grow across the sun. Soon, only the very edge of the sun would be visible and the earth would be covered in darkness for a few moments. How awesome an eclipse must have appeared to early humans. Even today a full solar eclipse is an event of worldwide interest and sometimes fear.

In the village of Khijuri, in the state of Rajasthan, India, people were staying indoors, even though it was the middle of the day. Many of the villagers lit candles. Many had forgone food for the previous twelve hours. Pregnant women avoided holding knives or anything sharp. They were experiencing a complete solar eclipse that was visible for ten thousand miles. The date was October 24, 1995.[13]

Eclipses have always reminded people that things are never entirely as they seem. The blackening of the sun was seen as a terrible sign of a world gone out of control. It was all so unnatural. The Lettish peasants of Latvia thought that the sun and moon were being devoured during an eclipse. The Buriat people of eastern Siberia thought that a monster, Alka, had swallowed the sun or the moon. In the basin of the Volga the Altaic Tatars thought an eclipse was caused by a vampire who lived on a star. For Hindus the demon Rahu swallowed Soma, the moon, causing a lunar eclipse.

For many the eclipse was an unnatural sign of ill happenings. The misfortune had to be checked. The Ojibwa Indians of North America shot lighted arrows into the air to keep the sun from being extinguished. The Peruvian Indians shot arrows to frighten the beast attacking the sun. The Guarayú Indians of Bolivia shot arrows at the heavenly Jaguar attacking the moon, making loud noises while they did so.

An eclipse had to be reversed and forestalled. The Chinese created a noisy uproar to scare away the evil forces consuming the sun while the Orinocan Indians of South America attempted to bury fire to keep some fire hidden. The Babylonians repeated incantations. And the ancient Mexicans sacrificed humpbacks and dwarfs. If the light was lost, life was lost. For ancient peoples around the globe, the eclipse became a critical sign. One simply did not know whether the sun would return.[14]

Even more frightening than the eclipses were comets. These were much

less common and often awesome in their unnaturalness. From the ancient Israelites to the Chinese to the Aztecs and Incas of South America, people saw
a comet as an omen of ill fortune. A sign of disaster to come, it was definitely
not part of the natural order of things.

Eclipses and comets were out of the ordinary. They were very different
signs than extra fur on the feet of an animal or the turning of the leaves before
a storm. Eclipses and comets were menacing reminders that disaster could be
just a heartbeat away.

At the same time that humans were reading the flights of birds and the
scattering of mice, they were also watching for the unexpected. The ancient
Chinese saw anything abnormal, irregular, or violent in nature as a rupture of
normal patterns. This included not only comets and eclipses but earthquakes,
unexplained sounds or voices, and the spontaneous upheaval of rocks and
trees.[15]

In recorded history this awareness of abnormal signs dates back to
Mesopotamia, three thousand years before the birth of Christ, where official
diviners spent their lives analyzing the significance of abnormalities. For the
ancient Mesopotamians the omens of importance were those involving freak-
ishness, such as two-headed babies or three-legged calves.[16]

As people saw deviations from the natural as omens, they began to connect omens with foreboding. Omens, once quite natural indications of the
human connection with the environment, were transformed into something
fearful. While omens were once the flight of birds, the blowing of leaves, and
the shape of the clouds, they became terrifying signs of things to come.

Official Omens: From Fear to Belief and Superstition

Fear can be power in the hands of the elite. Over three thousand years ago
the ancient Babylonian rulers had official diviners and an official book of
omens. And when ancient Sumeria emerged as the first political state, it became the birthplace of official superstition. This marked the transformation of
omens from the observation of the natural to the political tool of the ruler
class.

"If a ewe gives birth to a lion, and it has two mouths—the word of the
land will prevail over the king."[17] Although it is doubtful that a Babylonian
king ever had to face a serious threat from the "land" because of a ewe giving
birth to a two-mouthed lion, there were thousands of such entries in the Babylonian book of omens, and only those who had been carefully trained (and who
could read) were able to interpret the omens.

It seems likely that there is a connection between the rise of political states and the rise of superstition. There is a connection between the rise of states and the ordered interpretation of signs. For one thing, states can only exist when there is enough produced to support them. When our ancestors were hunting animals and gathering food, they were constantly faced with either feast or famine.

All this changed with the development of agriculture. There was a greater certainty than ever before. The seeds would be sown, the plants would grow, and the crops would be harvested. Even more important, when people started to farm, they produced more than enough for their own needs. For the first time in the history of the human race, there was surplus food.

By the days of ancient Sumeria, humans had developed a sophisticated agricultural system. There were large surpluses stored in granaries that could support the king, the priests, and the entire community. When people were moving in small groups, hunting for their survival, each clan was responsible for reading the signs of the times. But when a large agricultural system was established, as in ancient Babylon and Sumeria, there were specialists. The interpretation of signs became the special province of an elite group of priests.[18] The Hittite King Mursilis II reflected upon this in a prayer: "Either let me see it in a dream, or let it be discovered by divination, or let a 'divinely inspired . . .' declare it, or let all the priests find out by incubation whatever I demand of them." [19]

Much of the reading of signs in these ancient times concerned sacrificial animals. From the ancient Middle East to China to Greece, the reading of the livers and intestines of sacrificial animals became a common practice. In ancient Babylon a diviner was *mas-su-gid,* "one who stretches his hand into the sacrificial animal."[20]

Once the reading of signs became the province of a special group of people, omen reading became official. Once people no longer read their own signs, omens became fixed and rigid beliefs. It is at this time that omens became superstitions.

What is superstition? It is the reading of a sign according to an interpretation that is rooted in the past. For example, a child would probably not be frightened of a black cat crossing his path. He might be more frightened of a spider. A superstition is a learned reading of a sign. A superstition is a fossilized omen.

Once upon a time in a hut in South India a man of the Coorg culture was having his dinner. Suddenly, in the midst of the dinner, the lights in his hut flickered out. The man saw this as a sign. A thousand generations later the Coorg people consider it a sign of disaster if the lamp in a person's house goes out in the middle of dinner. If such an event occurs, the diner will get up from his meal, clean his dish, and wash his hands. He will then sit down to dinner again a few minutes later. This will make it a different meal and not the one that was interrupted. Disaster will have been averted. What was once a spontaneous sign has become, through time, a superstition.[21]

In Madagascar, if a boy is wounded during circumcision, superstition dictates that his mother has been unfaithful. Among the ancient Ouigour people of Turkey, there are omen texts that tell you if you cut your fingernails on a certain day, there will be a great danger. But if you cut your nails on another designated day, you will meet someone who wishes you well.[22] Like omens, superstitions give us a sense of control, or at least an illusion of certainty about what is going to happen.

But the reading of signs and omens is the opposite of superstition. An omen is alive. It is rooted in the here and now. A sign is a momentary thing. We see it. We reflect. We understand. A sign that appears at one moment will mean something different to someone at a different time. There is no superstition involved in the interpretation of signs, only the moment of reflection.

The human fear of the unknown and a craving for certainty gave birth to superstition. And it was the use of that fear to control and manipulate that gave rise to official books of omens and a privileged group of those authorized to interpret these omens. With the rise of this group, people no longer read signs for themselves. Instead, they looked to others to tell them what was real and what was unreal. Instead of knowing the signs of the times, people had to believe in the experiences and interpretations of others.

The death of omens is the birth of belief. Once we rely on other people's interpretation of reality, we have to believe in it. When we no longer trust ourselves to see the world, we have to believe in other people's experience. Belief and superstition are twins. Both are taught and conditioned. Neither comes from direct experience.

Belief and knowing are opposite. The Navajos recognize this in their word for divination, *bil 'ihosini.h,* which translates as "that which he knows." The Navajo diviner does not believe. He knows.[23]

From the time of ancient Babylonia, books have been ways of perpetuating the official superstitions. The Sinhalese, for example, have a book of omens that goes back centuries. This book has spread to the surrounding areas as a textbook of how to read signs.[24] Ancient Indian omen books divide signs into eight categories and may be read only by the select few. These categories involve the interpretation of earthquakes, droughts, plagues, eclipses, and comets. Others deal with throbbing of the limbs, moles, dreams, palmistry, and even the correct way to interpret snoring or the breathing through one nostril or the other.[25]

This ancient tradition of official superstition has carried on through the present day. Among the Konku people of South India, every day of the week and each month of the year is either auspicious or inauspicious. The designation of these days is in the hands of Brahman priests who refer to printed handbooks, and there is absolutely no room for spontaneous interpretation.[26]

Today few westerners consult books of omens, yet superstition still survives and thrives. We still like to latch onto beliefs that help us face the unknown, and sometimes we even like to create our own superstitions.

Making Superstitions

Every time that I travel by plane across time zones I have a ritual that I like to observe. I never, ever adjust my watch to the new time zone until the plane has landed. This is one of my pet superstitions. It's mine, all mine. And I would have to give myself a little time before I changed it. On January 27, 1996, on a flight from Dannam, Saudi Arabia, to Muscat, Oman, I finally risked changing my watch in midair. And I lived to tell the tale. It only took me twenty years to do it.

This game eases us gently into the awareness of our own superstitions. The more we are aware of them, the less hold they have on us. One way of becoming aware of superstitions is to create some new ones. Then, perhaps, we can drop them if we want to.

NEEDED: paper and a writing implement.

I. Make a list of all the superstitions that you have ever observed. This can be anything from the more common black cat, crack in the sidewalk, and broken mirror to those that are uniquely yours.

II. Choose one of them.

III. Turn it around and observe it as its opposite. For example, if one of your superstitions dictates that walking under a ladder will bring you bad luck, you might create a new one: Walking under a ladder brings good luck. Then walk under a ladder. (Don't feel obliged to pick the superstitions that you are most afraid of.)

IV. See if there are any changes in your life as a result of changing your superstition.

V. Practice this new superstition for a week.

VI. After a week go back to the old one for a day, then alternate the new one with the old one every other day.

VII. Make Sunday a superstition-free day.
VIII. Take notice of yourself and all of your superstitions on Sunday but don't practice any.
IX. How did you feel when you violated the old superstition? Be honest!
X. When you feel comfortable with this process, try a more precious superstition—one that means a bit more to you—and follow these same steps.

The Superstition Supermarket

Here we try to re-create the ways in which omens became superstitions. If we are playful with superstitions, they lose their power. Since superstitions are always quite serious, a playful superstition is indeed an oxymoron.

This game can be played alone or with a group.

NEEDED: Paper and a writing implement.

I. Close your eyes for a moment.
II. Think of meaningful occurrences in your life that were heralded by some event. For example, you unexpectedly saw an old friend right after eating chocolate mousse. It happened again later on with a different friend.
III. Make this into a superstition. In this example, chocolate mousse indicates the arrival of an old friend.
IV. Create ten new superstitions and write them down. The more outrageous the better.
V. If playing in a group, compare and combine these new superstitions.
VI. Pick one of these new superstitions and practice it for several days.
VII. How does it feel? You might feel silly at first. Watch yourself, you might find yourself believing these new superstitions. Are you becoming fearful? Anxious? Are these new superstitions having a specific impact on you?

Omens: Our Infinite Heritage

People have continued to read signs despite the rise of official superstition. In many societies omen reading remained the province of the people. For example, among the Shoshone Indians there has been no class of priests to interpret signs.[27] Likewise, the Ute Indians always emphasized the role of the individual in seeking visions. They have accepted claims of those who "see" clearly—they are called "vision recipients." Yet no single vision recipient has been recognized as the sole possessor of all truth and all power. For the Utes the individual determines his own interpretation; there is no one truth. As a consequence, the Ute Indians have always been particularly unwilling to accept the beliefs of those missionaries who claimed that one Christian sect prevailed over all other religions.[28]

From Lapland to China to Africa to South America omens have continued to be part of the heritage of all people. The reading of signs has been open to every person, and the connection to nature has been a basic element of all omen interpretation.[29]

The variety of omens is infinite. Some are manipulated by the seer. Others are presented by nature. Often people have seen signs in nature as reflections of human life. For example, although the people of the Tanala tribe of Madagascar generally do not use omens, if one comes across an *antsangoa,* an insect that looks like a walking stick, it is seen as a sign of death in the family. This is because the legs of the insect stretch out in front and behind like the poles of a funeral bier.[30] And while this has become rigid over time as a superstition, it is still a reflection of nature.

The Murias of India use eggs to find signs. They feel that eggs are favored by the gods because an egg is like a virgin whom no one has touched or a pregnant woman who holds two souls at once. The eggs are thrown and the resulting patterns are interpreted at that moment.[31]

"At that moment"—once again that phrase is the key to the difference between an omen and a superstition. An omen—a sign—is something that is read *in the moment,* is spontaneous and transitory. A superstition is something that is rooted in the past, either the distant past of cultural tradition or the personal past of our own creation.

The Celts have long utilized spontaneous signs. For example, there is the practice of *deuchainn,* or first sight. In this, a person with a question goes up a hill too steep for an animal. On the way down, the first creature he meets indicates the answer to the question. If someone wanted to know what kind of a year it would be, he would walk outside with eyes closed, go to the end of the house, and then open his eyes. The first thing he saw would be his sign.[32]

In the western Highlands of Scotland those people with sight were called *frithirs.* The *frithir* would fast on the first Monday of every quarter and stand on her doorstep just before sunrise, barefoot, bareheaded, and blindfolded. She would then hold onto the doorpost and remove the blindfold. She would take the first thing that she saw upon removing the blindfold as the sign and would interpret it.[33]

The Frithir *You Go, the* Frithir *You See*

The ancient Celtic practices of frith and deuchainn were rooted in the spontaneous interpretation of the here and now. In a sense, we do this all the time. We are constantly taking in signs around us and interpreting them, usually without thinking about it.

Sometimes we think too much. That is, we cogitate, work things over in our minds, and often don't see what's right in front of us. Unless we force ourselves.

Sometimes all we need to do is to open our eyes in new ways to the world around us. That's what the ancient Celts did when they practiced frith. That's what we are doing in this game: We look at things suddenly with a view toward finding a meaning for ourselves and our lives. The game can be played inside or outside.

I. Go to a place either in your living space or outside.
II. Stand still with eyes closed.
III. With eyes still closed turn around a few times in a circle.
IV. Open your eyes.
V. Focus on the very first object you see when you open your eyes.
VI. If it has a use, like a chair or car or window, think of the use and what it says to you about your present life situation.
VII. Concentrate on all the meanings of the object in question.
   a. What does it sound like?
   b. What feelings does it evoke in you?
   c. What associations do you have with it?
VIII. Think about some way in which this object is telling you something. Be imaginative.

The frithir is often interested in finding the answer to a specific question. So can we. Once again, be playful.

IX. Ask a specific question of importance to you.
X. Repeat the whole game.
XI. How does this answer the question?

If done with two or more people, the "frithir" can be blindfolded and led to a spot and then told to open her eyes.

Signs in the Aztec Year of the Twelfth House

The Aztec empire had reached a peak of power. While there were civilizations to the south and to the north, the Aztec society and culture had grown and thrived with little interference. It had subdued neighboring states. The Aztecs had emerged triumphant and expansive. Their power was assured. And, of course, there was no thought of a threat from the seas, either to the west or to the east. Certainly there was no thought of conquest from a foreign power. All the powers were known and manageable to the rulers of Aztec Mexico.

Then, in the year 1509, the year of the Twelfth House, strange things began to occur. First, there was a sign in the sky. It was like a flaming ear of corn, a fiery signal, or the blaze of daybreak. It seemed to bleed fire, drop by drop, as if the sky were wounded. It shone in the eastern sky in the middle of night and burned on until the break of day. This continued for a full year.

Then the temple of Huitzilopochtli burst into flames. There was no cause that the people could see for such a conflagration. And the attempts to put out the fire with water only made the flames grow worse. Shortly after this, another temple was destroyed by a lightning bolt. There was a light drizzle that day but no thunder, no other lightning, no storm. The people said that the temple was "struck by a blow from the sun."

A fourth sign occurred during this year of the Twelfth House. Fire streamed through the sky even as the sun was still shining. The fire was divided into three parts and flashed out from where the sun sets and ran straight to where it rises, giving off a shower of sparks. When the people saw the long stream of flame in the heavens, there was a great outcry and much confusion and a sound like a thousand little bells.

A fifth sign occurred during this year of the Twelfth House. The wind lashed the waters of the nearby lake until it seemed as if it were boiling with rage. It seemed to want to shatter itself in a frenzy. The waves began far off, rose high in the air, and dashed against the walls of the houses. The flooded houses collapsed into the water.

A sixth sign occurred during this year of the Twelfth House. The people of the town heard a woman weeping night after night. She continued to pass night after night wailing and crying out, "My children, we must flee far away from this city!" At other times she would cry, "My children, where shall I take you?" She could not be found or questioned, but her lamentations continued.

The seventh sign was a mirror on the head of a strange bird caught by fishermen. In this mirror the emperor Montezuma saw stars and the night sky in the middle of the day. He saw a distant plain with warriors moving across it, spread out in great ranks and coming forward making war. He saw strange and alien soldiers riding on the backs of animals resembling deer. He, Montezuma, saw this, but his magicians and wise men saw nothing.

The eighth and final sign of this year of the Twelfth House was the appearance of monstrous beings in the streets of the city. These were deformed men with two heads. These beings were taken to be shown to Montezuma, but the moment he saw them they all vanished.

Eight strange signs appeared in this Aztec year of the Twelfth House. Eight strange omens that were unprecedented. Eight omens that marked the approach of apocalypse.

Ten years later, in 1519, the Spanish armies of Hernán Cortés, unannounced and unexpected, struck out from Cuba and landed on the Mexican shore. The conquest of Mexico had begun. Two years later, in 1521, the Aztec state surrendered to the steel-coated warriors who rode on strange and fleet four-legged creatures, resembling deer.[34]

—A contemporary Aztec account translated from the Aztec

The Omen Body

Our bodies are rich sources of omens. Since the beginning of time people have looked to the body for signs. In the mountains of Colombia, diviners or shamans look to their bodies to provide them with information about their patients. For example, the rise of unusual sensations on the outer side of the shaman's right foot that proceeds to the ankle is an indication that the medication prescribed is having a beneficial effect. A sign from the right hip to the foot indicates that a woman patient will menstruate. While these body signs have become ritualized, there is no doubt that they are rooted in practical observation over time.[35]

The Mescaleros and other Apache groups are more fluid in their interpretations of body signs. The Apaches feel that involuntary muscular tremors are warning signals of good or evil events to come. For example, the Apaches see a muscular tremor under the eye as symbolizing misfortune and tears. Various other tremors are open to individual interpretation. When a person notices a muscular tremor in some part of his body, he makes up his mind about what kind of a sign it is. Some Apaches consider such signs to be a message from their guardian spirit or a source of supernatural help.[36]

For the Navajos, twitching of the skin, snapping of the nose, and tracheal rumblings are omens. There is no set way of interpreting these signs. Rather, the afflicted person discusses the possible interpretation with family members. If this doesn't lead to a satisfactory result, various methods of divination are employed. In any event, the meanings of the body signs are fresh and changing.[37]

It was a poetic metaphor for the African Americans of the Georgia coast in the 1930s to see an itching left palm as a sign of incoming money or an itching right palm as a sign of a forthcoming handshake with a stranger.[38]

Many societies "read" sneezes. Ancient Indian texts have identified all kinds of auspicious and inauspicious sneezes. Many African cultures believe sneezes are omens. Each sneeze has a variety of possibilities and meanings. When the sneeze occurs, where it occurs, and with whom it occurs are all part of the sneeze interpretation.[39]

Poetry and metaphors are the language of signs and omens. Reading signs is not a science, let alone an exact science. Body signs are as varied as the bodies themselves. Yet some metaphors have lasted because they hit the mark so well. A situation can be a "pain in the neck" or a "pain in the ass." Often, we can even feel that pain in our bodies. If we are involved in a consistently stressful and annoying situation, we might well develop symptoms in our necks. People who are constantly carrying burdens for others, both real and metaphorical, often develop back problems. The body is a rich source of signs about ourselves.

The Chinese have long seen the psychological and the physical as inextricably linked. They have always regarded body signs not merely as indications of sickness but as reflections of the entire person. Today, with the greater acceptance of holistic medicine, body signs have become more and more accepted as omens that help us see the whole person.

Looking Through Our Bodies

Many of us have become separated from our bodies. We don't think much about our bodies unless we have aches and pains. Then we often become worried if not downright hypochondriac. This game is not a substitute for a meaningful physical examination. It is merely another way of looking at signs and at ourselves. We can find out all kinds of things about ourselves by simply listening to what the body is telling us.

NEEDED: paper and a writing implement.

I. Find a comfortable place where you will be undisturbed for at least thirty minutes.
II. Think about every unusual feeling that you have had in your body for the past six months.
III. Write these down.
IV. Think of these as metaphors instead of just physical events. For example, if you have had a pain in the neck, think about what has been giving you a pain in the neck. If you have had a hard time digesting food, think about what in your life you have had a hard time digesting.
V. Write down what these symptoms relate to in other parts of your life.
VI. If these unusual feelings have disappeared, when did they disappear? What had changed in your life?
VII. If you do this over an extended period, say one or two months, see if you find a pattern to these feelings. See if you can relate them to other events that come and go in your life.

Body Language

The Apaches took body language seriously. Each person would pay attention to involuntary signs such as sneezing, muscular twitching, and tearing of the eyes. Each person would find out for herself the meaning of these signs by paying attention to the events that followed.

I. For two or three days, pay attention to your body.
II. Watch for any unusual involuntary signs.
III. Pay attention to how these can be seen as symbols of other things going on in your life.
IV. Watch for what occurs in the period of time following these signs.
V. Anything unusual?
VI. Is there a pattern? For example, are there things that occur every time you get a twitch?
VII. Make a list of these occurrences and follow them through for a month.

Auto Diagnosis[40]

The Navajos, Apaches, and Chinese have looked to the body as a source of signs. At the end of the twentieth century, technology is often an extension of our bodies. For us, in this age of the communications highway and magic pictures in little boxes, the omens can be a bit more technological.

One of the most common instruments of technology is the automobile. We can see signs in our autos.

I. Relax. Take a few deep breaths through your nose and exhale through your mouth.
II. Think of your automobile. Is there anything that needs fixing at this time? If there is nothing that needs fixing, think of your most recent repairs.
III. Think of what human qualities relate to these parts and functions. For example, what do we do in our lives that is similar to the function of a brake in a car?
IV. See if you can find a connection between the ailments of your car and what is going on in your life at this time.
V. See a good mechanic.

A variation of this game looks at problems with your house. You can play this game by yourself or in a group in which people write down their experiences and then share them with the others.

Fortune-telling is a hype that has reached its peak in this century. It comes from a notion of time that is two-dimensional. Fortune-tellers read the future and tell us about the past. Omens are much more interesting because they tell us about the present moment.

We have been taught to believe that omens are scary. That is superstition. So how do we reclaim our natural ability to read the world, signs, and omens? One way is to take them out of the closet and play. Another is to avoid our temptation to predict. Prediction, which is fortune-telling, is often a disguise for superstition. It is an attempt to control the unknown. Omens are about something much larger than that.

We need to remind ourselves, however, that reading signs has little to do with death or plane crashes. The signs we see enable us to see ourselves and our world more clearly. As long as we are aware of that, we can avoid getting into the habit of fearing and worrying that we will see things that are scary.

The key to any sign or omen is what we make of it. The world's religious literature is replete with images of burning bushes and bolts of lightning. To be sure, signs can take dramatic forms. However, it is often in the everyday that we can find our signs.

Omens have always been gateways into expanded consciousness and into our imagination. They reveal our creativity. Omens provide us with ways in which we can see ourselves in the mirror of a changing universe—and that's much more fun than superstition.

CHAPTER 2

Mirror, Mirror on the Wall (and Plate and Pool and Crystal Ball)

Mirrors

It is the early 1700s. The place is the northern part of the colony of New York. The man leaves the confines of his village and walks to a secluded but familiar place. It is late evening, the moon is new and the sky is dark. The man carries only a cup of water and a blanket. Carefully he places the cup of water on the ground. He then squats down, throws the blanket over his head, and stares into the cup of water in the double blackness of the night and the blanket. For this Waswanipi Algonquin seer, the practice has its own name. It translates as "he sees the soul."[1]

The Algonquin seer is scrying, a practice as ancient as human society. In fact, there are few other practices that are as common to so many cultures. From Australian aborigines to ancient Greeks, from Africans to Indians, from Muslim to Jew to Christian to Hindu, scrying is a universal method of discerning signs and omens.[2]

The scryer is one who "descries," or far-sees. Scrying is a method of gazing into a crystal, pool of water, mirror, or any transparent object in order to see beyond normal sight. It is "far seeing" because it sees beyond the object that is scried.

Crystals, plates, pools of water, and mirrors all have two things in common. First, they all have refractive surfaces. Second, they are all vehicles whereby we may see ourselves reflected and then reflect upon ourselves more deeply than the surface image. Traditionally they allow us to go beyond the mere image that shines back at us into a deeper part of ourselves and our consciousness.

Mirrors, crystals, and water—all are vehicles for second sight. All are tools for scrying. However, the number of ways in which people can stare into the beyond are almost limitless. Just about anything can be transformed into a medium for scrying—everything from fingernails to kerchiefs have been used.[3]

In India an ancient practice was to cover the fingernails of a prepubescent boy with oil and soot. He would then turn his nails to the sun, and the diviner would see answers to questions in the reflections in the boy's nails.[4]

Despite their variety, all forms of scrying are similar in that they all allow the observer to see "beyond" the object of gaze. The mirror, the crystal, the pool of water, or the kerchief is simply the object through which we see something else. The mirror, the crystal, the pool of water, and the kerchief function as gates to another kind of seeing.

The whole notion of "seeing" changes with scrying. What we "see" in the mirror is more than a mere reflection. What we "see" in a crystal is more than the faceted planes of clear stone. We see something that is inside of us. What we see is a reflection of our own deeper sight in the same way that a dream gives us insight that we would not find in our waking consciousness.

In America scrying has become a caricature of what it once was. When many of us think of crystal balls, we think of the Wicked Witch of the West in *The Wizard of Oz*. Her ball showed events on a sophisticated psychic movie screen. Divining mirrors evoke images of the Wicked Queen in *Snow White*. Wicked witches using mirrors and balls—that's what scrying has become in Western mythology. But the practice of scrying is very much alive and well outside of the world of Disney.

The mirror is the most common way of seeing our reflection. It is also the most common vehicle for scrying. On the simplest level, mirrors allow us to reflect upon ourselves. From earliest times, people have been fascinated with their reflections in pools of water or polished metal. With reflections, things aren't always what they appear to be. Is that really us that we see in the mirror?

A child who looks at his mother in a mirror realizes that there is something "wrong" with the way she looks. Everything is backward. A nose turned so slightly to the right is turned ever so slightly to the left. But that inconsistency is a shocking reality. The reflection is real, but not real. It reminds us that there is a difference between appearance and reality.

When the Algonquin diviner looked into "his mirror," he saw more than five o'clock shadow or a blemish on the skin. He was seeing beyond the reflection. He was allowing the mirror to reflect his inner being—his inner soul and sight. So it is with mirror gazing.

Throughout our lives we don't see ourselves as others see us. This is true even in the mirror. Our reflections in the mirror show us the way we see ourselves as we look in the mirror. We all have a "mirror look"—a way of look-ing that we reserve only for those times we approach our reflections. To scry with a mirror, we must go beyond mere reflections. To do this we must see that reflection clearly.

To See Ourselves as Others See Us

> O would some power the giftie gie us
> To see ourselves as others see us.
> It would frae mony a blunder free us
> And foolish notion.
> —Robert Burns

Day after day, we see ourselves in the mirror in pretty much the same way. We think this is the way we look. We don't realize that the rest of the world sees us differently. The strange truth is that we see ourselves as no one else sees us. The mirror tells us secrets that we do not generally reveal.

Who's That I See in the Mirror?

NEEDED: a mirror that you can stand in front of.

I. Stand in front of the mirror so that you are facing full-on.

II. Look at yourself.

III. Make a smile. Make a frown. Stare blankly. Look snobbish. Look meek. Make a scary face.

IV. Watch yourself in the mirror watching yourself in the mirror.

V. Look at yourself as if you are watching yourself for the first time.

VI. What are you doing?

VII. What are you feeling?

VIII. What strikes you about the reflection that you are seeing in the mirror?

IX. Close your eyes.

X. Think about an event that affected you deeply.

XI. With eyes still closed let the feeling fill you up. Let yourself relive the experience.

XII. Open your eyes suddenly.

XIII. What do you see? What is different about the person that you see so suddenly?

Others Seeing Us as We See Ourselves

To see ourselves as others see us is the flip side of others seeing us as we see ourselves. That's what this game is all about. At least two people are required for this game. If there are more than three participants, then players can divide into groups of two.

NEEDED: a mirror that you can stand in front of.

I. Decide which person is going to be the observer and which is going to look in the mirror.

II. The mirror person looks at her reflection in the mirror.

III. The observer watches how the mirror person looks while she is looking in the mirror.

IV. How does she change?

V. What expression does she have on her face?

VI. What does she appear to be feeling?

VII. Switch roles.

VIII. Repeat the game.

Scrying is found from pole to pole. Sometimes the harsher the lifestyle, the more developed the abilities to see far. The Labrador peninsula can be a cold and desolate place. This is not an environment for which human beings are "naturally" fitted. The polar bear has a warmer skin. The seal can stand freezing temperatures in relative comfort. Human beings are physically ill adapted for either the whipping arctic wind or the hunting of prey. Survival often requires the greatest attunement to the forces of wind and snow, ice and rain.

For people living in such adverse environments, an ability to read signs in the air and snow becomes essential. The Naskapi hunters of Labrador have lived on that cold and distant land for thousands of years. They have survived over time by tuning in to all that is around them. A simple thing like the rising of ice-covered kelp from the sea would be "read" by the Naskapis as a sign of mild weather to come. Mosquitoes bite worst just before a rain. The signs around them are a constant series of lessons.

It is no surprise that the religion of the Naskapis involves divination—reading and interpreting the myriad signs about them. For the Naskapi hunters each method of divination has its own purpose and name. When they want to find out where game animals have gone, they consult the scorched bones of animals. They read the mosquitoes, the rain, the seaweed, and the play of the wind upon the land. Everything is a key to understanding themselves and their world.[5]

Gazing into a mirror has a special name among the Naskapis. It is called *waponatca kwoma'u,* "he sees his soul." Gazing into a reflecting surface, the Naskapi diviner concentrates until an image—*atca'k,* or "soul"—is perceived.[6]

From northern Canada to New York, Native Americans have consulted their mirrors. The Fort Hope Algonquins used a clean dish, which they called *ni wabamowin,* or "my mirror." The Abitibi Lake Indians used a clear dish in a dark place when they feared something. The diviner would consult the mirrored surface. The name of the practice was *wabamo,* "he looks at himself."[7] Once again, this did not mean that the diviner was simply looking at his reflection. The mirror became a vehicle that allowed him to see his inner self.

Mirrors are a window into another side of reality. There is probably no divination practice more common than consulting mirrors. From Snow White to the Gwembe Valley in Africa, people have used mirrors to find the source of misfortune. Judges, from the Mayan civilization of Central America to the royal court of the Mossi people of Sudan, have used mirrors to find and convict transgressors. In the Sudan the royal diviner would use a mirror to find out if the royal wife was adulterous.[8]

Tezcatlipoca: High Priest of Reflection

In Mayan his name was Tezcatlipoca. It meant "Shining Mirror." He was Tezcatlipoca—God of the Shining Mirror. He was the High Priest of the Below—that which is beneath the surface. And, in recognition of his role, his temple in Mexico was lined entirely with mirrors made of obsidian and pyrite.

To the house of the God of the Shining Mirror the priests would come. To the temple of Tezcatlipoca the Mayan priests would come to seek deeper reflection. For the God of the Shining Mirror was everywhere and all around in the surfaces of the walls and ceilings. They would look into a mirror made of polished obsidian to seek and pronounce judgment on criminals. There they would seek answers to questions that they could not find in any other place. The God of the Shining Mirror provided accurate reflection to those who sought his guidance.[9]

—Mayan legend

Who's the Fairest of Them All?

There is no secret to seeing in a mirror. All we have to do is approach the mirror with new eyes. The dark of night seems to be the most helpful for seeing things in new ways. At night the sharpness of details is muted. Our minds and sight can play and we can see forms that we would not see in the brightness of day. Diviners, from the Algonquins of northern New York to the Mpongwes of French Equatorial Africa, use the mirror in darkness so that new light may emerge. This game is an adaptation of an Algonquin divining practice.

There is no "right" way of doing this. The main objective is to allow your mind to wander. If we allow our minds to wander, they might just wander into new and unexplored areas. For the Algonquin scryer and for us the idea is to let ourselves see beyond the apparent. That's what this game is all about. If little happens the first time, don't worry. It takes a little practice.

NEEDED: small, pocket-sized mirror.

I. Wait until it is dark.

II. Go into a place where there is virtually no light. A closet is fine if you can be comfortable.

III. Sit with the mirror in front of you.

IV. Take a few deep breaths with eyes closed.

V. Open your eyes and stare into the mirror. You can think about anything. Just let the thoughts pass as if you were viewing a film sequence.

VI. Be patient. Just continue to concentrate on the mirror.

VII. Let whatever forms or pictures or feelings come to you while you are staring at the mirror.

VIII. Make a mental note of whatever comes to you during this time.

Do this for three or four days at the same time of night. Experiment by asking questions and seeing what kinds of things occur. Be patient with yourself.

Crystals

Thou hast been in Eden the garden of God; every precious stone was thy covering, the sardius, topaz, and the diamond, the beryl, the onyx, and the jasper, the sapphire, the emerald, and the carbuncle, and gold: the workmanship of thy tabrets and of thy pipes was prepared in thee in the day that thou wast created.
—Ezekiel 28:13

The Greeks called them *krystalos,* meaning "frozen light." To this day the slang word for diamonds (a rare form of crystal) is "ice." Indeed the structure of both the diamond and frozen water is crystalline and more similar than different. The Cherokees called crystals "lights."[10] For as long as people have inhabited the earth, crystals have been seen as powerful and mystical. Before biblical times, people wore crystals as amulets and talismans. In ancient South America a shaman would prove his power by striking a large mallet against a giant crystal. Even then, humans knew of the mysterious crystalline electrical force.

Every crystal generates electrical energy when subjected to pressure. This unique property of crystals is called "piezoelectricity." The pressure of a large hammer on a giant crystal could generate enough energy to electrocute a person. Every society and culture, from the mists of ancient Atlantis until the present, has respected the power of the crystal.

In some societies crystals were a part of government. Among the people of Tecpán, in Guatemala, crystals were used by civil and military authorities alike. For the civil authorities crystals were used in criminal cases. The judges would gaze into a large block of quartz. A demon would appear and attest to the guilt or innocence of the accused. Military authorities, on the other hand, would consult the crystal before engaging upon their campaigns.[11]

Today more than ever, crystals are an important part of everyday life. Specifically, computers would not exist in their present form without crystals. Where would a computer chip be without the crystalline silicon? In our time the scientific and the mystical are joining hands. The computer-mystical-crystal connection is personified in crystal specialist Marcel Vogel. As a senior researcher for IBM in the 1950s, Vogel became entranced with crystals. After years at IBM, Vogel left and devoted his life to research on the exciting properties of crystals.

Next to mirrors, crystals have been the most common vehicle for scrying. And there are as many different forms of crystal reading as there are cultures that produce them. Native Americans have a special connection to crystals. The Navajos, in particular, use crystals in a variety of ways. A Navajo stargazer uses the light of the stars to illuminate a quartz crystal held in his hands. The stargazer then uses his crystal to find the source of an illness. He sings songs to the star spirit while staring at the light of the star reflected in the crystal. Soon the star emanates a beam of light through the crystal, and the stargazer sees the cause of the illness visually and graphically as in a picture.[12]

Sometimes the stargazer actually applies the crystal to his body to enhance his vision. The Navajo shaman grinds up some crystal into a fine dust, mixes it with the eye water of an eagle, and rubs it under his eye. Then he fixes his gaze on a star until a vision comes. He is aided by the vision of the eagle and the clarity of the crystal.[13]

The Crystal Growing Inside

Then he took out the crystals which he had to see by. Those are crystals which a man keeps inside his breast. They are little shining things, as long as a finger joint but they cast light like a fire. Some medicine men dream where to find them and they go out in the bare mountains and see them lying there, burning in the sun. Then they swallow them and keep them safe in their hearts. But some men never have to find them. Their crystals grow inside them as a worm can grow. Even if you suck it out, still it grows again. Those are the men who have great power.

Our medicine man had crystals which he had picked up, but he told my father that when he swallowed them, they leaped into his mouth out of his hand and went down his throat like water. He never took them out again because he could see even while they were in his body. While he was sitting there in the house he could see things going on outside and inside, too. Even if someone was coming far away, he could see. . . .

"You could be a medicine woman." "That cannot be," said my father. "We have one medicine man in the house and it is enough." So the medicine man said he would take out my crystals. He leaned over me and sucked them out of my breast, one by one. They were as long as the joint of my little finger, white and moving a little. He said: "Look, I have taken them out before they got big." Then he made a hole in a giant cactus and put them inside. Then he looked at me and said: "They will grow again, for it is a gift."

—Ruth Murray Underhill,
"The Autobiography of a Papago Woman"[14]

The southern Alleghenies of the old Cherokee country abounded with crystals. They lay along paths traveled by Cherokee hunters. They lay in fields cultivated by Cherokee farmers. They were part of the everyday life of the Cherokees. Some of these crystals were special. One was called *ulufisu'ti*. It was triangular, transparent, and had a single red streak running through the center. According to legend, one who owned such a crystal could call one of the Little People (similar to those of Ireland) to him at any time and make him do his bidding.[15]

The Eastern Cherokees experienced crystals, or "lights," as part of both their physical and spiritual environment. Cherokee diviners used special crystals to determine the best time to wage war. There were special crystals for purification. Other types of crystals were used to find the causes of illness. They were also used to find game, as well as things that had been lost or stolen. And the Cherokee diviner used the smallest ones to determine the time allotted for anyone to live. These were all crystalline quartz.[16]

Cherokee elders would use crystals for major decisions. The Cherokee national council would reckon the number of nights from the last new moon and would consult a divining crystal to determine the appearance of the first spring new moon. Similarly they would use a divining crystal to determine the time of appearance of the new moon for autumn.[17]

To determine health, the Cherokee diviner would consult his crystal. If the crystal stayed clear, health would reign. If it became cloudy, sickness would come. The Cherokee priests would even use crystals to determine the fate of their apprentices. The young boy would apprentice for seven days of training and fasting. Then his teacher would consult a crystal to see the boy's future. The stone would be set in the sun. If an old man appeared in it, success was assured, but if a man with black hair and beard appeared, the boy's career would be a failure. For Native Americans crystals were manifest light and vision. They were a sparkling invitation into the world beyond ordinary sight.[18]

Move then to the plains of the American Old Northwest of the eighteenth century, now called the Midwest. An Ojibwa shaman sat alone. There was war in the air and the warriors of his tribe were anxious to move. The shaman sat still, and then out of his pouch he pulled a piece of smoky quartz. He gazed into the crystal for a few long minutes. Reflected in his mind's eye through the quartz he saw the enemy. Their numbers were small enough for his tribe to manage. Their position was vulnerable. The Ojibwa shaman stood up. The message seen in the smoky quartz crystal was clear: The tribe could attack.[19]

Across the plains and to the south, in the desert plains of the Southwest, ponies were missing. These were more important than gold and almost as important as water to the survival of the Apache people. Were they stolen? Were they lost? Where were they? One did not simply start looking across the expanse of desert. The services of an Apache medicine man were required. Finding lost or stolen property was one of the main functions of the Apache diviner. It made sense to ask him to locate the missing ponies. After all, it was part of his job.

The Apache diviner sat quietly with eyes closed. It was always necessary to clear the mind. He then lifted a clear quartz crystal from his pouch and gazed into it. Flashing before his mind's eye were the ponies. Among the shadowy shapes were other shapes of men, braves. The ponies were being herded north and east by thieves. The shaman communicated the message to the elders.[20]

Crystal light shines on the Yucatán peninsula of Mexico, where descendants of the Maya Indians divine with crystals. The name of their stone is *zaztun,* or "stone of light." The light of the candle brings forth the light of the stone and gives the Mayan shaman the light to find the will of the gods or a cause of illness.[21]

Crystal light also shines in Madagascar. There the earth offers one of the richest and most varied sources of gems and stones. The Madagascans use all kinds of crystals—quartz, topaz, aquamarines, amethysts, and opals—for scrying.[22]

Throughout the continent of Australia crystal light has been used for thousands of years. In the northeastern part of Australia an Euahlayi diviner uses pieces of quartz about the size and shape of small lemons. The diviner holds up the lemon-shaped stone, gazes into it, and sees visions of the past, of far places and of what is yet to be. The Euahlayis feel that a spirit inhabits the crystal and goes forth to find the answer to questions and then returns to present the answer in the crystal.[23]

Crystals have shined their unique light on the entire world. Their very name has indicated the lightness and light bestowed by these gifts of nature. They are, indeed, frozen light. Crystals are as varied as they are beautiful. From Africa to Australia, from the Malayans to the Mayas, they have been a source of insight and sight. They have been a source of light and healing. So can they be for us.

The Crystal Tribe Instructs the Others

The animal tribes were concerned. One tribe, that of the human beings, was killing without sense. That tribe of two feet and standing up was cutting down forest homes and destroying other animal tribes not even for food.

The Bear tribe, chief among animals, had called the meeting. All animals knew that the Bears were slow to anger but sharp when their wrath was sparked. The Bears were brave and suggested that they, the Bear tribe, shoot back when attacked by the two-legs. Sadly it was clear that a bear would have to die to provide the bowstrings of each bow. Even then the claws of the bear would become entangled.

The Deer tribe knew not the strength of the Bear nor even its courage. For the Deer tribe, the idea of fighting the two-legs with their own weapon was unclear. The Deer tribe was gentle and clearsighted and offered to bring disease into the world. The Human tribe was destroying the balance of food and shelter. The human beings were living out of balance with the land, the sea, the air, and all other creatures.

The Deer tribe, long familiar with how to evade and confuse an enemy, volunteered to bring disease into the world. The humans, they said, were living out of balance with the earth, the air, and the water. As the humans lived out of balance so they would become sick. The Deer tribe brought rheumatism and arthritis. With rheumatism the humans would be struck in their heart. For only in heartlessness could the humans slay another animal not even for food. With arthritis would the very limbs become painful so that the two-legs would have to reflect upon their actions.

After the Deer tribe, the other animals took heed. Each of the tribes of Nature followed the Deer tribe. Each saw disease as the lesson for the two-legs. Each animal tribe created a new disease.

The Plant tribe, vast and varied, had suffered much with the humans. But the Plant tribe was far older than the Deer and far wiser than the Bear. When the Deer and the Bear were still spinning in the stars, the Plant tribe lifted its face to the sun and sucked nourishment from the Earth Mother.

The animal tribes had meted out harsh punishment to the humans. Diseases would fly down among the two-legs like grasshoppers, sand in the wind, poison in a stream. They would live with pain.

The Plant tribe felt the need of balancing the other animal tribes. The Plant members were skillful. They had traveled to the depths of the deepest waters and lived just below the bowl of heaven.

The Plant tribe offered that, for every disease a human suffered, a plant would be present to cure it. All the humans would have to do to cure their ailments would be to use their eyes, their noses, their ears—their intelligence.

All of Nature supported the Plants. It was then that the Rock and Mineral tribe agreed to help.

They were the oldest, the members of the Rock and Mineral tribe. They were the oldest and often the clearest. They were close friends of the Plant tribe.

Each mineral spoke for the power that it would give the two-legs to regain health. The Ruby, the color of blood itself, declared that it would heal the heart of the stricken humans. The Emerald, green as the rolling fields, volunteered to heal the liver and the eyes.

When Quartz, the chief of the Mineral tribe, spoke, all tribes took heed. For Quartz was as clear as frozen light and Quartz was the oldest and the most patient.

"I will be the sacred mineral," spoke Quartz. "I will heal the mind and help the humans see the origin of their diseases. I will help to bring wisdom and clarity in dreams. And I will record the spiritual history, including our meeting today, so that in the future if the humans gaze into me, they may see their origin and the way of harmony."

So it was.

—Cherokee legend[24]

Within the Crystal Within Us

In North America Native Americans have consulted crystals from the dawn of time. Among the Iroquois a diviner called ya-ku-wi-sat was said to possess, within himself, a live crystal which he could call from his mouth or nose.[25] But others, like the Cherokees, were able to leap into the crystal to see what it told.

In this game, which is an adaptation of several Native American divining practices, the crystal is not within us as it was with the Papago woman. Rather, we are within the crystal.

NEEDED: one quartz crystal that you can hold in the palm of your hands.

I. Spend a few minutes discovering your crystal. Hold it. Run your fingers over it. Feel its rough spots and its smooth spots. Note its planes and edges. You may close your eyes while doing this if you wish.
II. Find a comfortable spot with natural light.
III. Close your eyes. Take a few deep breaths.
IV. Let yourself get smaller and smaller and smaller.
V. With your fingers and with your imagination find the spot in the crystal where you may enter it.
VI. Let yourself enter the crystal.
VII. Explore the crystal from the inside. Touch it. Feel it.
VIII. What kind of light is there?

IX. What kind of feelings do you have inside?

X. What do the surfaces feel like on the inside?

XI. Explore the crystal to your satisfaction.

XII. Take several deep breaths.

XIII. Find the spot where you entered and leave the crystal.

If you find this difficult the first time, don't worry. It's just a matter of using your imagination. You did it as a child. It takes a little practice to get back to it. Allow yourself to "see" things with your mind's eye, as in a dreamlike state.

Blind Crystal Game

We have forgotten how much we know. We think that we have to learn all kinds of methods, techniques, and approaches to survive in the world. Yet we know much more than we realize.

This game shows us just how much we intuitively know about crystals, rocks, and ourselves. It is best played with five or more people and can be an exciting party game.

First, gather about twenty different stones or rocks. The best are the small polished rocks and minerals that are available in a rock and mineral store. It is important that the rocks be roughly the same size.

Have one person act as group leader for each game. Everybody should sit in a circle.

NEEDED: twenty small polished rocks and stones.

I. With eyes closed each person picks a rock from the collection of rocks in the center of the circle.

II. The group leader makes a notation of which rock each person takes.

III. Each person takes time to feel his rock, hold his rock, and generally become acquainted with his rock with his eyes shut.

IV. After about five minutes all the players return their rocks to the center of the circle.

V. With eyes open or closed each person feels the rocks in the center of the circle and retrieves his own.

Alternatively the group leader can give each person a rock.

Listening to Crystaltalk

Crystal balls have existed for thousands of years. These perfect spheres have been the source of many legends. Andrew Lang, an English scholar and spiritualist, spent a great deal of time looking into the properties of crystals. In a typical no-nonsense British way, Lang described a simple technique of scrying a crystal ball: "It is best to go, alone, into a room, sit down with the back to the light, place the ball, at a just focus, in the lap on a dark dress, or a dark piece of cloth, try to exclude reflections, think of anything you please, and stare for, say, five minutes at the ball."[26]

In this game we begin with Lang's technique, but end with a twist.[27]

NEEDED: a small polished crystal.

I. When it is dark, go into a room that is quiet and relatively undisturbed.
II. Sit with candle at your back so that there is no reflection.
III. Hold a crystal quietly in your hands.
IV. Feel the crystal, its nooks and crannies.
V. Hold the crystal up to either ear.
VI. Close your eyes.
VII. Let your mind's ear listen to the crystal.
VIII. What is it saying?

At first this may seem difficult. Remember, you are using your mind's "ear." If you actually hear sounds, that's fine, but let whatever words you hear permeate your mind's ear. Remember, nobody can record the voices that we hear in our dreams, yet that does not mean we do not hear voices in our dreams. We hear these voices with the mind's ear, and in this game we try to do this in a waking state.

Pools of Water and Other Reflections

Three-quarters of our bodies, three-quarters of the earth's surface, is water. Little wonder that water has been used as a medium for scrying. The very fluidity of water suggests that it is a perfect vehicle for seeing shifting reality.

Pools of water present us with both two and three dimensions. Reflection is perceived on the surface of the water—in two dimensions. But there is the third dimension, depth, that lies below the surface of the water. It is in the depth of water that its mystery lies. It is in this dimension that the seer focuses.

Humans have replicated just about everything, including natural pools and lakes. Pools of water have been replicated in miniature—in bowls of water. In the Southwest, among the Tewa people, a medicine bowl becomes a lake in miniature. It becomes both the vessel and the vehicle of clairvoyance. It is called the *pokwi,* which means "lake" or "pool." According to the Tewas, the spirits of the lake follow the road to the ceremonial chamber, and from the ceremonial chamber they enter the bowl. The bowl is filled with water from the sacred springs: the white lake, the blue lake, and the red lake. The New Mexican Tewa shaman gazes into the medicine bowl filled with the sacred water and imbued with the essence of the spirits.[28]

The spirits speak through the water, through the vessel, and through the diviner. In Zimbabwe the Ila tribe also uses a bowl for scrying. For the practice of *Kuteka,* the Ila diviner fills a bowl with water and dissolves a substance in it to make the water black. In this case, it is both the blackness and the water that provide the vehicle for scrying. The inner vision of the diviner plays upon the water, and he sees things that are happening, will happen, or have happened at a distance.[29]

On the other side of the world, in Honduras, light and dark, solid and liquid interact to provide the medium for the diviner. A Honduran "seer," or *gariahati,* half fills a calabash with water. Then, by the light of a candle or a full moon, he can see a distant scene just as if it were a moving picture.[30]

For the islanders of the world, water is the most natural medium for scrying. In the Pacific, among the native Marquesans, there is a folk legend about the cultural hero Kena. In the story, the mother of Kena fills a taro leaf with water, looks into it, and seeing the lower regions, dives into the water and arrives at the nether lands. In modern times one of the most common methods of second sight for Marquesan diviners is to gaze into liquid. Sometimes the diviner fills a taro leaf with water, gazes into it, and detects thieves.[31]

There is a mystery to water. It can flow endlessly through the crevices of mountains and wear them down to plains. It can be solid and impenetrable. It can become gas and vapor and disappear before our eyes. It is in clouds, rivers, and icebergs. The scryer uses the medium of water and works with the darkness of night or the light of a candle or the moon. Sometimes the diviner looks at both the water and the material suspended in it to see clearly. In Madagascar, for example, diviners put water in a clear glass bottle and shake it vigorously. The Madagascan seer will then study the movement of the water, its cloudiness, and the way in which sediment collects. The variations are endless and each diviner has his own set of practices and rules.[32]

Sometimes the natural liquid of the scryer, such as saliva, is combined with the liquid of the vessel to create the divination vehicle. Among the Wolof people in Gambia, a great hunter is a student of divination. And one method of divination among this African people is called *njamba*. The hunter places special roots in a bowl of water, recites a spell, and spits into the water. He then looks into the water for game, and it is said that he sees the eyes of the animals in the immediate vicinity.[33]

In the frigid northland, water constitutes even more than three-quarters of the surface. For these islanders of the Arctic, ice, the solid form of water, is also a means of scrying.

Vision on the Lake: The Dalai Lama

A high lama of the Gyu monastery in Lhasa was sent to look for the reincarnation of the Dalai Lama. In Tibetan Buddhism, oracles and visions are necessary to find the boy who has been brought into this world as the embodiment of the previous Dalai Lama.

The lama set out from his monastery to the Heavenly Lake of the Goddess Pan-Dan Lha-Mo. Arriving at the lake, the lama found it covered with snow. The winters of Tibet lasted many months of the year and were hard and icy. The lama stared at the snow-covered lake, searching for a sign. The tempestuous Himalayan winds came to his aid. Within moments a high wind arose and dispersed the snow, leaving the ice clear before the lama. Staring into the ice of the sacred lake, the lama saw an image. It was an image of a house and surrounding land. He saw a peach tree in flower, even though the season of peach blossoms was several months past. In the ice of the Heavenly Lake of the Goddess Pan-Dan Lha-Mo the lama had seen the location of the boy who was the reincarnation of the Dalai Lama.

The lama soon found the house he had seen in the lake. And with it he found the peach tree, strangely blooming out of season. He also found the future Thirteenth Dalai Lama. All this did the lama from the Gyu monastery see in the frozen water of the sacred lake.[34]

—Sir Charles Bell, *Portrait of the Dalai Lama*

Mixing Oil and Water

Everybody knows that oil and water don't mix. Long before the time of Aladdin, ancient Middle Eastern psychics, called baru, mixed oil and water to see what they could see. These baru were a skilled and respected group in ancient Babylon. They were not fortune-tellers. Rather, they were people who would use their imaginations and their inner sight to "alchemize" water and oil into a vision. These Babylonian and Hittite seers would pour water into a cup of oil or oil into a cup of water.[35]

In this game we mix oil and water and watch as they unmix. This is best done in a quiet atmosphere either at night with a candle lighting the glass or during the day with the light of the sun.

NEEDED: a large clear glass bowl or very large glass such as a brandy snifter, water, and salad oil.

  I. Wash the bowl or glass in warm water and let the water just flow over it.
  II. Fill the bowl or glass with water, leaving about a finger joint of room at the top.
  III. Take a pure grade of salad oil, like olive, corn, sesame, or canola, and pour a thin film on the water. Be sure not to cover the entire surface of the water.
  IV. Close your eyes, roll your eyeballs up toward the top of your head, and think of a rainbow fountain of water coming out the top of your head. (That's an ancient method for instantly clearing the mind).
  V. Take several deep breaths in through the nose and out through the mouth.
  VI. Open your eyes and look at the water and oil.
  VII. What patterns do you see?
  VIII. What shapes do they suggest?
  IX. What feelings are you experiencing?

An alternative way of doing this is to ask a particular question and see how the shapes correspond to an answer. Still another alternative is to use candle wax and drop it carefully in the water and check out the shapes.

Well, Well, Well

In this, we take what we get from a well or a pond. It is based on an ancient Greek form of scrying that involved gazing into the water of a well.[36]

NEEDED: a clear glass bowl, paper, and a writing implement.

  I. Take a clear glass bowl to a well or a pond.
  II. Find a comfortable place to sit down near the well or the pond.

III. Take in the air, the earth, the water. Breathe deeply.

IV. Close your eyes.

V. Think of a question, if you wish, or imagine that you are putting all your thoughts in a little box and putting the box at the end of the pond.

VI. Dip the bowl into the water so that it is at least half-full.

VII. Let whatever is in there become part of the picture.

VIII. Look at the surface of the bowl.

IX. What patterns do you see?

X. Look deeper into the bowl.

XI. What is going on under the surface?

XII. Make a list of ten words that describe what you see.

XIII. Put the words together in a meaningful sentence or phrase.

Scrying the Bear in the Tracks

It was deep in the middle of winter in the icy reaches of Labrador. The old hunter was looking for traces of a bear. It was deep in the middle of winter and the traces of the bear had been swept away by the icy winds and lost in a deep snowdrift. All that the old hunter saw were the footprints of the bear immediately around him. But the footprints led nowhere. It was deep in the middle of winter and the old hunter needed to find the bear without its traces and with only the few tracks surrounding him.

The old man squatted down next to the bear tracks. He pulled his blanket over his head, creating darkness. In the darkness, under his blanket, the old man concentrated his gaze on the footprints. He began to see beyond the tracks in front of him. He began to see deeper than the "reflection" of the bear in front of him. After a while he saw prints leading from his place, leading in a certain direction. The old man followed the prints that he had seen and soon found the bear and killed it.[37]

One for the Road: If at First You Don't Succeed, Scry, Scry Again

The number of vehicles for scrying is almost infinite. The object is not so important as the way in which we gaze into it. In this game we create our own vehicle for scrying.

NEEDED: an object that has some meaning for you. It must be smaller than a bread box and preferably shiny.

I. Place your chosen object in a position where it can remain safely for a few days.
II. At twilight sit down and face the object.
III. Focus on an imaginary spot a foot or two *beyond* the object.
IV. Let your thoughts wander.
V. Gaze "through" the object for at least ten minutes.
VI. What thoughts go through your mind? What do you "see"?
VII. Repeat this again in the morning.
VIII. Ask a question that is important to you.
IX. Gaze through the object.
X. What images or thoughts or feelings come to you?

When we scry into an object, the object becomes a vehicle. We are looking beyond the object and our reflection in it. We are looking beyond appearances into a deeper reality. In a sense, any shiny or reflective object can be a vehicle for scrying. Seeing beyond appearances is key to scrying. It is also the essence of all intuitive sight.

We scry when we look beyond our surface reflection, past the image of our face. There is a contradiction here. For, in order to look beyond our reflection, we need a surface that reflects us.

Humans are a curious race. We have always wanted to see what is beneath and beyond the surface. We have learned that there is a difference between appearance and reality. Scrying helps us to go beyond appearance. It helps us see our own reality more clearly. Mirrors on the wall, pools, plates, and crystal balls are all vehicles for us to see by using different sight. These reflective objects help us to reflect. And, in so doing, we can see the world in a new light with our individual vision.

CHAPTER 3

Stars, Stones, and Bones:
Skeletons of the Universe

There is nothing permanent except change.
—*Greek proverb*

I went to the rock to hide my face
The rock cried out "no hiding place!"
—*American spiritual*

THE natural world is changeable. Flowers wilt. Summer turns into snow. Children grow up, grow old, and wither. There are few things in this world that have the appearance of eternity. From the time that people realized that they were mortal, they have searched for signs of permanence.

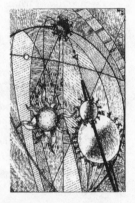

For the earliest humans the stars seemed to be eternal. Their patterns were predictable and appeared to be unchangeable. On earth, the stones, rocks, and sands of the beaches seemed to have a certain permanence. Rocks were the symbol of the eternal. In Greek and Latin the word for rock is *petra,* which also translates as the name Peter. Jesus, in one of the most famous puns of history, said to his foremost disciple, "thou art Peter, and upon this rock I will build my church."

Stones seemed to last for all eternity. A stone marking might remain in the lore of a people for generations without changing. By contrast, flesh is soft and weak. It has come to represent change and impermanence. But bones are something else. The only thing that remains of our bodies and the bodies of other vertebrates after the rest is gone is the bones.

We find stars when we look upward; looking down we find stones. When we look within we find bones. Stars, stones, and bones—these are the symbols of permanence.

The Fixed Stars of Heaven

> *The bay-trees in our country are all withered*
> *And meteors fright the fixed stars of heaven*
> *The pale-faced moon looks bloody on the earth*
> *And lean-looked prophets whisper fearful change . . .*
> *The signs forerun the death or fall of kings.*
> —*William Shakespeare*, Richard II

> *We have an entire sky within us, our fiery strength and*
> *heavenly origin: Luna which symbolizes the continuous motion*
> *of soul and body, Mars speed and Saturn slowness, the Sun God,*
> *Jupiter law, Mercury reason, and Venus humanity.*
> —*Marsilio Ficino, fifteenth-century Florentine astrologer*[1]

> *Science, then, draws us into that unity with nature, the*
> *sensation of which has long been regarded as a quality of art,*
> *and shows us why the universe might appear to be both*
> *intelligible and beautiful. As a matter of cold empirical fact, as*
> *independent from our mystical yearnings as we know how to get,*
> *the universe presents itself as all of a piece and tells us that we*
> *are part of it. The big bang was about as unified an event as one*
> *could imagine, and we were* there. *Every electron in the synapses*
> *of every human (and inhuman) thought, every atom of our blood*
> *and bones, every* here *was* there. *That was a long time ago, but*
> *the unity of the universe remains with us, if only as a species of*
> *remembrance, sensed through art and articulated through*
> *science.*
> —*Timothy Ferris,* Space Shots:
> The Beauty of Nature Beyond Earth[2]

An ancient philosopher once said, "You are another world in miniature and have in you Sol and Luna and even the stars."[3] We do have an entire sky within us, and a galaxy as well. We have a universe within us. And we are also the microcosm of that universe.

This is not just poignant poetry or philosophy. It is scientifically true that we are the universe. We are made up of that same material that makes up our universe. Most scientists accept the idea that the universe was created in one big expansive bang. Everything that came into existence at that time still exists. It exists in different forms, perhaps, but it still exists. We are physically part of that instant of creation.

The sky probably still glowed red well before the setting of the sun in those evenings of our ancient ancestors. The meteoric dust that surrounded the earth during the age of dinosaurs was still present when our forebears looked to the heavens.

Nomadic Siberian tribes wandered the Northern Hemisphere. In the evening they tried to figure out the language of the planets and the stars. During the day they read the language of the clouds. As their lives were intertwined with the sun, the moon, the clouds, and the seasons, so did our ancient relatives try to see all of this as one and inseparable.

For these nomadic tribes all was in flux. They wandered from place to place and learned from the world around them. It was out of the wandering of our nomadic ancestors that the oldest book in the world came into existence, the *I Ching,* or *Book of Changes.*

For the last several millennia the Chinese have seen the reflection of their world in the stars. The ancient authors of the *Book of Changes* looked at the world around them—tides, animals, cycles of the seasons, stars—and sought to find how all of these related to patterns in families and society.[4] Later it became a function of a state bureaucratic office to determine the way in which the stars affected society. A group of officials called *Pao-chang* came into existence. These men were responsible for reading from the stars the fate of the earth.[5] Out of this came Chinese astrology and an entire system of divination that saw Heaven and Earth, society, and nature as an interrelated whole.

For the ancient Chinese everything on earth was a reflection of divine form. To the Chinese the sun was the male principle in the heavens, the moon the female, and the stars and planets examples of their earthly representatives. Thus, the heavens were a textbook that was meant to be deciphered.[6]

Long before modern physics, the ancients knew that we were born of the stars. The world was but a reflection of the cosmos, a universe in miniature. To see the earth as a mirror of the heavens is a concept shared by many peoples. On the highlands of Guatemala, diviners lay out patterns with grains of corn. The most basic earthly treasure of these Mayan descendants is used to re-create galaxies on the earth. These circles and shapes of corn are then used as instruments of divination.[7]

From earliest recorded history, people have used the stars as a way of understanding themselves and their times. This is the origin of astrology, which literally means study (*logy*) of the stars (*astro*). Perhaps no practice of divination is more widespread than the various practices of astrology.

In ancient Ireland diviners constructed mounds at Newgrange that accurately showed the times when the sun was highest in the sky—the winter and summer solstices. The ancient Irish looked to the skies to conduct both their spiritual and their temporal affairs.[8]

It is the Chinese and Indian people that have developed the most ancient form of star study. In China, as early as the twelfth century B.C., official diviners looked at the position of the stars, the clouds, the sun, and the moon as indicators of conditions on earth.[9] In India astrology was developed alongside the study of natural phenomena. The observation of the stars was connected to the study of the weather, the birds, and the trees.[10] From East to West astrology spread. It is found in ancient Peru and Guatemala in the Aztec and Mayan civilizations, where it developed to a sophisticated level. Perhaps the use of the stars as a divinatory tool was the first major global exchange.[11]

First Light: Our Time of Birth

First impressions are important. Almost all astrology is based on the time of birth when we take our first breath. What we take in is important. When we breathe in, we inspire the universe. After all, "inspiration" is just another word for taking breath.

We come into the world as living and breathing antennae. We feel the world around us. To be sure, we may not be able to make much rational sense out of that world in those first few moments of our lives. But we feel it.

We have first impressions of the sun, moon, seasons, and climate. We take it all in. Here we try to replay our first impressions of that time when we arrived on this earthly scene. This game works best when two or more people participate.

NEEDED: paper and a writing implement.

    I. Write down the date of your birth.

    II. Using single words, write down the characteristics of that time of year as you know it. (For example, if you were born on August 4, 1968, concentrate on August.)

    III. What is the temperature?

    IV. What is the sun like?

    V. What feelings do you associate with that time of year (other than your birthday)?

    VI. Draw a line down the center of the page and create two columns. At the top of one write "positive," and at the top of the other write "negative."

VII. In the positive column write down all the things that you like about that time of year.

VIII. In the negative column write down all the things that you dislike about that time of year.

IX. Do this for at least ten minutes. Do not stop to check or edit—just keep on going.

X. Now examine your notes and describe what kind of person would be characterized by this period of time.

When you have finished your first lists, you might compare them with another person's lists and see how they are different. Two players born during the same time of the year should compare their lists as well.

A variation of this game is to have a group of people focus on the birth time of one person in the group. Everybody then offers impressions of that time of year and the qualities of the person born at that time.

Let the Sun Shine[12]

In this game we find that the energy of the sun is not only outside of us but inside as well. As the ancients saw humans as microcosms of the universe, so we can find the sun within us. This can be played on a clear summer day or a cloudy autumn afternoon. It can be played rain or shine.

I. Go outside during the day.

II. Focus your energy on the sun and get a sense of its energy. (If the sun is bright, look at it indirectly.)

III. Feel the qualities of the sun.

IV. Does it nourish? Soothe? Stimulate?

V. Close your eyes.

VI. Feel the sun in your heart.

VII. If it could speak to you, what would it say to you now?

VIII. What part of you is sunlike?

IX. What parts do you like?

X. What parts do you dislike?

This could be an enjoyable ritual to play on your birthday. After all, our birth date was when we first drew breath and first saw the rays of the sun.

Try it on the night of a full moon. Then you would focus on the moon and its energy instead of the sun.

How the Pleiades Were Born (or the Boys Kept on Dancing)

Once there were seven boys. They were fine lads, honest and true of heart. But they used to spend all of their time dancing. All day long they did nothing but dance around in a circle beating their drums, singing, leaping.

The parents of the boys were concerned. At first they tried to get the boys to stop their ceaseless dancing. They told the boys to obey and stop dancing. The boys continued to dance.

At last, the parents decided that it was time to do something about this continuous irresponsible dancing. They determined that they would force their sons to stop.

It was in the black of night when the parents went in force to where the boys were dancing. The boys always danced in the same place.

It was in the black of night. Even the moon hid her face when the parents came to stop their children from dancing.

The boys were dancing around and around. The drum beat swifter and harder than a thousand hearts. The boys danced faster and faster. And the drum beat swifter and harder than the hooves of a thousand horses.

The will of the fathers was strong as they approached their dancing sons. They would stop the dance with the force of their very arms. They would see that the boys returned to the ways of their parents.

As the parents drew close to the dancing place, they stopped as suddenly as a deer that scents the danger of the nearby panther. The parents stopped but the boys continued to dance.

The parents stopped because the boys began to rise into the air. They danced and rose into the air. They rose and they danced. They danced and they rose. The parents watched as their sons danced and rose into the black sky, lighting it up with their drum and their dance. There, in the dark umbrella of night the boys would stay for all time.

The boys still dance in the black sky of night. The smallest star is said by some to be the drum. But others think this star is only the smallest of the boys.

—A tale told by the Cherokees[13]

Reflect Yourself in the Sky: Creating Our Own Constellations

There are thousands of stories about the constellations in the night sky. For centuries people have seen themselves in the stars. They have told stories of men and women, gods and goddesses, who have lived their lives and struggles on earth and were borne to the heavens as stars. Such stories depict the origin of the zodiac, or astrological symbols.

Often, the constellations seem to only faintly resemble what they are supposed to represent. Recently, on Candolim Beach in Goa, India, I looked up to the sky and saw a fantastic sprinkling of stars. There was Orion's belt. For years, I had tried to picture just how the constellation portrayed Orion. Then, in a flash of insight, I realized that the three stars of Orion's belt resembled the top of Bart Simpson's head. Now I will never forget the Constellation Bart.

In this game we create our own stories, symbols, and constellations.

NEEDED: paper and a writing implement.

   I. Wait for a clear night with a star-filled sky.
   II. Pick three or four groups of stars. These do not have to be a recognized constellation.
   III. Do a rough sketch of the group of stars on a piece of paper.
   IV. Create a figure (animal, vegetable, mineral, or whatever) using your rough sketch as the general framework. This is similar to the children's game of connect the dots.
   V. Make up a story for each one of the figures that you have created. Tell how each figure came to be and how it came to find its place in the sky.
   VI. Create a story that connects the various figures.
   VII. How do the stories reflect your life at this moment? Or what do these stories have to do with your life up to now?
   VIII. Check on the sky periodically to find the positions of your constellations.
   IX. How do they change?

Since there are millions of stars in the sky, this game might seem overwhelming at first. One suggestion is first to identify the stars that are brightest. Sketch them on your paper, then connect the "dots" and see if a picture evolves.

Whichever way a falling star travels the wind will follow.
—Ojibwa saying[14]

Since the stars have always been symbols of permanence, people become alarmed when there are changes in the heavens. Eclipses, comets, and falling stars are reminders that the appearance of permanence is quite different from the reality.

In India, ancient texts such as the sixth-century *Brhatsamhita* codified various celestial and atmospheric disturbances into a clear manual of omen interpretation.[15] A special branch of Indian omen reading called *ulkapata* specialized in reading atmospheric events such as solar and lunar eclipses, comets and shooting stars.[16]

Comets became an irregular reminder that even the heavens were subject to the forces of change. Halley's comet, in particular, became a source of foreboding from ancient times to the present. To be sure, Halley's comet did appear at peculiar times. It appeared in A.D. 218 preceding the death of the Roman Emperor Macrinus. In 451 it foretold the death of Attila. And in 1066 it foretold the Norman invasion of England, and its likeness was woven into the Bayeux tapestry.[17]

When we look into the sky on a clear night, we see thousands of little lights that illuminate the heavens. There are stars that have shined down on earth when it was still a mass of raging gases. They lit up the forests and swamps as giant reptiles looked for prey. They shined on the sleeping armies of Alexander the Great. They shined over the Hanging Gardens of Babylon. Shepherds watched them long before the birth of Christ. Ancient sailors guided their small boats by the lights of these stars.

When we look into the sky on a clear night, we are looking into the past. Much of the light of the stars we see takes thousands, even millions, of years to reach us. Some of these stars have exploded into astral dust and no longer exist. Others have burned out and exist in space as dead masses. Yet we see them still. We see that which no longer exists. The light we see is ancient. We see the past in the present.

Even in our very bodies the past is manifested in the present. Even in our physical being is the persistence of memory. DNA is the building block of life itself. It is both a genetic memory of our ancestors within us and the basic physical unit of our bodies. It is the "then" within now.

Albert Einstein showed us that time is not a line. It does not go chugging along from past to present to future. It folds and bends and curves. The past exists within the now. In our universe. In our planet. In ourselves.

Astronomers are cosmic historians. The galaxies that they see are millions of years old. The photographic plates that they develop are sensitized by light older than the bones of dinosaurs. Astronomers call this "look-back time." For, in looking out across the universe, in looking out at the stars, they are looking back in time.[18]

Light from the Stars—Footprints in the Sand

Many years ago I lived in the gardener's cottage on an estate on Long Island. It was unique in that there were two hundred acres of virgin land in my backyard. I would walk in the fields and dunes behind the house at least four mornings every week. There were pheasants and field mice, tricolored blackbirds, and every kind of northeastern American bird imaginable.

One warm day in late April as I was making my morning constitutional I saw footprints in the sand. I felt a bit like Robinson Crusoe when he saw the footprints of Friday on the beach. It was my backyard and someone else had been there. Had been? Was? I was confused for a moment. The footprints were there but the person wasn't.

It was an archaeological discovery. The person was still there in the form of his or her footprints. It was another case of the presence of the past. We all leave our footprints and live among the footprints of those who have gone before us. We live in a universe of footprints. Some are invisible. Many are accessible. If we allow ourselves, we can see the footprints. We can feel them.

The stars give us the wisdom of their light. They show us the presence of the past in the moment. We can find examples of the presence of the past all around us. Walking along the beach, you can see footprints in the sand which are tangible reminders of the presence of another who has passed by.

Old houses are perfect subjects for this exercise. Basements of old houses are excellent. Old barns are good, too. Use your imagination and find a place where there is a clear presence of the past.

NEEDED: paper and a writing implement.

    I. Find a spot where you can be relatively undisturbed. Close your eyes and take a few deep breaths. Be aware of smells and how the air touches your skin.

    II. Visualize this place before now.
       a. Imagine hearing people who might have been here before.
       b. Imagine hearing other sounds from this place.
       c. Do you have any feelings about this place?

    III. Re-create a time when this place was much younger.
       a. If it is a building, imagine how it was when it was new.
       b. Populate it with people.
       c. Let other sensations come to you.

    IV. If you are doing this alone, write about this place as it was and what the people were like. Do this as if you were there.

V. If you are doing this with someone else, take roles and, for a
moment, pretend that you are in this place long ago.

Under the clear crystal nights of the American Southwest, a Navajo diviner sits quietly. When all murmurs of the night have ceased and there is nothing but silence, he places a crystal in his hand and chants. He prays to the Gila
monster and holds his arm and hand outward in line with the moon or a star
and gazes unblinking at the crystal. Soon he sees something. He closes his
hand upon what he has seen. He sees a line of light, a ray of "lightning" from
the star to the crystal, so that the ground around him appears light. The diviner
is a stargazer. His mission is the diagnosis of illness.[19]

The stars are a source of wisdom and guidance to the Navajo people. They
use stargazing to find the source of misfortune or disease or even where stolen
goods have gone. The stargazer will use rock crystal, translucent flint, pieces
of bottle glass, colored broken marbles, or cut glass to scry the sky. The gazer
will gaze at stars of first magnitude and might even call upon others to help.
All fires in the Navajo dwelling are extinguished and all are asked to stare at
a particular star. No blinking is allowed. Finally a vision is seen in the star.[20]

The reclining group of stargazers might see the outlines of a distinct picture of a place. Or they might see a house or a rider. Any image is then interpreted in accordance with the question that was posed.[21]

Stargazing can be practiced by anyone who wants to learn. An intelligent
person can learn it in a day. All that is needed is a star to "steer" the diviner.[22]

Gazing Through the Stars

*The Navajo stargazer is an ordinary person. He has trained himself to focus
on a star and trust his vision. That's what divination is about: focus and trust. Here
we try a similar technique to that of the Navajo stargazer.*

NEEDED: a piece of clear crystal, glass, bottle, or a marble.

I. Wait for a clear night with lots of stars.
II. Find a comfortable place and lie down facing the stars.
III. Think of a question.
IV. Pick a star, any star, the first star that grabs your attention.
V. Focus on that star.
VI. Close your eyes and take a deep breath through the nose and ex-
hale through the mouth. Do this about ten times.
VII. Open your eyes and focus on that star again.

VIII. Take the clear piece of crystal or glass or marble and hold it at arm's length between you and the star.

IX. Look through the crystal at the star. Focus your eyes on the star through the crystal so that the crystal is out of focus.

X. Try not to blink.

XI. Let whatever images come to your mind.

XII. How does this relate to your question?

The Stones Alive

> Now! Now You Provider, who made the Stones alive, I have just come to question You.
>
> —Cherokee shamanic prayer[23]

For Native Americans the earth, sky, plants, fish, animals, and stones all speak. Nearly five hundred traditions and tribes of Native Americans exist in North America and all of them have their own medicine wheels and ways of interpreting them. Roughly speaking, a medicine wheel is a representation of the forces of the cosmos and the earth depicted in a circle laid out on the ground. The medicine wheel of the Senecas, for example, features twelve directions laid out like the face of a clock, with each direction symbolizing a certain color, cycle of truth, and birth month. Each direction represents a pathway any human may follow to find inner peace. A medicine wheel can also act as map or dictionary that will allow a person to understand the languages of Plant People, Stone People, Creature-Beings, and the elements of nature as well as objects that nature gives to each person who requests them.[24]

Native Americans feel that the stones are alive. They are a tribe unto themselves. Every person is connected to other members of the Planetary Family, such as the Stone People and Plant People. And thus, we are never alone.[25]

For Native Americans the Stone Tribe is the oldest and most enduring of all those who have lived on the earth. They are the record keepers. And since, for Native Americans, age and wisdom are connected, it is no surprise that the stones are the wisest of the tribes. In this tradition we look to the stones to find out where we have come from and where we are heading.

Native Americans feel that the Stone People provide signposts and have their own simple language that is written all over the earth. Stones are present everywhere and provide direction for those people who are interested in examining them.[26]

It is not only the Native Americans who have a tradition of watching stones. The Greeks felt that all nature was alive. Every stone, every tree, contained a living spirit. So, too, did Chinese natural science consider the stones to be living things.[27]

Stones on the Road

Have you ever walked along a road or path and stubbed your toe on a stone or rock? Rarely would we consider that to be a gift. However, there are cultures that take such chance meetings to be gifts. For the Thonga people of southern Africa, a stone found in a road or distant place was a sign of fortune. Such stones were used in divination practices by the Thongas.[28]

For Native Americans the markings of a stone give direction to the person who discovers it and reveals hidden talents that the person may possess. The actual markings on found stones are used by some Native Americans to find meaning in their lives. For example, a straight vertical line on a stone can mean the power to conquer challenges in the material world. The outline of a square can represent firm foundations, and so on.[29] In this game we read the markings of the stones.

    I. Spend a day just being aware of stones that you find in your path.
    II. Pick up two or three of these.
    III. Notice their markings. Study their shapes. Notice if there are lines and indentations.
    IV. What pictures or images are evoked by these lines and shapes?
    V. Imagine the stone to be a creature—a stone creature.
    VI. How do you relate to this stone creature?
    VII. Imagine that this stone creature is coming to you with a specific message for you.
    VIII. What would it be?

Many Native Americans felt that some of the Stone People could be used for healing or for fuel. Others still for protection. Some would be used as brilliant colored gems. But all stones were also repositories of wisdom for those willing to learn.[30]

There are stones all around us. We cannot avoid them. Indeed, we can sometimes trip over them. The natural geology of our area presents us with the stone tools of divination. And with no culture has this been truer than with the Native American.

In Cherokee tradition stones were instruments of divination. For the Cherokees of the southern Alleghenies stones abounded. The Cherokee shaman would use crystals and small stones of various shapes and colors to discover lost articles.[31] The Eastern Cherokees used five different sizes of divining stones. Each size had its own purpose, from the largest, used in war divination, to the smallest, used for determining the time allotted for anyone to live.[32] The Oklahoma Cherokees still use two small stones, about the size of acorns. The diviner clenches one in each hand and a small prayer, or *i:gawe:sdi,* is recited four times. The diviner then opens his hands and observes the stones. If the one in the right hand moves, the answer is favorable. But if the one in the left hand moves, there is bad news.[33]

Among the Punyaro Indians of Ecuador, stones are a basic part of a diviner's repertoire. Four stones are used, each painted a different color. One of the stones has a face of a person, another the face of a bull, a third the face of a pig, and the last the face of a sheep. The reader puts the stones in the form of a cross and lights a candle at each one. By looking into the candles above the stones, he will see the answer to the questions posed.[34]

People can collaborate with stones to bring fortune. The Navajos place a stone or piece of turquoise on cairns along trails throughout the surrounding country. Over time, these stones accumulate to form hills. These hills of stones are visible for miles in the flat high desert lands. They mark the trails and are often as high as a man on horseback.[35]

As the Navajos use stones to guide them along the trails of this world, so have stones been used as guides to the outer worlds. The Neolithic Irish, for example, built stone mounds in the Boyne Valley over five thousand years ago. They are among the world's oldest remaining buildings. One of these mounds aligns with the rising sun in the winter solstice. At that time, the light of the rising sun enters through a hole into an inner chamber of the structure. At another stone site the rays of the setting sun enters the chamber. These were stone observatories that allowed humans to connect their earth with the stars. Similar stone structures have been found throughout the world from Easter Island to South America.[36]

Stones are oracles. Among the Mandans of the west-central United States, medicine rocks foretold what was to happen during the year. A group of Mandans would visit the medicine stone every spring and sometimes in the summer. They would consult it, pray, smoke, and retire for the night. The next day they would take down on parchment the message conveyed by the stone and bring it to the village where the elders would interpret it.[37]

The Rock Cried Out

Tara was the ancient capital of Ireland. One day, Conn, a renowned king of Ireland, was in Tara after the other kings had left. As was his custom, Conn went on to the highest point of the city. He mounted the rampart of Tara preceded by his three druids, Mael, Block, and Bluiccnu, along with Eochu, Corbb, and Cesarn, his *fili,* or poet-seers. Conn regularly climbed the rampart every day lest the people of the fairy mounds take Ireland unawares.

This day, as Conn mounted the rampart, he saw a stone at his feet and trod upon it. The stone screamed so loudly that it was heard throughout Tara. Conn asked his *fili* why the stone had screamed and what manner of stone it was.

After a period of meditation and reflection, the poet-seer answered his king. The name of the rock was Fal. It had come from Inis Fail to Tara in the country of Fal. It would go to Teltown where a fair of games would always be held. Any prince who should not find it on the last day of the week of the Fair of Teltown would die within the year. Further, said the *fili,* the number of cries that the stone had uttered under Conn's feet signified the number of kings of his seed who should rule Ireland. Conn asked his poet-seer to tell him how many of his descendants the stone had said would rule Ireland. But the seer, wise in the way of stones and kings, told him, "I am not destined to tell them to you."

—Ancient Celtic tale[38]

Them Bones: The Voice of the Turtle

> *Them bones, them bones, them dry bones*
> *Now hear the word of the Lord.*
> —*African American spiritual*

> *Let us reverently consult the tortoise concerning the king.*
> —*Oracle bone incantation, China, ca.1400 B.C.*[39]

> *And he burnt the bones of the priests upon their altars, and*
> *cleansed Judah and Jerusalem.*
> —*II Chronicles 34:5*

Picture this: The elder of the family sits quietly and meditatively at a table. It is getting dark and the evening meal is finished. The rest of the family sits quietly around the table. The elder gets up and goes to the window. There, drying in the sun, is a bone from the fowl that was consumed by the family the day before. It is a specific bone, taken from the sternum of the animal. It is the same kind of bone that was used by his father, his father's father, and his father's father's father, back through countless generations.

The elder takes the bone and walks over to the youngest member of the family. The child already knows the ritual, having participated in it numerous times, and takes hold of one end of the distinctively bifurcated bone. Both father and child close their eyes for a moment. Then they both pull hard on the bone. It breaks. "My wish! My wish!" shouts the child as she sees that the larger part of the bone broke off in her hand.

The instrument of divination is the "wishbone" of a chicken. Everybody recognizes the wishbone ceremony. Practiced in millions of households throughout the Western world, it is one of the many such rituals that have involved bones as instruments of divination.

Bones have been instruments of divination throughout recorded time. In the midst of World War I a westerner rode along the south bank of the Yuan River in China, north of Chang-te in the province of Hunan. It was there that he came across some bone relics that had been around for three thousand years. These were the oracle bones of China. These were mostly the plastron, or underbody, of a tortoise.[40]

The art of bone consultation was already an ancient practice a millennium before the birth of Christ. The Chinese *Shu Ching,* or *Book of History,* told of how the shell of the tortoise was cut and a red-hot metal rod applied to the shell. This caused cracks to form on the surface of the shell. The diviner would then read these cracks to find the answer to a question.[41] The scorching of the shell of the tortoise became synonymous with divination. To this day, the Chinese character for divination, *pu,* is a vertical line with a shorter lateral branching from it—an actual illustration of the cracks in the tortoiseshell.[42]

It was from the observation of the world and cosmos that the ancient Chinese formulated their principles of divination. But it is significant that it is from the cracks in the shell of a tortoise that the *I Ching* was supposed to have evolved. According to the legend, the Emperor Fu Hsi studied the patterns on the shell of a tortoise and came up with the first eight trigrams, or ideograms, that became the basis of both the book and the divinatory practice.[43]

Tortoises were not always available. Soon Chinese oracles were using the scapulae (shoulder blades) of deer and other animals, and once again, the bone was dried out with heat and the pattern of the cracks was read.[44] By the third millennium B.C. there were specialists in bone-crack reading, and diviners used deer, sheep, pigs, and cattle in addition to the traditional tortoiseshells.[45]

The practice spread throughout Asia. Tibetan shamans still read the scapulae of sheep.[46]

Throughout the world the bone of preference has been the scapula. The practice has become known as "scapulimancy," or the reading of the scapula.

Central Asia has always been a center of scapulimancy. In Turkey there were specialists called *yagrinci* who read from the scapulae of sheep. In Mongolia the scapulimancers were known as *dallaci*. The Kazakhs used the shoulder blade of a goat, the Yakuts used a stag. Among all of these, the bone was considered to be the essential organ, the source of life and resurrection.[47]

Scapulimancy is also found in Celtic tradition, where the Gaelic word *slinneanchachd* means "signs from the shoulder." The Celts would slaughter a black sheep or pig and study the marks on the shoulder blade.[48]

Bone reading still takes place in Asia, Africa, Europe, and the Americas. In the mountains of Greece, for example, Christianity and scapulimancy intertwine. The sheep is an instrument of the divine. The markings on the shoulder of a sheep are interpreted as a message from God. The Greek diviner, or *sarakatsanos,* pours out the blood of his sheep in the same way as Christ poured out his blood to open a way between people and God. In Christian tradition the sheep, and particularly the lamb, is symbolic of innocence and purity. The sheep becomes a means of establishing a relationship between man and God. Eating its flesh is a form of communion. And, for the mountain Greeks, God communicates with men through the markings on the shoulder blade of the sheep.[49]

The reading of bones has traveled across continents separated by bodies of water. The practice of scapulimancy in Mongolia is almost identical with its practice by the Naskapi Algonquins in Labrador, where the reading of bones reached its most complex and intricate form. Among the Naskapis scapulimancy is a basic part of everyday life. The Naskapis live by hunting caribou. Over the centuries, reading the scorched bones of caribou has become a fixed part of Naskapi divination. It is not an art restricted to the few; it is practiced by the hunters of the tribe.

The Naskapi diviner uses the bones of friendly animals. For him, as well as for diviners in many other cultures, the spirits of the animals live in the bones. Given proper respect, the animal spirits can act as guides. The Naskapi hunter takes the shoulder blade or pelvis of a fur-bearing animal and subjects it to heat. The blackened spots, cracks, and breaks are interpreted as a kind of map that features rivers, trails, and valleys. The hunter might take the pelvis bone of a beaver to coincide with the shape of his trapping ground. The hunter would then ask which river he should follow to obtain big game. The cracks on the bone would indicate the answer.[50]

The use of bones as maps is one common function of scapulimancy. Throughout the Arctic and northern Asia, diviners read the cracks and fissures with all the clarity of an American Automobile Association Trip-Tik.[51] For the Reindeer Chukchis of the Arctic Circle, the burned shoulder blade of a domesticated reindeer can indicate where the community should move. Mountains, land, sea, and underground are represented by the various parts and shapes of the bone.[52]

Ham Shanks and Turtle Cracks: Trip-Tiks from a Bone

It is not often that we can find the shoulder blade of a large animal. However, the pork, lamb, or beef roast is not that uncommon, unless you are a vegetarian. The next time you have such a roast, save the bone. Or, if you are a vegetarian, simply go to a meat market and ask for a large bone.

This game is adapted from practices of the Naskapis, Mongolians, Iranians, Greeks, Celts—and just about every other culture that practiced bone reading.

NEEDED: a fire in a fireplace or a bonfire, a beef, lamb, or pork bone, and a responsible adult.

    I. Focus on a question that is important to you concerning direction in your life.
    II. Close your eyes.
    III. Throw the bone in the fire.
    IV. Wait for the bone to heat and crack.
    V. Remove the bone from the fire (carefully).
    VI. Look at the burns and cracks and fissures.
    VII. Check out the bone as if it were a topographical map. Pay attention to the bumps and depressions.
    VIII. What picture can you draw from this?
    IX. What direction is indicated?
    X. You have your answer.

The use of bones as maps is only a small part of bone divination. There are as many methods of using bones as there are cultures. Among the Inland Tlingit people of the Arctic, a young girl might listen to the ear bone of a salmon to find out whom she should marry. A Tlingit girl on the coast might throw the humerus of a seal in the air and watch just how it lands to find out who her husband will be.[53]

In Mongolia, among the Torgut people, one could use a bone as a listening and divining device. If you had a question, you would take a burned shoulder blade and hide near a stranger's tent and then listen through the bone to what the people inside were saying. The Torguts thought that the people inside the tent would give the answer to your question in the course of their conversation.[54]

Bone reading is common all across the continent of Africa in a variety of forms.[55] Among the Zulus in southern Africa, a specialized group of bone diviners, *amathambo,* use the bones of wild animals in their consultations. The elephant, the lion, and smaller animals provide their bones for the oracle. If, for example, the bone of an elephant comes to rest on the bone of a hyena, the diviner will ask what the elephant and hyena have to say to each other and to humans at that point.[56]

Many other African diviners use the knucklebones of sheep. From below the Sahara to Mozambique the position of knucklebones in a reading determines the direction in which an individual is going.

The Thonga tribe of South Africa has an intricate system of using bones of domestic animals to indicate people in the village. The Thongan diviner uses the bones of five kinds of he-goats, from an old castrated male goat, representing an old man, to a suckling kid, representing a little boy. In the same way, he uses five bones from she-goats, ranging from an old she-goat, representing an old woman, to a suckling she-goat, representing a virgin.[57] The diviner throws the bones and reads their position. The variations are almost infinite. The reader looks at how the bones have fallen, in which direction they face, the disposition they take with respect to each other, and the relation of male and female bones to each other.[58]

In a variation of the Thongan bone reading, another South Africa group uses only four bones. These represent an old and young man and an old and young woman. Once again, the diviner reads the pattern created by the bones after they are thrown to the ground.[59]

Throwing Your Life Away: Bone Reading Adapted

Bone reading is part of our heritage—it's in our bones, so to speak. However, much of the Western world has lost its connection with the natural world. Most of us do not hunt or fish for our food. Bones come wrapped in plastic in the supermarket.

The basics of bone reading are still within our grasp. As the Thongan reader would find bones to represent aspects of life, so we can find objects that do the same. The key here is to find objects that are as basic to our lives as the bones of the caribou are to the Naskapis or the bones of the sheep to the Thongas.

NEEDED: 6–12 small household objects (see description below), paper, and a writing implement.

   I. Think about objects that are an essential part of your life. These objects should be small and portable.

   II. Choose between six and twelve of these objects. It helps to use objects that are physical opposites: something hard and something soft, something sweet and something sour, a seed and a flower.

   III. Have each object represent a basic aspect or issue that has an opposite. Male-female, old-young, laughter-sadness are some time-tested possibilities. Have one object for each polarity; that is, one for male, one for female, etc.

   IV. Find a place that is quiet and relatively undisturbed.

   V. Either think of a question or just allow for a general reading.

   VI. Close your eyes.

   VII. Throw the objects on a flat surface.

   VIII. See how they fall.

   IX. How are the opposites positioned with respect to each other?

   X. How are the categories positioned with respect to each other, for example, female and laughter?

   XI. Make up a paragraph using the categories as the subjects of each sentence and the relationship with each other as the verb. This is similar to stone readings. Just look at how the objects lie with respect to each other and describe it.

   XII. What does this say with respect to your life?

"To see the world in a grain of sand" or a bone or a stone or a star has been a common goal from the dawn of time. It is as old as the race.

The permanence of stars, stones, and bones has always given people a sense that there is something more permanent than the flesh of the body. Yet there is more than the search for immortality here. We are all of flesh and bone. And of the stars. And of the earth. To seek answers in the stars and bones and stones is to seek answers within ourselves. Stars, stones, and bones are the skeletons of the universe. They are also that which links our mortal and immortal being.

CHAPTER 4

Air, Earth, Fire, and Water: Everyday Alchemy

Unless the bodies become incorporeal, and the spirits corporeal, no progress will be made. The true beginning then of our work is the solution of our body, because bodies, when dissolved become spiritual in their nature, and are yet at the same time more fixed than the spirit, though they are dissolved with it. For the solution of the body means the coagulation of the spirit and vice versa; each gives up something of its own nature; they meet each other half way, and thus become one inseparable substance, like water mixed with water.

  —Marsilio Ficino,
    fifteenth-century Florentine alchemist and astrologer[1]

A<small>IR</small>, earth, fire, and water are part of our daily lives, whether we live in a penthouse in New York City or on the bush in central Australia. This is obvious. We breathe the air. We walk on the earth. We cook with fire and receive sustenance from the fire of the sun. As for water, three-quarters of our planet and our bodies are made up of water. Air, earth, fire, and water: They are the sources of life.

Wherever we are in the world, we face these four elements. We can never escape the air we breathe, the ground we tread, the fire from the sun and from our stoves, and the water we drink. We share these elements with all other living beings on this planet.

In the West those who sought to wrest basic truths from earth, fire, water, and air were called "alchemists." But in elementary school we were taught that alchemists were misled men who tried to turn lead into gold. We laughed at the stupidity of these greedy old wizards. However, it is this perception that is childish. Turning lead into gold was a metaphor.

The search to transform lead into gold was often a "cover story" for a deeper and much more dangerous and heretical search: the transformation of consciousness from its base "metal" into the sublime, into the divine. The alchemists strived to extend the spiritual realm of light by pushing back the world of matter.[2]

Basil Valentine was a Benedictine monk at the end of the sixteenth century. He was also a closet alchemist. In a work that was secretly published, Valentine put things in their proper order. "All things," he said, "proceed from a heavenly influence, elemental operation, earthly substance, from this mixture arise the four Elements, water, air, earth, which engender by the help of fire hid therein, in a warm digestion, producing a Soul, Spirit, and Body."[3]

A century before Valentine, another alchemist and astrologer, Marsilio Ficino, spoke of transforming the "inner gold," the golden self. Alchemists used heating, cooking, boiling, and baking. They used them literally, to experiment with changes in the form of matter. They tested various substances and watched them change. In this, they laid the basis for the development of modern chemistry. But the alchemists also used boiling, baking, heating, and cooking as figurative terms to discuss the change of consciousness from the "base metal" to its higher form.[4] The alchemists were seekers. They were the folks who tried to find the connection between material and spiritual transformation.

Traditional tarot and astrology make use of the four elements of Western alchemy. In the tarot the suits are divided into four elements: Wands are fire; Pentacles are earth; Swords are air; and Cups are water. In Western astrology the signs of the zodiac are also divided into the four elements. Aries, Leo, and Sagittarius are fire signs. Pisces, Cancer, and Scorpio are water signs. Taurus, Capricorn, and Virgo are earth signs. And Gemini, Libra, and Aquarius are air signs.

On the other side of the globe a sophisticated study of alchemy developed in China. In Chinese alchemy there were five elements: metal, wood, water, fire, and earth. These elements were interrelated. For example, wood burns and produces fire. The fire produces ash or earth, from which is mined metal, which melts, becoming like water, which nourishes wood. Each of the five elements produces another element and destroys yet another. For example, while wood produces fire, it destroys or absorbs earth. And while metal produces water, it destroys wood. (Axes, for example, are made of metal.) Earth destroys or absorbs water and water destroys fire. Fire destroys metal.[5]

The study of alchemy in China began as early as the seventh century B.C. It was called *wu-hsing*, which aptly meant "the quintet." At first the quintet signified only the five elements. Soon, however, it came to have a spiritual meaning and was used in broader terms: the five ways of righteous conduct, the five social relationships, the five virtues, five tastes, five colors, five tones.[6] For later Chinese alchemists the five elements were universal. They could be found in the body of human beings, in the earth, the heavens—everywhere.

Despite a difference in the number of elements, Western and Chinese alchemists had one thing in common. Both felt that the smallest aspect of material reality was a reflection of a larger cosmic whole. For the monk Basil Valentine the human body was a microcosm of the universe. For the Chinese, too, everything on earth was a reflection of its divine form.[7]

It's Elemental: A Western Alchemy

For Western alchemists the four elements were present everywhere. They were part of our material, spiritual, emotional, and mental worlds. We are part of this tradition even if we are not aware of it. We think of people as "earthy" or "fiery." Some people are "grounded." Others are "airheads." We talk about "going with the flow."

The four elements are part of our consciousness. They are also part of our unconsciousness. Just viewing things in terms of the elements can fundamentally change our entire perspective.

   I. Take a few minutes to think about earth, air, fire, and water.

   II. Close your eyes and think of the characteristics of each.

   III. Think of the elements as adjectives. For example, what is "watery"? What is "fiery"? What is "earthy"? What is "airy" or "ethereal"?

   IV. Think of people that you can associate with each of the four elements.

   V. Go through the elements one by one.

     a. Take the element of earth.

       I. Think of all things earthy.

       2. What feelings are connected to this? For example, the feeling of security might be associated with the earth.

       3. What time of year do you associate with this?

       4. What are the pluses of this element? For example, you might see being grounded as positive earthiness.

     5. What are the minuses? For example, being stuck in one place is negative earthiness.

    b. Do the same thing with the elements of fire, water, and air.

VI. During the course of the week keep an eye on all things with the view of categorizing them according to their elemental state. Don't be disturbed if some things are a combination of elements. The idea is simply to play around with the way we look at reality.

Transforming Your Metal into Gold

The alchemists were not really trying to change lead into gold. Of course, that story kept them employed by monarchs who didn't understand what they were trying to do. Gold is the highest metal. It can represent our highest aspirations. The base metals are what we are given. They are "base" in that they are basic and commonly found.

In this exercise we try to find out some of our base elements and see how they can be transformed into gold.

NEEDED: paper and a writing implement.

    I. Make a list of the four elements—air, water, fire, earth.

    II. Write down at least two qualities that you have that would apply to each.

    III. Look at how your "elements" work with each other.

    IV. Evaluate how these elements are positive and how they are negative.

    V. Try to find other ways of mixing them together.

When I first tried this, I came up with the following:

AIR:
My active mind
My thoughts

FIRE:
My anger
My creativity

WATER:
My feelings
My adaptability

EARTH:
My habits and routines
My structures

I then needed to see just how each of these was a help and each a hindrance to me. When assessing my negative qualities, I came up with the follow-

ing: My anger definitely blocked my creativity (fire). My routines (earth) some-times became mindless. My feelings (water) could become overwhelming. And my active mind (air) could easily become obsessive.

On a more positive note, my creativity (fire) and my mind (air) worked to-gether especially if my feelings (water) were allowed to surface and if I disciplined myself to focus within a structure (earth).

The Living Earth: Geomancy

I am the revealer of secrets; in me are marvels of wisdom and strange and hidden things. But I have spread out the surface of my face out of humility, and have prepared it as a substitute for earth.

—Islamic geomantic tablet, seventh century [8]

Where to live? Where to build a house? Where to raise a family? These are questions that people have been asking ever since the dawn of civilization. There are right places and there are wrong places.

In Germany in the 1920s it was found that people living in certain houses in a particular area contracted cancer. This occurred from one generation to the next. When a new family moved into a "cancer house," they, too, would be stricken. People were at a loss to explain this strange incidence of cancers, which was apparently connected with the houses and not the people. Neither physicians nor scientists could explain this.

Finally dowsers were called in to evaluate the situation. These dowsers were specialists who could, among other things, locate water veins. They found that significant numbers of underground veins of water crossed under the houses where the cancer occurred. Since that time, dowsers around the world have found that living above crossing veins of water can induce all kinds of degenerative diseases, such as cancer and arthritis, as well as sleeplessness and colic in babies. [9]

In 1948 my father died in our family house after a three-year bout with cancer that he contracted during service as a physician in World War II. A little over a year later, my mother, little brother, and I left the house and moved to New York City. I visited the house several times over the next few decades. Subsequently, three more times the man of that house died, leaving a wife and two sons.

Then, over forty years after my father's death, I visited the house once more with my daughter. The town, in Westchester County, New York, had grown from the small country village of my youth to a sprawling mall town and bedroom community. The house still loomed at the top of the winding driveway. The road that ran past it at the bottom of the hill had been fenced off, leaving the house much the same as it had been when I was a child.

We drove up the driveway in late October. Leaves cluttered the long drive up the hill, and at one point I thought we would become stuck. When we reached the top, we saw that there were two cars parked in front of the house. But, to all appearances, the house was completely empty. A grayish light glowed from somewhere in the interior of that house. I felt that the house had reclaimed itself. There was no longer any life within. I turned the car around and left.

Now, my tale is the stuff of which ghost stories are made. All of those dead fathers—a curse. Yet there is often something to be said for such stories. Much of the time they are based on real experience, unexplained but real. There are right places to build a house. And there are wrong places. There are right places to stay and there are wrong places.

Another example of energy in the land concerns electrical power lines. There are indications that high-power electrical lines are profoundly harmful. In January 1995 researchers from McGill University in Canada reported there was a tenfold risk of lung cancer for those people living near high-frequency electrical power lines.[10]

The scientific link between cancer and electromagnetic fields began in 1979 with a report on childhood deaths from cancer in Denver, Colorado. Since that time there have been links between proximity to high-voltage electric lines and breast cancer in men, childhood leukemia, the breakdown of DNA, and a host of other ailments. In Sweden the studies of such connections has been thorough and alarming.[11]

There are right places to live. There are wrong places. The study of the harmony between humans and Mother Earth is called geomancy. It is a study of the earth that goes beyond geological formations. It is a study of the spirit of the earth. It is a study that is as diverse as the cultures of the world.

The people of Celebes live on four mountainous peninsulas on the Indonesian archipelago. These people, the Toradjas, have long used geomancy to find out whether to build in a new area. Four or eight strings are carried by the Toradjas. They are knotted in pairs and are carried hanging down. The questioner strokes hanging strings repeatedly with the right hand in a downward direction, invoking the gods. If the knots fall together, like people doing a round dance, then the answer is favorable. If they fall separately, the sign warns building in a new area.[12]

In rural Vietnam, people care a great deal where a house is built. The front of the main building should never be in a line with a road, nor should it face the angle of a pond. With rare exceptions the main front of the house always faces south. For the Vietnamese this is all based on sound geomantic principles.[13]

Whether in Vietnam, Indonesia, North Africa, China, or England, geomancy has common themes: It is the study of the earth element as alive and organic and it also deals with the energy of the land.

During the early years of this century an Englishman named Alfred Watkins discovered that ancient sacred sites were connected along straight lines in the land. Watkins called these lines "leys." Since then, many Western dowsers have discovered ley lines in Europe, America, and Asia, and these leys signify energy lines along which many sacred sites were placed. Native Americans and Celts alike placed their sacred sites on ground that was truly charged.[14]

The earth lives. It has energy. It has positive and negative forces. It is a microcosm of the universe just as humans are. Geomancers have understood these ideas for thousands of years. In China the geomancers have been called *feng-shui xianshang*, "doctors of the earth."

Sometimes people see the energy of the earth in the form of invisible spirits. For the Bambara people of western Sudan, there are invisible spirits in the land. The spirits are all around. They haunt rocks, thickets, or trees near a village. The work of the geomancer involves finding the place where the spirit resides.[15]

Merchants of the Mossi people of Upper Volta often make sure to consult a geomancer before establishing a market. For the Mossi, invisible spirits are everywhere, behind the house, under the trees, in the fields and groves.[16]

The Mundurucú people of Brazil move their village every ten years. Before they move to a new spot, a diviner checks for *yurupari*, which are malevolent spirits that can live below the surface of the ground and create mischief and disease. The diviner checks the spirits in the earth before the villagers choose their site.[17]

Outside of China, it was the world of Islam that developed geomancy to its highest form. Islamic geomancy goes back at least twelve centuries. Three hundred years before the Normans invaded England, an Islamic holy man, Ja'far al-Sadiq, wrote a treatise on the practice of geomancy, which he called *ilm-al-rami*, "the science of the sand." A complex system of sand patterns, Islamic geomancy required a great deal of experience to read the sixteen various designs. As early as the thirteenth century, a metal tablet dictated the proper throwing of a geomantic reading and the correct interpretations.[18]

Humans have always sought to formalize their intuition. What begins as an intuitive reading of earth energy becomes a complex form of reading, removed even further from the practice of the everyday person. So it has been with the Islamic branch of geomancy.

The science of the sands spread throughout the Islamic world. In Iran people would examine new sites with the help of a geomancer specialist. Dice were thrown and the geomancer would look up the sequences in a book on geomancy and work out the correct answer.[19] As Islam spread, so did this particular branch of geomancy. From Madagascar to Sudan, from Nigeria to Iran, people sought to read the earth through the interpretation of sand patterns.[20]

Places Everyone!!

Geomancy is all about finding the right place. It is about invisible forces that make for comfort or disease. Whether it be a Mundurucú shaman looking for the site of a new village or a merchant of the Mossi tribe seeking to establish a market, geomancy has to do with finding the right spot. This is something that we do without thinking about it.

Did you ever go into a room and feel immediately uncomfortable? Did you ever go into a house and feel that you belonged? Did you ever try to get to a new place and find your way as if by magic?

We all have special places. As kids, sometimes we are lucky enough to have a tree house. Maybe it's a room that we went to all by ourselves when nobody else was around. It could have been under the porch or in the bathtub. Or perhaps under the blankets when the room was bathed in the light of the moon and nobody else existed in the whole world.

In this game we tune in to our special places. It can be played with anywhere from two to twenty people (or fifty if the room is big enough).

NEEDED: blindfold(s).

    I. Everybody picks a partner.

    II. Decide which partner will be the guide and which partner will be blindfolded for the first circuit. The sighted partner helps the blindfolded partner to maneuver around the room, but does not exert any influence on where the blindfolded partner should go. The sighted partner asks questions (see below) but tries to interfere as little as possible and steps back to let the blindfolded person feel her space.

    III. The blindfolded partner is to find the place in the room where she feels the most comfortable standing up.

    IV. The blindfolded partner should take time feeling each space and moving from one space to the other. Check out the smell, the touch. The sighted partner can ask the blindfolded partner the following questions:

    a. What thoughts come to you?

    b. What feelings come to you?

V. The blindfolded partner makes a mental note of the space that is the most comfortable.

VI. The partners continue to explore, but then return to *the* place.

VII. When the blindfolded partner is ready, the sighted partner takes her away from the special place and the blindfold is exchanged.

VIII. Repeat all the steps.

IX. With blindfolds removed, each person finds her space using eyes and any other sense.

X. Spend a few minutes in your space with eyes closed. Record your feelings.

The Next Time You Go to a Public Place ...

I. Take a moment to look around a place, such as a restaurant, a nightclub, or the room where a party is being given.

II. Determine which areas of this place are ones that you might like to be in.

III. If possible, try them out. For example, in an uncrowded restaurant you should have a choice of tables with all kinds of views or non-views. Give yourself permission to try some out before you decide where you want to sit.

IV. Pick the place that is most comfortable for you. (If you are doing this with a partner, you both have to agree to either work together to find a place or assign one person to pick it.)

V. When you decide on a place, notice what it feels like and why it feels comfortable to you.

VI. Try this again in other public places and notice what similarities there are among the locations you have chosen. For example, some people always like to be against the wall facing the "action."

We play this game more often than we think. We all do this without thinking about it. More often, we don't follow our instincts. The key here is tuning in to where you want to be and taking note of it.

You can play this game in any area that has a variety of seats. Watch for patterns.

Taking the Pulse of the Land

When we visit a place, we feel something. Sometimes this feeling is stronger than at other times. Where I live, in Woodstock, New York, the entire area is reputed to be sacred land. I can tell when I return home. It just feels different. It has nothing to do with town boundaries or any other legal fictions—it's something in the land.

There is life in the land. That's what geomancy is all about. In this exercise we try to feel the life in the land.

I. Go to an outdoor place that you like to visit.
II. Give yourself a few minutes of silence with eyes closed.
III. Absorb whatever sensations come to you. Smell. Taste. Touch. Hearing.
IV. How does it feel?
V. Other than memories, what is it about this place that you like so much?
VI. Open your eyes and take in the surroundings.
VII. What are the natural surroundings? Water? Hills? Trees?
VIII. Where is the life in this place? What lives? In the air? In the ground? All around?

Water: The Mother of the World

Riverrun, past Eve and Adam's . . .
—*James Joyce*, Finnegans Wake

You could not step twice into the same rivers. For other waters are ever flowing onto you.
—Heraclitus

The water that bears the boat is the same that swallows it up.
—Chinese proverb

Wade in the water,
Wade in the water, children
Wade in the water,
God's going to trouble the water.
—*African American spiritual*

Water flows. Water comprises three-quarters of our bodies and our planet. We are immersed in water for the first nine months after we are conceived. Our blood contains the same chemical composition as the sea. And, as the moon pulls the waters of the sea, so does it exert its force upon us.

As a college undergraduate, I fulfilled my science requirement with a course in geology. What impressed me the most then, as now, was the power of water. The giant mountains that were thrown up by the molten forces of volcanic fire are the same mountains that are slowly worn down to a level plain by water.

In Africa the Bushongo people of Zaire look to water as the primal substance from which all things spring. Their story of creation starts, "In the beginning, in the dark, there was nothing but water."[21] The Yoruba people of Nigeria tell of a universe created by the High God Olodumare. When he sent his beloved disciple Ifa to Earth, the planet was completely covered with water. It was part of Ifa's job to create solid land so that people could thrive and reproduce.[22]

The Kamchatka peninsula lies far in the frozen north. It extends southward from the mainland of eastern Siberia and lies between the Sea of Okhotsk and the Bering Sea. The territory is ruled by water. It is bounded by the seas and sliced through by a mighty river. The people live by water, and the primary livelihood is fishing. For seers on Kamchatka, water is considered to be the door to the divine. Water is considered an opening where the lower regards the higher in reflection.[23]

The element of water has long been used as a means of divination. In the West this practice came to be called "lekanomancy."[24]

Water Knowledge

NEEDED: paper and a writing implement.

I. Spend an entire day watching water in your life.
II. Watch how water presents itself to you. How are you touched by it? How do you think about it? How do you use water images in your language?
III. Identify the various ways that you connect with water.
   a. How do you use it?
   b. Where is it around you?
   c. What does it feel like to satisfy a thirst with water? How does it differ from other liquids?
IV. Describe the qualities of water as you experience them during the day.
   a. Hot.

  b. Cold.
  V. Jot down a list of words used for describing water. They may be adjectives, nouns, verbs, adverbs: watery, ocean, sprinkle, wetly, etc.
  VI. What feelings do you associate with water? Make a list of these feelings.
  VII. Put the lists together and make up some phrases using the words on the lists. For example, "Her *watery* eyes betrayed an *ocean* of sorrow. I tried to *sprinkle* the conversation with humor in hopes that the sadness would simply *vaporize*. But she only watched me, her lips *wetly* glistening. Was it *tears* or was it desire?"

Welcoming the Water Spirits . . . And Life Began

The Earth Mother called her tribes together. There were the Stone People, the Plant People—all the tribes that inhabit the planet. The Earth Mother spoke of the tribes and of their function.

The Stone People were the most ancient. Some of the Stone People would be used for healing. Others would be used for fuel. Still others for protection. But all would be libraries of earth records.

All members of the Earth Tribe had talents. All were tempered by volcanic heat. Now it was time for a new tribe, the Water Spirits.

The Earth Mother spoke, telling of this new tribe, filled with liquid, which would cool her surface. She spoke of this tribe which would bring the Rain People, who would permit things to grow upon her surface. She spoke of the spirits that the Great Mystery had placed in her care. She spoke of the seeds of the Plant People that would grow into trees, fruits, herbs, flowers and vegetables to feed the Children of Earth.

The Earth Mother spoke. She told of how the mountains had grown deep and sloped wide so that they could hold the bodies of the Water Tribe.

And so the Water Spirits came. They came upon the parched earth. They came and filled the spaces that the other tribes had created for them. And all over the earth there were running brooks, wide rivers, deep lakes, rapid streams, ponds, and creeks. They created steamy pockets of water that touched the soil.

Time and again the Water Spirits returned to the sky. They returned and created the Cloud People, who blessed the Earth Mother with gentle rains, until her surface had cooled. And life began.

—Native American story[25]

Shapes That Move upon the Water

It's New Year's Day in Tibet. The household gathers round for a traditional ceremony that happens every year at this time. A bowl filled with water is brought over to the head of the household. He takes a ladle filled with hot butter and pours it into the water. There, on the surface of the water, shapes begin to form and the pattern of the coming year can be seen.[26]

In Czechoslovakia it is Christmas Eve. This is a time where traditionally divination games are played. One of the most popular involves young people dropping melted lead into bowls of cold water and reading the shapes.[27]

In Malta, on June 24, the Feast of St. John, people pour melted lead into a vessel of water. The shapes that the lead assumes when it solidifies indicate the direction of the person's life. Young girls can see their mates.[28] In Denmark young women melt lead on New Year's Eve and pour it into water. If the shape looks like a pair of scissors, they will marry tailors. If it looks like a hammer, they will marry smiths, and so on.

The southern Slavs have a more serious use of water. The diviner will use melted lead dropped in a bowl of water to read the source of illness in a patient. The sounds of the lead dropping into the water are also read.[29]

NEEDED: a large clear glass bowl or very large glass (like a brandy snifter), water, and a candle.

   I. Wash the bowl or glass in warm water and let the water just flow over it.

   II. Fill the bowl or glass with water to within an inch of the top.

   III. Light the candle, and drip some wax into the water. Be sure not to cover the entire surface.

   IV. Close your eyes, roll your eyeballs up toward the top of your head, and think of a rainbow fountain coming out the top of your head.

   V. Take several deep breaths in through the nose and out through the mouth.

   VI. Open your eyes and look at the water and wax.

   VII. What patterns do you see?

   VIII. What shapes do they suggest?

   IX. What feelings are you experiencing?

After you feel comfortable with this game you might try it again. This time ask a particular question and see how the shapes correspond to an answer.

There are other alternatives to wax. You might take some salad oil and drop it carefully in the water and check out the shapes that form. Or, like the ancient

Greeks, you might take some water from a well or stream, leaving the particulate in the glass and watch how the particles move. There are countless possibilities. Just go with the flow.

Immersion in Water—a Game for Two

We spend the first nine months of our lives surrounded by water. For most of us, the adjustment from the water within our mother's womb to the air of the outside world is harsh and shocking. Recently a French obstetrician named Leboyer rediscovered that babies adapt easily and wonderfully to the world of air if placed in a warm tub of water immediately after birth. It makes sense that immersion in water has been a symbol and ritual of rebirth from long before the time of John the Baptist. In this game we immerse ourselves in water. The game is best played with two people who are beloved to each other.

    I. Fill up a bathtub with water that is roughly the same temperature as the body.
    II. One bather gets in and gets comfortable, with the water covering him up to his shoulders.
    III. He closes his eyes.
    IV. The other partner gently scrubs him as if he was a baby or small child.
    V. The bather lets all feelings and memories pass gently through his mind.
    VI. After about ten minutes the other partner leaves the bather alone.
    VII. The bather plays in the water with eyes closed.
    VIII. He notes what memories and feelings arise and then lets them pass.
    IX. He gets out of the tub.
    X. He dries between his toes.

Fire, Fire, Fire!

Fire is like a person who doctors. There is a fire in every home, and fire is like a person. We cannot live without it.
        —Navajo shaman[30]

Fire is the purest and most worthy Element of all, full of unctuous corrosiveness adhering to it, penetrating, digesting, corroding and wonderfully adhering, without visible, but within

invisible, and most fixed; it is hot, dry, and tempered with Air. Its
Substance is the purest of all, and its Essence was first of all
elevated in the Creation with the throne of Divine Majesty.
    —Michael Sandivogius, seventeenth-century alchemist[31]

The Bible tells us that after the great Flood, Noah looked into the sky. There God had placed a mighty rainbow as a sign of the covenant between Him and humans. It stood as a reminder that next time there would be no flood, but fire.

Fire is a symbol of both purification and destruction. For the Zoroastrians it is the arm of Mithra, the god of the sun. For humans fire provided heat and light for cooking and warmth and allowed us to see with new eyes while the rest of the world was dark. It was a weapon that allowed us to drive animals toward killing stands.

Fire and light. Fire and heat. Humans are the only animals that are able to control the power of fire. In conquering our fear of fire, we achieved a power that no other animal has ever achieved. Fire allowed us to keep dangerous animals at bay. It allowed us to sharpen our hunting weapons, and bake clay pots that would last beyond the season. And it allowed us to smelt metals.

Maui Tricks His Grandmother

Maui was a small fellow, one of the more diminutive gods. From Hawaii to New Zealand he was the essence of trickster. He had been unwanted and abandoned. Reared by the sea gods, Maui was educated by his ancestor in the sky, Tama-nui-ki-te-rangi. But soon he returned to earth.

Of good heart, Maui was also a trickster. At that time the world was without fire. Maui's grandmother, Mahuika, was the underworld goddess of fire and earthquakes.

Maui approached his grandmother for fire. Mahuika conceded and gave her grandson her fingers one by one. Each one contained fire. But Maui quenched each one with water. She then gave him her toes, one by one. Each one contained fire. But Maui quenched each of the toes with water, except one.

Down to her last toe, Mahuika, goddess of fire, used her last toe to start a grand fire. It was a fire that burned mountains and valleys. It burned lakes as well as forests. It threatened to burn up the world.

The joke was over. Maui had to use all of his powers to invoke the rain and the snow and the hail. Finally the fire was put out, but not entirely, for fire still continued in the highest branches of the trees.

Since that time fire exists in the trees. It may be liberated from the trees by rubbing together pieces of wood.[32]

—Hawaiian folk tale

Watching the Flames, Tasting the Smoke, Hearing the Fire

The ancient Finns saw fire as a means of determining the direction of peace—or war. They would throw twigs into the fire and watch the sap. If sap flowed from the twigs, then war would follow.[33]

A fire is more than just hot. It can be red-hot or blue-hot or white-hot. It has countless sounds, shapes, and colors. In Albania, on the eve of the first of March, women take a special leaf and throw it in the fire at the same time that they pronounce the name of a person they wish to divine. By the sounds of the leaf in the fire they determine the fate of the person.[34]

God spoke to Moses in the crackling of a burning bush. Fire reading is probably as old as the human race. Back when people sat huddled around a warming fire they certainly listened to the sounds of the flames.

NEEDED: paper, a writing implement, and a fireplace.

I. Find a fire, preferably at night. A large fire is preferable, like a bonfire or fireplace fire.

II. Find a comfortable place to sit down and let the fire in.

III. Use all of your senses (except touch, please) and let yourself feel the fire.

IV. Smell it, taste it, hear it, and, of course, see it.

V. Close your eyes and continue to let the fire in.

VI. Open your eyes and see what else you can experience.

VII. Take a sheet of paper and make four columns. At the top of each column mark down one of the senses you have used—that is, one for taste, smell, sight, and hearing.

a. What did the fire say? Can you make words out of the sounds?

b. What images did you see in the fire?

    c. Close your eyes and smell the fire. Does the scent evoke any memories or thoughts?

    d. Close your eyes and "taste" the fire. Is it acrid or sweet?

VIII. Under each of these headings put down between five and fifteen words that describe your senses of the fire.

IX. Make at least two sentences out of the words you have listed.

X. You have gotten to know a fire.

Blazing Cinemas

In the mountains of Colombia a horse is stolen. The victim has no recourse but to go to a diviner. The diviner will take a cigarette or a firebrand and light it. In the wisps of smoke and the way the flame devours the article, the diviner finds the culprit.[35]

Watch a little baby watch a fire. Her eyes will go wide and she will stare and stare and stare. It almost seems as if she is seeing something in the fire. She is. And you can, too. In this game we see things in the fire.

NEEDED: a candle, a match, paper, and a writing implement.

I. Wait until it is dark and turn out all the lights in the room you are in.

II. Light a candle.

III. Get comfortable in a seat about two feet from the candle.

IV. Look at every part of the candle. Note its shapes and colors.

V. How are the shapes moving?

VI. What are the colors?

VII. Close your eyes.

VIII. Imagine as many things as you can that have these colors.

IX. Take the shapes of the candlelight and imagine things with those shapes.

X. Open your eyes and stare at the candle again.

XI. Let the shapes and colors mix up in your mind.

XII. Close your eyes again and let a scene come into your mind.

XIII. Fill it up with motion, colors, and shapes.

XIV. If you wish, write down your impressions of the scene you have conjured. You have seen a blazing cinema.

The Wind and the Air

> *Down in the valley*
> *The valley so low*
> *Hang your head over*
> *Hear the wind blow*
> *—American folk song*

The wind is mysterious. You can never see it, yet it can lift mammoth trees into the air and throw them to the ground. It is invisible, yet you can see it play upon the leaves on a gentle summer's day. You can smell it as it bears the scents of a thousand flowers or the whiff of a memory. You can hear it as it shrieks from the mouth of a hurricane. You can feel it as it softly rattles your window as you doze off to sleep.

For tens of thousands of years the wind has transported ships to their destinations. For tens of thousands of years it has dashed them against rocks.

Fire can be seen. Water can be seen. The earth can be seen. But air and the wind are different. The wind has power. It has a voice, but it has no form. It is little wonder that our ancestors have regarded the wind with awe. For what better describes a divinity than a being with a power and a voice cloaked in invisibility?

For the ancient Chinese the wind was the breath of the universe and therefore was connected to natural phenomena like crops and famines. But it was also connected to human passions and migrations. Thousands of years ago the imperial Chinese government decreed the formation of a state institute. The institute would be responsible for the observation of the winds and was mandated to perform divination rites with regard to the winds.[36]

Among many cultures the wind was associated with the dream world. Indeed, there is something dreamlike about the sound of the wind. Often, we are most conscious of its presence as we drift off to sleep.

In the old Celtic world the wind was a basic force. A seafaring people, the Celts relied upon the wind to power their ships. Legions of fishermen went to sea with the aid of the wind. Occasionally a ship would not return. There was a special ritual among the ancient Celts used to find lost ships. A virgin was selected. She would then go to sleep. And, while she dreamed, her spirit left her body and searched for the ship. When her spirit returned to her body, she woke up and reported where the ship or its wreckage could be found and what had happened to the people aboard it.

There was only one catch to the dream ritual of the Celts. The woman selected to search for the ship in her dreams had to be of strong mind. For if the wind changed while her spirit was absent from her body, she stood a chance of losing her reason.[37]

For many Native Americans the wind, dreams, and divination are linked. In an age-old Navajo legend, Younger Brother learns the Star Ceremony and Chant. This is one of the important curing ceremonies. He learns this in the sky from the Star Spirits. The Black, Blue, Yellow, and White Stars attend the ceremony, with the Black Star presiding. It is the Black Star that gives Younger Brother the Wind Spirit. The Wind Spirit is inside of Younger Brother and speaks to him in dreams.[38]

For the Washo Indians of the Southwest, the Wind Spirit also speaks through dreams. It is through dreams that Washo shamans achieve their power. And it is often the wind that speaks through the dream.[39]

The Answer, My Friends, Is Blowing in the Wind . . .

The ancient Israelites used the wind directly as a means of divination. The wind spoke to them through its motion in the trees. Like many other literate cultures, they would cast words "randomly" to find answers to questions. In this game we combine both and use the wind as the vehicle.[40] The game is best played when there is a gentle breeze.

NEEDED: paper and a writing implement.

    I. Make a list of thirty to forty words. They may be nouns, verbs, adjectives, and adverbs. A mix is best.

    II. Pick ten to fifteen of these words.

    III. Write each of the words that you have chosen on a separate piece of paper.

    IV. Take the pieces of paper outside when a gentle breeze is blowing.

    V. You may either ask a general question or just see what happens.

    VI. Place the pieces of paper on the ground.

    VII. Let the wind scatter them.

    VIII. Decide beforehand how you will pick up the pieces (clockwise, counterclockwise, etc.).

    IX. Pick the pieces up, one on top of the other.

   X. Read them from top to bottom and write them out in the order you have picked them.

   XI. What does this say to you?

   XII. Now use the words in any order and make a sentence out of them.

   XIII. What does this say to you?

Hearing the Voice of the Wind

The Navajos take the wind most seriously. It is mentioned in Navajo chants and in the Origin Legend itself. Among Navajo diagnosticians are those who are called "listeners." These are diviners who listen to the wind for their messages.[41]

As children most of us played the game of telephone. We sat in a circle and one person whispered something to the person next to him. The message would be passed around the circle until the last person, who would speak it out loud. In this game we play a variation of telephone and then let the wind whisper to us. This can be played with three or more people.

   I. Go outside where there are trees or bushes and a breeze is blowing. In summer the breezes are gentle and the sound of the leaves is soft. In fall the rustling leaves make the whispers different. In winter's silence the voice of the wind may crackle some. In spring's time the sound of the wind mixes with the sound of the stirring land.

   II. Stand in a circle, everybody holding hands.

   III. One person agrees to be the game starter.

   IV. Drop your hands and close your eyes.

   V. Game starter whispers a statement in the ear of the person next to her.

   VI. That person whispers it to the person next to him.

   VII. The whispering continues at least five times around the circle with the whispers getting fainter and fainter. They must still be audible.

   VIII. Stay silent for a minute or so after the whispering has stopped.

   IX. Each person now composes a statement that has meaning from the last whisper they heard. *You must make meaning out of the last whisper.*

   X. What meaning does it have for your life?

   XI. Everybody turns around so that there is still a circle but everybody is facing outward.

   XII. Listen to the whispering of the wind.

   XIII. What is it saying?

   XIV. What is it saying to *you*?

A variation of this can be played at the beach, where the waves and the surf become the whispers that we listen to. Or it can be played on a mountaintop. Remember, you will hear sounds, not voices. But you can loosen up your mind and hear the words in these sounds.

The air and the wind are inseparable. Without the air there would be no wind. Without air there would be no breath. Without breath there would be no life. Psyche was, among other things, the Greek goddess of breath. Psychic ability is as natural and as easy as breathing itself.

In many cultures breath and soul are seen as synonymous. Even in the English language we see the connection between breathing and much deeper issues. For example, inhalation means the same thing as inspiration. And exhalation means expiration. To be inspired is literally to be taking breath, taking in air. Similarly, to die is to expire—to let the breath out. We are inspiring and expiring every moment of the day. Our bodies are constantly in a state of life and death.

Spiritual traditions of Japan and India have long recognized the importance of the breath. One of the simplest Japanese Zen meditations consists of simply watching the breath.

It Won't Leave You Breathless

This game is based on meditative techniques that are ancient and effective.

I. Find a comfortable place to sit. Keep your back straight.
II. Close your eyes.
III. Take a deep breath through your nose.
IV. Exhale through your mouth.
V. Inhale and exhale deeply for about a minute.
VI. Breathe normally.
VII. Count your breaths: "one" inhale, "two" exhale, "three" inhale, "four" exhale, etc.
VIII. Whatever thoughts come to you, just watch them in your mind's eye and let them pass.
IX. Just count and watch and count and watch.

There is no right or wrong way to do this. You may do it for two or three minutes or up to an hour. Even doing it for one minute will make a difference. You might try this at a regular time each morning or afternoon for a week or so and see what difference it makes in your day.

Airing Our Nose

> *Smells are surer*
> *than sounds or sights*
> *To make your*
> *heart-strings crack.*
> *—Rudyard Kipling*

Borne by the air and wind, our most powerful and earliest sense is that of smell. We smell our mom long before we are able to focus our eyes. Smell evokes our earliest memories. It is smell that connects us to times and places before our conscious memory. It is smell that brings back the rushing torrents of our own history.

Smell allows us to taste the difference between an apple and a potato. Smell arouses us. We smell each other, our loved ones, and our homes. In this game we don't take smell for granted.

NEEDED: paper and a writing implement.

I. Give yourself a whole day to play this game. Of course you can do other things during the day. This doesn't involve doing anything special. It merely requires maintaining a certain awareness.

II. When you wake up in the morning, spend a few minutes with your eyes closed and focus all your attention on your nose. (This is the day you will be led by your nose.)

III. Identify the most important smells that come to you at this first moment.

IV. What feelings do you associate with these smells?

V. What memories come to you?

VI. Be aware of smell at all times during the course of the day.

VII. Note any feelings or memories.

VIII. During the course of the day, find at least four more moments when you spend a minute or two concentrating on nothing but smell.

IX. At the end of the day try to list smells and memories.

This is one of those games in which keeping written notes could be both helpful and fun.

Air, earth, fire, and water—there would be no world without them. Just as the very atoms of our bodies carry the first cosmic explosions of eons ago, so do our bodies mirror the four elements. However, it is not only on the physical plane that we reflect the elements. It is also in the very nature of our being. That is why the alchemical search was profoundly spiritual. It was a search for higher consciousness, for our own higher being. And it is through our awareness of our elemental nature that we are able to see signs in our physical universe that are reflected in our emotional and spiritual universe. In our elemental nature we may see the signs of our times and thus be able to transform ourselves. That is, after all, the nature of alchemy.

CHAPTER 5

Tuning In to the *Qi*

> *All things are microcosms of the Tao;*
> *the world a microcosmic universe,*
> *the nation a microcosm of the world,*
> *the village a microcosmic nation;*
> *the family a village in microcosmic view,*
> *and the body a microcosm of one's own family;*
> *from single cell to galaxy.*
>
> —*Lao Tzu*, Tao te-ching[1]

Two thousand years before the birth of Christ, the Chinese saw the universe as an organism at once unified and complex called "Sky-Earth," or *T'ien-Ti*. Human beings were situated in between the sky and the earth. They were the intermediaries between the two realms, and at the same time they contained within them their families and societies, a microcosm of the universe.[2]

Until the twentieth century people believed that the continents had always been separate and fixed, pretty much the way they exist today. When in 1912 a geologist named Alfred Wegener postulated the earlier existence of a single giant continent, which he called Pangaea, scientists in the West thought he was mad. When he further speculated that the continent not only had broken up but had drifted away in segments that formed the continents we know today, people thought that they were reading fiction.

Today it is an accepted fact that the earth has been growing just as humans grow, just as plants grow. It grows much more slowly, to be sure, but it grows nonetheless. The scientific community has come to accept the notion that giant shifting plates make up the surface of the globe. These leviathan earthen plates shift and move, colliding with each other and creating spaces in the planet where molten liquid erupts from volcanoes. Today we know that Africa and Europe were connected as one continent and that Asia is presently moving toward America.[3] What was once a fantasy is now an accepted scientific fact. The earth is a growing, breathing organism. It lives. And it dies.

A century ago it would have been considered sheer fantasy to think that one's actions in, say, the United States would affect the climate in Brazil. Three decades ago people in the United States welcomed air conditioners into their automobiles. And aerosol sprays came in all shapes and forms. Nobody in his right mind would have thought that the air conditioners in cars on the highways of America would affect the melting of glaciers at the north pole. Few people would have seriously thought that the fluorocarbons released by aerosols would affect the climate of the planet.

Today it is accepted by most reasonable people that the use of aerosols and automobile air conditioners in New York State affects the melting of the glaciers, and most reasonable people see that the destruction of rain forests in Amazonia contributes to the warming of the planet. Yesterday's fantasy is today's reality. Still, the notion of an action in Brazil affecting the climate in Alaska is hard for many to accept. Similarly the notion that pressing a point on a person's foot can affect his heart or lungs or intestines is one that most people on this side of the globe find difficult to entertain.

In the East it has long been understood that the universe is one. "The world is a microcosmic universe," says the ancient spiritual text *Tao te-ching*. Everything is connected. Everything is a microcosm of the whole.

For the ancient Chinese the understanding of the earth and its ways was part of survival. In the mists of time a group of people appeared in China who developed their understanding of the earth into an art and a science. These were people who saw the connection between the land and the air, between the rivers and the sun, even between the seasons and the feelings, the clouds and the spirit. These gifted diviners/scientists came to be known as *feng-shui* masters, or "doctors of the earth."

Feng-shui (pronounced *fung shway*) literally means "wind and water." It is the oldest practice of ecology. It is probably the oldest form of geomancy in the world. The first known textbook on the subject appeared in the ninth century A.D. However, the practice goes back to the Chou dynasty in China, a thousand years before the birth of Christ. By the Yuan dynasty of the thirteenth century, the practice had become so well established that *feng-shui* masters chose the site of the capital, Beijing, according to their principles.[4]

As with all forms of geomancy, *feng-shui* deals with the earth as a living whole. What works in a small scale works in a large scale. In the Chinese worldview everything is related. You can't cut down a rain forest without affecting the weather. The universe is a delicately balanced ecosystem. Relationships, not absolutes, are key in the practice of *feng-shui*. Based on traditional Chinese philosophy and the experience of dealing with the environment for thousands of years, *feng-shui* is a most potent form of geomancy, perhaps the mother of all geomancies.[5]

It's all about *qi*. Without *qi, feng-shui* would not exist. More important, there would be no life. For *qi* (pronounced chee) is the very breath of the universe. In fact, it can be translated as "breath of nature." It is that vital energy that operates at every level of existence. On the human level it is the energy that drives the body. On the earth it is energy carried by the wind and through water. So, wind and water are the main elements in traditional *feng-shui* ecology.

In the human body, when *qi* is abundant, the body exudes health and strength. When it is exhausted, life ends. Similarly, on the earth, a barren plain is where life energy—*qi*—is scattered. On the other hand, a location where there is an abundance of *qi* is an auspicious place to live. Therefore, for *feng-shui* practitioners, the essential goal is discovering where the greatest amount of *qi* can be found.[6]

Feng-shui has been very much alive in China for the past several millennia. It is a tool as well as a way of looking at the world. When the colonial powers of the West moved into China at the end of the last century, the *feng-shui* were mobilized by the Chinese government to fight the barbarians.

The Manchu (or Ch'ing) was China's last imperial dynasty, which was overthrown in 1911. But the middle of the nineteenth century marked the beginning of the end of this dynasty. For two centuries the Manchu rulers had brought a surge of expansion and a flowering of culture. At the time that the American colonies were struggling to achieve their independence, the empire of China had reached the farthest boundaries in its history. Yet, within a generation, the empire had begun to crumble.

Drugs began to infiltrate China. British merchants has drugs to sell—opium in particular. The Chinese market was a potentially rich one for the British merchants. However, the Chinese government proved to be uncooperative. The Manchu rulers felt that opium was bad for their people and refused to allow the British to bring it into China. The Manchu rulers wrote a letter to Victoria, "Queen of All the Barbarians," to plead with her and her government to cease their pressure upon the Chinese to accept shipments of opium.

The pressure escalated. The British government would not allow the Chinese to restrict British opium merchants. The government of Queen Victoria declared war on the Chinese and forced them to allow the importation of opium, missionaries, and the British colonization of Chinese ports. It was open season on China. Soon the French got a piece of the action. They, too, got opium privileges and a few Chinese ports. The Russians followed and then the Germans.

There was little the dying Ch'ing dynasty could do to retaliate. They had to relinquish land to the foreigners. The Manchus called in old and wise men to select the sites for the foreigners. The old wise men came with their strange apparatuses and funny-looking compasses. They chose the sites and the foreigners occupied them.

Strange things occurred on these sites selected by the old men. Illnesses erupted among the foreign occupiers. The population deteriorated rapidly. The housing built on the island of Shamien was overrun by ruinous white ants. The old men had chosen well. They were *feng-shui* masters instructed by their government to pick the worst sites for the foreign barbarians. They did.[7]

A century and a half later *feng-shui* masters are routinely consulted by the most reputable of Western banks. In Malaysia leading stockbrokers consult *feng-shui* masters for the most propitious times and places to invest.[8] One American bank listed "geomancy fees" of several thousand dollars for a new office in Hong Kong. The most celebrated recent marriage of *feng-shui* and commerce was the Crédit Lyonnais Fung Shui Index developed by Gary Coull and Martin French using hired *feng-shui* practitioners. At first it was viewed with great skepticism by the Crédit Lyonnais clients. But at the end of 1992 the conservative *Far Eastern Economic Review* reported that this *feng-shui* index had established "a clear correspondence with the Hang Seng Index,"[9] the Hong Kong stock market's leading index. From Bangkok to Tokyo and from Ulan Bator to Jakarta, *feng-shui* is rapidly gaining acceptance as a powerful tool.[10]

Recently Western ecologists have developed complex scientific methods of testing use of the land based on the most modern ecological techniques. One of the most well known of these ecologists is Bruce Hendler, who has applied modern ecological principles to landscape design.[11]

In the Harvard University Graduate School of Design, Ping Xu, a Ph.D. student, compared the traditional use of *feng-shui* with these most advanced contemporary methods of landscape analysis. Utilizing state-of-the-art computer graphic programming and analysis, he concluded that the ancient methods of *feng-shui* and modern Western techniques compare identically 80 percent of the time.[12]

Plus Ça Change[13]

Plus ça change, plus c'est la même chose. *The more things change, the more they stay the same. It's an old French adage. While it is a somewhat cynical statement, it is generally true. Feng-shui is about a certain awareness. It is about awareness of our environment, our living space, our immediate world. There are so many things that we do without thinking—without awareness. Often, I will consciously create a habit (like always putting my keys back in my pocket) just so that I won't have to think about it. And then there are times that I have put things in the most sensible place and have forgotten where.*

This is an awareness exercise. It helps us to get in touch with ourselves and our environments, especially those environments we create. In this exercise we consciously change our normal routines. In the process we become aware of just how much we do that we are not aware of.

At least once a day every day for at least one week change something about your daily routine. Change something that you do the same way all the time, like putting on your socks starting with your left foot or brushing your teeth after you go to the toilet first thing in the morning. Change the way you get up in the morning. We all have a way.

Change something. It does not have to be something big. It just has to be something that you do the same way all the time. If you drive to work the same way, maybe you could drive a different way. If you wear the same combination of clothes, you could change that. If you use a certain expression when someone tells you something exciting, you could change that. You know what your routines are. We have millions of them. Change one.

It's amazing how many little habits make up our day. It's amazing how little consciousness we bring to bear upon everyday activity. Simply watching this is a revelation.

You might want to write down some of your observations in a journal. These will be most revealing to you. Guaranteed!

Checking Out the Qi

The qi, or life force, is all around us. We can see it in obvious places, like in a tree that is green and growing. We can feel it in the motion of a breeze through our hair on a summer's day. We can hear it in a child's laugh. We can smell it in a crackling fire. We can touch it in a running stream. It is life energy. It is all around us. This game is about seeing it, hearing it, and feeling it around us.

    I. Stop wherever you are.

    II. Look around you.

    III. Without thinking about it, note all that is around you that is moving in even the slightest way.

IV. Note which things or beings have the greatest amount of energy. (Don't think about it much.)

V. Which things make you feel comfortable (even slightly)?

VI. Which things make you feel uncomfortable (even slightly)?

VII. What colors have more energy for you?

VIII. What colors have less energy?

IX. What shapes have more energy?

X. What shapes have less energy?

XI. Make some notes on the above, if you wish, and try this in different environments.

This does not require training. All we have to do is trust what we see and hear. As I sit here at my window in early spring, I hear the chirping of birds. That's life energy. I see the trees swaying with the wind. That's life energy. It's all around us. This is just about noticing.

The notion of *qi* may seem mystical. To an extent it is. Acupuncture is based on the same principles. The flow of vital energy through the human body in defined lines, called "meridians," allows the acupuncturist to work. The effectiveness of the practice of acupuncture was belatedly acknowledged in the West three decades ago when James Reston of the *New York Times* wrote an article about having had his appendix removed in Beijing without the use of anesthesia. Strategically placed needles manipulated *qi* and eliminated any feeling during the operation.

Just as *qi* flows through acupuncture points in the human body, so does it flow through points in the earth. The basics are simple. Nothing is absolute. For example, when *qi* is blown by the wind, it will be scattered. A mountain area where the wind blows hard will scatter *qi* and be cold and barren. On a flat plain, however, dead *qi* can accumulate and a gentle breeze will blow it away.

Proof of the presence of living *qi* can be seen in a flourishing area. If living *qi* abounds in an area, the trees and grass will turn green earlier and die later than in areas with less abundant *qi*.

Shapes are important. A straight line will generate evil *qi*, or *sha*. These lines are called hidden arrows. All kinds of straight lines apply. A straight rushing water source like a river will bring hidden arrows. Water running off in a straight line is a malignant breath that takes away the force of the area. Think of a house located on a barren plain. There are no trees or shrubs and no flowing water. The wind blows across the plain. The house receives the blast of the wind in straight lines or hidden arrows. The presence of wind without water makes it the ultimate inauspicious location.[14]

Curved lines are favorable for accumulating *qi*. Meandering streams are preferable to rushing rivers. A rounded hill would be preferable to a sharply rising mountain. Imagine a house in an area that is sheltered by hills. Gentle breezes blow off the hill and clear out the area around the house. A meandering stream flows near the house. This would be considered a positive site.

A *feng-shui* master can choose a site where there is the most accumulation of *qi*. For example, consider the house surrounded by a plain where the wind rushes by in a straight line and robs the area of life energy. One can counteract this by planting trees in back of the house and keeping a tank or pond with a constant supply of fresh water in front of the house.

There are four steps in the *feng-shui* master's search. One must find an open space surrounded by good hills and water. Second, one must find a suitable area in the open space. Third, one must arrange the *qi* so that the life *qi* is accumulated and the dead *qi* swept away. And, finally, one must find a "true dragon."[15]

Dragons in the hills? When the *feng-shui* practitioners speak of a dragon, they are referring to a form within the land. They are also speaking of the *qi* itself, which is seen as the "dragon's breath." Dragons are different in China than in the England of King Arthur. Anybody who has seen a New Year's parade in a Chinatown or in Hong Kong can attest to that. While in the West we tend to characterize things as either good or bad, the Chinese dragons cover a wide spectrum of positive and negative.

A "true dragon" in the land must begin with a peak—a mountain. Along the ridge of the mountain are at least two other peaks. As the elevation drops, the contours of the mountain correspond to certain shapes that relate to the five Chinese alchemical elements of wood, fire, metal, water, and earth. The dragon mountain should have a sinuous profile. Finally the true dragon always stays close to its partner, water.[16]

Open spaces surrounded by hills are ideal *feng-shui* sites. From the open space the peak of the mountain is seen in the distance. In front of the open space is a lake or running water. The true dragon provides the ideal enclosure of vital *qi*. The surrounding mountain lets the *qi* in. The water refreshes and revitalizes it. And, given this landscape, gentle breezes will sweep away the dead *qi*.[17]

The Qi to What's in Tune

Sometimes things just don't "feel right." We walk into a place and feel uncomfortable. Or we enter a house that we have never been in before and feel immediately at home. We see something that jars us. We see something that soothes us. We are experiencing the qi—life energy. All of this is part of being tuned in.

Humans are naturally tuned in. What we learn is something else. We already have the powers that allow us to pick up energy around us. We don't have to go to the mountaintops of Tibet. We can go into our own living spaces and become aware of how we feel. In this exercise we rely on our natural attunement.

    I. Walk around your living space room by room.

    II. Stand in the middle of each room.

    III. Close your eyes and take several deep breaths.

    IV. With eyes still closed how does the room feel?

        a. Do you feel comfortable? Can you put it into words?

        b. Do you feel antsy? Can you put it into words?

    V. Open your eyes.

    VI. Look around the room.

    VII. What furniture, pictures, objects seem like they belong where they belong?

    VIII. What objects seem like they don't quite belong?

    IX. Do this with each room in the house.

You might actually do some rearranging just to see how it feels. We do this all the time. This time you will be doing it very playfully. The whole point is to see how different things feel in different places and how you feel about this place-ment. There is nothing to "learn"—only to experience.

Where Are Your Shoes?

He was a Zen Master. And it was not easy being a Zen Master, for many would-be disciples came from all parts of Japan to seek his guidance. But he lived in a modest cottage in the mountains and let the aspiring disciples come as they would.

One day a young man arrived at the Master's cottage. This was a young man who was quite serious about his spiritual path. This acolyte had studied much, meditated much, and felt that he was quite ready to become the right-hand disciple of any Master.

It had been raining when the young man arrived at the Master's house. The Master was seated on a pillow in a small room. The young man carefully removed his shoes and placed his umbrella outside the door.

The young man entered the room and bowed to the Master. "I would like to become your disciple. I would like to become enlightened as you are, Master," the young man said.

The Master smiled.

"I have studied much and feel that I am on the path to realization," said the young man, growing a bit uncomfortable at the Master's silence.

The Master smiled with his eyes half-closed and nodded.

"Don't you feel that I could become an awakened one?" asked the youth, becoming exasperated at the Master's reticence.

The Master opened his eyes. The young man now felt hopeful. The Master would accept him.

"Do you know on which side of the door you placed your umbrella and on which side you placed your shoes?" asked the Master quietly.

"I—I—n-n-no," stuttered the young man, disconcerted. "Why?"

"Because," answered the Master slowly, "what you seek is awareness. And how can you be aware if you do not even know where you have put your shoes and umbrella?" [18]

—Zen story

Feng-Shui *Sampling*

Feng-shui *comes from the experience of thousands of years. Yet it comes from the experience of folks like us. We can tune in to our surroundings. We can become aware of how we feel in certain places. We can see how, in some places, things grow and in others they don't. Within each of us there is a feng-shui master who can be sensitive to our surroundings. In this exercise we use our ordinary senses to "feel" certain surroundings.*

I. Find a place that
   a. Is surrounded by rolling hills or gentle mountain peaks.
   b. Has a meandering stream or river.
   c. Has little wind but gentle breezes.
   d. Is a dwelling located on a flat place.
   e. Has water that flows from or is connected in some way to the mountains or hills.
II. When you have found a place that features all or most of the above . . .
   a. Stand outside the dwelling.
   b. Close your eyes.
   c. Take ten deep breaths.
   d. How do you feel? In your body? In your heart?

e. What thoughts come to you?

f. Does this remind you of anything else? Is it like any other place that you remember?

Once again, there are no "rights" and "wrongs" to this. You just have to trust whatever it is that you see and feel. And if nothing particular comes, so what?

A Trip Within a Trip—the Hidden Map

One branch of feng-shui, the Jiangxi school of geomancy, placed emphasis on physical forms. In this game we look at the forms of the land.[19]

NEEDED: a black felt-tip pen for each person playing.

I. When you are about to make a trip, get two road maps of the area. (One you will use to get there. The other you use to play the game.) Make sure it covers a large area like a state or province.

II. If you are not driving, pay attention to rivers, railroads, mountains, valleys and roads. (If more than one person is playing, people can take turns watching the scenery.) Pay attention to these features on the map as well.

III. Pay attention to different colors (for counties or subdivisions).

IV. Take the felt-tip pen and, using any features of the map that you choose, sketch out several creatures. This is similar to the child's game of connect the dots. You can connect towns and see what shapes emerge. You can use the roads.

V. How do these creatures stand with respect to each other?

VI. What is the creature that you are presently in?

VII. What creature(s) are you traveling through?

VIII. What part of the creature(s) are you traveling through?

IX. What creature are you heading toward?

X. Identify the different parts of the creature(s) (head, eyes, heart, mouth, etc.).

XI. What part of the creature are you heading for?

XII. What part would seem the most peaceful?

XIII. What part seems the most turbulent?

XIV. When you arrive at your destination, you might experiment by exploring the various parts of your creature. For example, does it feel different being in the stomach of the creature than the head?

XV. Note the different feelings in each part.

The Five Elements of the East

As Chinese as *feng-shui* may be, it has parallels in the study of Weastern alchemy. Western alchemists, as we have seen, identified four basic elements: air, earth, fire, and water. For the Chinese alchemist there are five elements: wood, fire, earth, metal, and water. All five elements are interconnected. *Feng-shui* cames from the play of these five elements.

The *Five Elements* is a literal translation of the original Chinese *Wu Hsing*, which may also be tranlated as *Five Phases*. It was a quintet of forces, a sacred "five" that permeated everything.

There was an order to this quintet. First there was water—the basic fluid of life, representing that liquid from which we all, as living beings, have emerged. Then there was fire. From the bowels of the earth, from the skies, and beneath the cooking pots, there was fire. Then there was wood. Then there was metal and then there was earth.[20]

Three centurines before the birth of Christ, Chou Yen, a Chinese sage, described the Five Element Phases as follows: "Water is that which is straight and crooked; gold [or metal] that which obeys and changes; and earth that which is of use for seed-sowing and harvest." In the Chinese worldview there are no "good" elements and no "bad" elements. All are necessary for existence.[21]

The relationship of the elements can be seen quite simply. Burning wood creates fire. Having consumed the wood, fire gives birth to ash or earth. The earth gives birth to metallic ore, or metal. The metal, when smelted, gives birth to liquid, or water. And water, finally, gives birth to trees or wood. The cycle is completed.

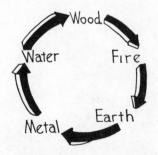

The Five Elements of Chinese alchemy and how they support each other

The elements can also operate to the detriment of each other. Wood, for example, when growing, exhausts the supply of energy in the earth. Thus, in Chinese alchemy, wood controls earth. The metal ax of the woodsman cuts the tree. Metal controls wood. Fire, used in smelting, melts metal. Therefore, fire controls metal. Water extinguishes fire, so water conquers fire. The earthen dam controls water, so earth controls water.

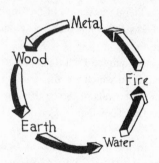

The Five Elements of Chinese alchemy and how they control each other

Scissors, Paper, and Rock: Feng-Shui Style

Many of us have played the game of scissors, paper, and rock. It is played with two people. Each person holds his right hand behind his back. On a prearranged signal each person puts his hand in front either as a fist (rock), flat out with palm down (paper), or with first and middle fingers separated (scissors).

Paper **Scissors** **Rock**

The winner in this game is determined as follows: Scissors cut paper. So, if you put out your "scissors" fingers and your opponent puts out his "paper" fingers, you would win. Rock smashes scissors. If you put out your "scissors" fingers and your opponent puts out his "rock" fist, you would lose. Paper covers rock. There are three ways to win. And lose.

As a boy I was both enthralled and fearful of this game since the winner would always get a chance to punch the loser. That is not necessary in the feng-shui version. It has more cooperative elements. Also unlike the Western version, three or four people can play this game.

The first thing that the group does is to agree on the hand signals representing the elements: Wood, Fire, Earth, Metal, Water. Then, on a prearranged signal, put out your hand with the chosen element's signal.

You can win in two ways. First, you can win by being the Element that controls the other. So, for example, if you put out the signal for Wood and your opponent puts out the signal for Earth, you would win. Or you can win by being the Element that supports your opponent's Element. Again, if you put out Wood and your opponent puts out Fire, you would win.

You can keep playing by keeping track of the points (wins) that each person gets.

Being in tune is the essence of Chinese alchemy. *Feng-shui* is part of that tradition. It is all about awareness. Basically it is quite simple. If we are trying to sail a boat, we would make sure that we knew which way the wind was blowing. Obviously it is easier to sail with the wind than against it. If we want to plant a garden, it is important to know what the natural growing seasons are. All of this involves being in tune—being aware of our surroundings, both internal and external.

Think of all life as existing within a multitude of currents. Unlike the current of the river, these currents are largely invisible. But, like the wind, they swirl around us. And through us. And within us.

Now, we can choose to ignore the wind. We can be unaware of the rain. We can be oblivious to the cold of winter. This does not mean that we will be unaffected by them. The hurricane can blow a tree on our heads whether or not we are aware of the wind. We will get wet in the rain whether or not we choose to pay attention to it. And if we go outside in the ice of winter without a coat, we will get cold no matter what your consciousness or belief system.

Similarly we can be unaware of the color scheme of a room in which we live or work. We can be heedless of the lighting of a work space. Or the construction of a house. Or a playroom. But that does not mean that we will be unaffected.

Feng-shui is one way of developing awareness of our surroundings. Such awareness then helps us to develop ways of working efficiently, comfortably, and successfully by following the patterns of nature. The key to the *qi* is awareness.

You Can Have Your Cake and Eat It: *Yin/Yang*

In the West we are taught to think of things as opposites. The old expression that "you can't have your cake and eat it, too" is an example of this kind of thinking. It is a way of thinking that conceives of the world in terms of either/or. It assesses things as good or bad, right or wrong, up or down, cold or hot. This is called a dualistic view of the world because it evaluates everything in terms of mutually exclusive opposites.

This can become so much a part of the way we think that sometimes we are not aware that we are even thinking this way. It's almost as if we are looking at the world through a pair of glasses and aren't aware anymore that we are wearing the glasses at all. We take it for granted that this is the only way to see the world.

But there are other ways of looking at the world around us. For thousands of years in the East, there has been a very different way of looking at reality. Three thousand years ago, China was beset by chaos. It was a time of conflict and war. It was a time of contesting warloads. This time was called "the Period of Warring States." Out of this period of chaos and conflict, of war and disunity, there arose a world that had order and unity.[22]

In the West we had a similar experience. Six hundred years ago a plague called "The Black Death" swept through all Europe and destroyed as much as half the entire population. Then, almost as swiftly as it had begun, it subsided. Out of this disaster—out of the Death—was born the Renaissance (which means "rebirth"). Out of the blackness of the plague came the light of Michelangelo and Leonardo da Vinci.

Out of the chaos came order. Out of the disunity came unity. Out of the aimlessness and uncertainty came direction and stability. Out of the period of Warring States came the Ch'in dynasty that laid the basis for two thousand years of a united China. And out of it all came the concept of *yin* and *yang*.

Yin and *yang* are the names for the opposites present in all reality. They are the opposites that move into each other, just as the death of winter moves into the life of spring.

Out of chaos, order; out of war, peace: out of darkness, light—the concept of *yin* and *yang* was applied to all reality. It was during the Chou dynasty that *yin* and *yang* came to be identified with everything from the weather to the state of the universe, from the connection between Heaven and Earth to the sexual connection between man and woman.

Yin originally referred to the shady side of a hill, and *yang* referred to the bright side of a hill. By mid–Chou period the terms had come to mean primal cosmic forces, with *yin* signifying all that is resting, receptive, contracting, moist, cold, and dark, and *yang* signifying that which is active, expanding, rising, hot, dry, and light. Soon they came to be seen as the constituent parts of life energy, of *qi*.[23]

Unlike the concept of opposites in Western thinking, the opposites of *yin* and *yang* do not cancel each other out. One is not "good" and the other "bad." They are not mutually exclusive. Man would not exist without woman. Cold would not exist without heat. Light would not exist without darkness. Each is contained within the other. Each coexists and interpenetrates the other. The symbol of *yin* and *yang* illustrates this:

Here the light is contained within the dark, and the dark is contained within the light. Each defines the other. Each transforms the other. From the ancient Chinese the universe itself was a relationship between *yin* and *yang*. Heaven was *yang* and covered the earth, which was *yin*.

Life energy reflected the principle of *yin* and *yang*. For example, *qi* that rises from earth to sky in the form of moisture and becomes a cloud is called *yang qi*. On the other hand, *qi* that falls down from sky to earth becoming rain is called *yin qi*. It was very much like people making love. An early manual stated the relationship quite clearly: "The intercourse of *Yin Qi* and *Yang Qi* produces everything."[24]

Checking Your Yin and Watching Your Yang

"The darkest hour is just before dawn," goes the old hymn. This is a recognition of the way in which opposites flow from one to the other. So often we find ourselves making choices between opposites: "This is good. This is bad. This is right. This is wrong." These moral choices permeate our entire world and we get ourselves into a mind-set of either/or.

Yin cannot exist without yang. In this game we check some opposites in our lives and try to see how they define each other. And we see how we tend to identify them as either good or bad.

NEEDED: paper and a writing implement.

   I. Make a list of at least twenty opposites (heat/cold, light/dark, etc.).
  II. Put them in two columns. For example, heat would go in one and cold in the other.
 III. Note with a little plus mark the ones that you judge to be positive.
  IV. Note with a little minus mark the ones that you judge to be negative.
   V. Think about how the member of each pair needs the other.
  VI. Spend a day looking for opposites in your daily life.

The aim of *feng-shui* is to find oppositions in the land. The *feng-shui* practitioners saw the landscape as containing one of two dragons, a *yin* dragon and *yang* dragon. The ideal spot would be where the two dragons come together and mate. At that point, the life energy would be the most vital. Just as when man and woman culminate the sexual act, life energy is released, so is *qi* released when the same principles are at work in the land.

There is a sexual nature to that spot where there is a sudden leap from male to female. The link between opposites of man and woman is merely a mocrocosm of the same link in the earth and the universe.

Mountains are generally considered to be *yang*. Water is considered to be *yin*. High land is *yang* and low land is *yin*. Sharply rising land is *yang* while flat land is *yin*. Stillness is *yin* and moving is *yang*. Sold is *yang* and the void is *yin*. The ideal places are those where the two forces come together and one becomes the other.

Take the mountains. The best place for prosperous *qi* is at that point where mountains and water come together. The *yang* mountains need the *yin* water. So the best spot in a mountainous area is by a water source. However, in an area where there is much water, the most valued spot is near a mountain. Another favorable spot is one that is enfolded by surrounding hills *(yang)*. At the same time a meandering river would be passing through *(yin)*.

The shape of the mountains and the nature of the water are also factors in *feng-shui*. If the opposites come together within the form itself, the production of *qi* is enhanced. For example, the nature of mountains is still *yang*. The valuable mountains are those that have a rising and falling shape *(yin)*.

The issue is balance. Precipitous *(yang)*, sharply rising *(yang)* mountains *(yang)* meeting a straight *(yin)* river *(yin)* would be extreme. It would be much more violent than the gentle meeting of dragons envisioned by the *feng-shui* masters, more like a rape than a lovemaking.

On the other hand, if the individual elements that make up the land site are balanced within themselves, then the "dragons" can mate. A gently rising and falling *(yin)* mountain *(yang)* has the two elements meeting within it. If this gently rising and falling mountain range meets a meandering *(yang)* river *(yin)* or still *(yin)* lake *(yin)*, then the elements are balanced within them-selves. In this case, the best spot would be that where a gently rising mountain meets a meandering river.[26]

A solid with form is considered to be *yang*. On the other hand, void without form is *yin*. The *yin* and *yang* dragons must be mating and moving for the *qi* to be produced. Mountains have form. Valleys are spaces. Once again the meeting of mountains and valleys is the mating of the two dragons. The ancient *feng-shui* texts always come back to the sexual symbolism. The main sites were at a center surrounded by enclosing hills that evoked the female body. And the favorable *feng-shui* site was called the "hole" or the "heart of the flower," both implying the vagina.[27]

Do-It-Yourself Feng-Shui

It takes twenty years of hard work to become a feng-shui master. Neverthe-less, there are some principles that all of us can follow. After all, feng-shui, like every other practice involving the tuning of awareness, comes from basic human percep-tions. And we are all basic humans.

Start with the following characteristics of yin: passive, water, cold, and humid. Use the following characteristics of yang: active mountains, hot and dry.

NEEDED: paper and a writing implement.

I. Go to a place of your choosing.
II. Using the above characteristics, find the *yin* aspects of the area.
III. Find the *yang* aspects of the area.
IV. Where do they come together and how?
V. Assuming you were all-powerful, what changes would you make in the area to the landscape, geological formations, and climate?
VI. How would these alterations change the nature of the *yin* and the *yang?*

> *To see a world in a grain of sand*
> *And a heaven in a wild flower,*
> *Hold infinity in the palm of your hand*
> *And eternity in an hour.*
>
> —William Blake, *"Auguries of Innocence"*

Three thousand years before the mystic and poet William Blake wrote about seeing the world in a grain of sand, Chinese mystics were hearing the universe in the whisper of the wind. For the ancient *feng-shui* masters the grain of sand, the wildflower, and the beating of lovers' hearts were all part of the same fabric.

The Asian sages perceived an integrated and interconnected universe. It was a cosmos where wind and rain, wars and flowers, were all governed by the same principles. Three thousand years before Greenpeace and the emergence of the modern ecology movement, Chinese scholars practiced the art of being in tune with the environment.

Fritjof Capra in his book *The Tao of Physics* shows how modern atomic physics has finally caught up with the principles known in the East for thousands of years. Perhaps there is nothing new under the sun. Certainly awareness of the earth and the relation of humans to their environment goes back two millennia before the birth of Christ. Perhaps we can draw upon these ancient perceptions to harmonize ourselves with our own environment.

CHAPTER 6

"That Which Hath Wings": Signs in Nature

*Curse not the king, no not in thy thought; and curse not the
rich in thy bedchamber: for a bird of the air shall carry the
voice, and that which hath wings shall tell the matter.*
—*Ecclesiastes 10:20*

*I am quite aware of the statement often used, "nothing is
holy now." We who still have faith in our religion know
everything is holy. How else can we live! The air we breathe is
holy, the natural spring is holy, childbirth is holy. Just thinking
of all the wonderful things nature provides, it is all holy.*
—*Tom Ration, Navajo Indian shaman[1]*

THE Seneca Indians listen to nature. They hear
voices. For the Senecas feel that all nature is conscious—the birds, the trees, the animals and plants—
even the rocks.[2]

The Senecas are not alone. It all began between
thirty and sixty thousand years ago when bands of no-
mads crossed the dividing line between northeast
Asia and the North American continent. These were
the wanderers of the Siberian steppes. The forebears
of the shamans of ancient China, they were the origi-
nators of the *I Ching* and the ancestors of the Native
Americans.

These ancient wanderers felt that the universe was a cosmic, harmonious
whole. They believed that everything was connected. Humans and animals
and plants and rocks and the fish in the sea were all part of a whole. To see the
part was to see the whole. To hear the part was to hear the whole.[3]

The spirits of nature have been with us from the time that the ancestors of
mammals crawled onto the land. Fifteen thousand years ago shamans in the
ancient lands of France disguised themselves as bison better to hunt among

their fellow animals. This was not merely a camouflage, but a way to gain kinship with the beasts. Many Native American cultures see the spirits of the animals, mountains, rocks, and plants as guides to those who are able to use them.[4]

It is the voice of nature that is heard by those who listen. Down through time, diviners and shamans have listened to the sounds of the natural world. The ancient Bulgars listened to the howls of dogs. The Turks interpreted the language of the beasts.[5]

Calling to the Four Winds: What Animal Comes to You?[6]

> Anyone can get to be a shaman by dreaming. In the dreams,
> spirits such as those from the eagle, bear, owl, snake, antelope,
> deer, mountain sheep, mole, or falling star appear. The spirit that
> comes in the dreams is the shaman's power.
>
> —Paiute Indian shaman[7]

Native American seers pay a great deal of attention to the animals that cross their paths in the daily course of life. The medicine wheel, which we discussed briefly in chapter 3, is an ancient and sacred American Indian tool of perception that allows us to understand the language of the animals. It is not something that can be popularized. However, the "reading" of animals as a door to understanding is something that we can all try.

Even those of us who live far from the country see animals on a regular basis. It is true that you won't find a wild deer in New York City outside of the zoo, but you will find dogs and cats and pigeons as well as spiders and cockroaches and mice. To participate in this game, we do not need a menagerie of beasts. All we really need to do is to pay attention.

Calling to the four directions for guidance is something that is found in Judaic and Christian as well as American Indian tradition.

As you play this game, try to be aware of the negative associations you have about certain animals. Lots of us don't like spiders and snakes, but there are beautiful aspects to each: The spider weaves wondrous webs and the snake continuously sheds her skin, becoming fresh and reborn each time. We don't have to be poets to make the connections with the animals that appear in our lives. For example, we weave our lives (and our illusions) as certainly as the spider weaves the web. And we shed the old and move into the new as the snake sheds her skin.

This game is not about judging, but about letting the animals be our guides.[8]

NEEDED: paper and a writing implement.

I. Find a place outside that is relatively undisturbed. This can be a little clearing of land in the middle of the woods, or a bare patch of land in a park.

II. Make a circle with a twig on the ground and mark out the four directions, east, south, west, and north.

III. Consider east as symbolizing the area of rising sun and rebirth; south as youth, summer, and new day; west as that which is within the heart and autumn; and north as winter, old age, and nighttime.

IV. Make a list of all of your own associations with each direction.

V. Spend some time alone with your circle.

VI. Close your eyes and call upon animal guides to come and help you.

VII. Pay particular attention during the course of the day and even during the week to the animals that come to you. This can be done either in waking or in dream states.

VIII. Notice which direction they are coming from and which direction they are heading toward.

IX. What is your reaction to the animals?

X. What qualities do the animals possess?

XI. What relevance do the animals have for your life at that moment?

If you don't know much about the animals that you see, find out more about them at the library. It's best to play the game over a period of time.

From the Druids and Scots of Britain to the Fang of West Africa; from the Ute, Blackfeet, and Crow Indians of America to the Samoans of the Pacific, people have sought answers to their lives in the spirits of animals. As often as not, these animal spirits appear in dreams.[9]

An old man leaves his village, carrying a pack across his back. It is the coming of nighttide. The hills are starting to redden with the glow of the setting sun. It is deep in the Highlands of Scotland, centuries before the birth of Christ.

The old man climbs high into the hills until he reaches his destination. There, pounding down into the river below is a waterfall. The man carefully climbs down a rock ledge into a small cave behind the waterfall. The plummeting water fills the cave with a deafening thunder. The man settles down into the cave and takes the pack from his back. He unfolds his burden. It is a large hide from a recently slaughtered ox. He takes the ox hide and fully wraps himself in it. He lies down and closes his eyes.

The old man is a diviner. He has been sent by his village to find the answer to pressing questions that involve the very future of the village. He is practicing *taghairm*. During the night, wrapped in his "cloak of knowledge," the diviner will find the answer in the roar of the water and the spirit of the slain animal.[10]

Native Americans see animals as both teachers and spirits. Each carries certain strengths, called "medicines." These power animals, or totems, are a reflection of our own animal nature. Our totems are a reflection of ourselves.[11]

The Ojibwa Indians gave the world the word "totem." Their word was *ototeman,* which meant "his sibling kin." The Algonquins adapted the word as *nto'tem* or "my kin." The Cree Indians developed the word as *ototema,* or "his kin." For all of them, the animal was our relative.[12]

The totem poles of the Northwest Native Americans show the connection between the animal world and the human world. These poles, often towering, represent animals who in ancient times dropped their animal form to reveal a human form. These animals are the relatives of the human families they represent. The totem poles are sculptural genealogies.[13]

Physiologically we are part of the animal kingdom. However, many cultures have recognized that our connection to the animal world is more than merely physical. Human beings have long related to their fellow creatures as both helpers and distant ancestors.

Totems for All[14]

We are animals, divine animals but animals nevertheless. From the dawn of human time people have looked at animals as guides, guardian spirits, and inner forces in their own lives. In this game we focus on the animals within. The key to playing this one is to relax. Don't judge.

    I. Focus on the heart. This is the area of love, intimacy, friendship.

    II. Place your hand over your chest.

    III. Let your hand feel the warmth of your chest. Let your chest feel the warmth of your hand.

    IV. Ask for the first animal to come to you through the heart.

    V. This is the animal for your heart.

    VI. Place your hand over your throat. This is the area of communication.

    VII. Close your eyes and let thoughts and images come into your mind's eye.

    VIII. What animal comes through your throat?

IX. Put your hand over your forehead. This is the area of creativity and intuition.

X. Close your eyes and let whatever picture comes.

XI. What animal comes through your forehead?

XII. Put your hand over the indentation right below the ribs in the center of the chest. This is the solar plexus or power center.

XIII. What picture comes to you? What animal?

XIV. Close your eyes and picture all four animals.

XV. How would they stand with respect to each other in real life?

XVI. How do they stand with respect to each other inside of you?

XVII. What conflicts exist among the animals? Which ones get along with which? Which ones do not?

Take your time with this exercise. You may decide to spend time with each animal separately before bringing them together. Discover what feels the best.

Follow the Rainbow

> *God gave Noah the rainbow sign:*
> *No more water but the fire next time.*
> *—African American gospel song*

It was August 1979. I was in India at the Rajneesh Ashram in Poona, where I participated in a prayer group. At first I was instructed to lie on my stomach with a rubber ball in my navel, then kneel with my arms outstretched in the Islamic prayer position, then stand quietly, then repeat the whole thing. I did this for eight hours. We assumed each of these prayer positions while a very serious German woman disciple read aloud quotations about how prayer was not asking for things but simply letting existence in.

I was a new disciple and very enthusiastic. But this group really irritated me. As my belly button got sore, so did my disposition. Let existence in? I just wanted to get out. Surprisingly, though, the eight hours went much faster than I had expected. Still, at the end of the day, I was overjoyed that the ordeal was over. Let existence in, indeed! I'll let existence in, all right.

I walked out the door to the din of thousands of parrots streaming through the sky to alight in two trees right next to the building I had been in. I walked out the door to see a brilliant rainbow arch down right across the street.

The rainbow has always been a source of wonder. After all, to look into the sky and see the seven colors of the spectrum arching over the earth is awe-inspiring whether you are living in a Neolithic cave or a modern penthouse.

The Marshall Islanders, faced with the fickleness of nature, saw the rainbow as a sign of hope. No matter how black the sky, a rainbow anywhere would indicate a break in the weather.[15] For the Shoshone Indians the appearance of a rainbow is a good omen as well as an indication that the rain will stop.[16] For the Navajo and the Norse the rainbow is seen as the bridge that carries heroes and giants between the human world and the other side. For the Irish, the Silesians, and the Malayans there is a treasure at the base of a rainbow.[17]

I have found that every time a rainbow appears, something significant is happening in my life: a marriage, the arrival of children, a change in career. All of these events have been preceded by a rainbow. Maybe I'm not the only one to experience this phenomenon.

NEEDED: paper, a writing implement, and one rainbow.

I. Write down the date of the rainbow.
II. What is going on in your life at this moment? Think of this time frame as specifically as possible.
III. How do you feel? Elated? Depressed?
IV. Check the entry a week or two later. Has anything in your life changed significantly?
V. Keep a record of every rainbow. You'll find that they are not such unusual occurrences. The sun has to be shining and the rain has to be falling.

The Voice of the Trees; the Whisper of the Leaves

It was one of many battles. The perpetual Philistine enemy had been defeated once before. The young poet king of Israel, David, had vanquished them in the battle of Baal-perazim. There, the king and his armies had destroyed the graven images and burned them. But now the Philistines had gathered their forces in the valley of Rephaim. Gathered in the heights above, David sought guidance from God. The Lord commanded him to attack the Philistines from the rear. God Himself would give the signal. A sound in the mulberry trees would be the signal to advance.

King David listened. He heard the sound in the leaves and attacked. That day the Philistines were vanquished.[18]

—Samuel 5:20–25, The Holy Bible

The Message of the Trees

Plants and trees. These are the source of the air we breathe and the food we eat. Native Americans have always viewed the trees and plants as guides. They hear the voices of the ancestors in the trees, the bushes, and the flowers of the field as well as the stones and animals.[19] The Chinese have long seen the life force, *qi,* as flowing through trees and plants and enhancing the life of humans.[20] In the mountainous regions of Guizhou, China, the Miao people feel the spiritual essence of the universe in the trees and vines that overhang the numerous cliffs.[21] From Asia Minor to the tip of Scotland, sacred groves of trees have been meeting places for seekers and diviners for thousands of years. Of the Germans at the time of the Roman Empire, the historian Tacitus wrote, "The grove is the center of their whole religion. It is regarded as the cradle of the race and the dwelling-place of the supreme god to whom all things are subject and obedient."[22]

Trees grow as we grow. But they stand quietly while the world around them changes. They have the wisdom of age and solitude. So it is that among the African Ashantis, a diviner will undergo rigorous training that involves listening to the voices of the trees.[23] The ancient Israelites also listened and noted the movement of the wind through the trees.[24]

The tree of life casts its shade across the oceans of the world. For the Celts the tree of life was the apple. For the Chinese it was the peach. For many Semitic peoples it was the date. For the Carib, Maskushi, Arekuna, and other Guiana Indian tribes there was a founding tree from which all other plants came and, indirectly, all life.[25]

Trees give us shelter from the heat and cold and rain. As the destruction of the tropical rain forests illustrates, they are a basic force in the regulation of climate itself. They are a source of life and a mirror for us as well.

Roots and Branches[26]

People have always been fascinated by trees. Mighty oaks and redwoods grow from tiny seeds. Their roots go deep into the nourishing earth. Their trunks reach higher into the sky. Their branches spread outward as hands reaching to the heavens.

We are like trees. Our lives are like trees. We begin as seeds within the womb. We spend our lives growing, branching out, and reaching upward. From the Druids to the Buddhists to the medieval Jewish Kabbalists, the tree of life has been a powerful symbol. In this game we try to see ourselves through the image of a tree.

I. Find a tree that feels right to you.

II. Walk around the tree.

III. Feel the tree.

IV. Sit down with your back against the tree.

V. Close your eyes.

VI. "Feel" the roots of the tree in your imagination.

VII. Imagine the sap of the tree rising from the roots through the trunk.

VIII. Let yourself rise with the sap from the roots through the trunk into the branches and leaves.

IX. What feelings come up as you rise with the sap?

X. If you saw your life in this moment as a tree, where would you be? In the roots? In the branches? In the leaves?

XI. Visualize that part of the tree and let yourself move into it.

XII. Imagine the "roots" of your life now.

XIII. What do they need for their strength and nourishment?

XIV. What is the status of their health now?

XV. Imagine the trunk of your life.

XVI. Looking at it as a gardener, what is its health?

XVII. Imagine *your* leaves.

    a. Are they healthy?

    b. What do they need?

XVIII. Take time for one more hello and goodbye to the tree.

If we think of ourselves as trees, we may think of ways in which we can be better cared for. Gardeners prune away dead branches. So, too, we may think of old "branches" that we would like to get rid of. Gardeners also nourish the roots and branches of a tree. How can we do this as well?

Wise Spider Finds Fire

In the beginning, fire was set in a hollow in the ground on an island. It was a challenge to all living creatures. Someone had to go and get the fire. A meeting of animals was held. They had come together to find someone to bring fire.

The possum was the first to volunteer. Possum was a courageous creature and came forth to offer to go. He went but tried to carry fire with his tail. His tail became so scorched and burned that he could not carry out his mission, and to this day Possum has a hairless tail.

Buzzard volunteered. But he, too, failed, burning his neck and head. All manner of bird and fowl followed. Eagle flew over the island but was burned to a dark color for his efforts. Raven tried but was burned so badly that he, too, turned black. Raven was followed by Crow and Turkey. They, too, were burned.

Some of the four-legged creatures thought that they would try. Bear was burned black. Skunk, who was a bit more agile, was only partially burned—in stripes. And one of the large family of fox tried his luck only to be burned black.

The last creature to attempt to get the fire was Spider. Everybody laughed when she offered. She was so small and light. She had no way of getting across the water and nothing in which to carry the fire. How could Spider bring fire?

Spider listened to the laughter of the birds and animals. She had made a decision. She would carry the fire. Spider got a small clay bowl, tied it behind her with her spiderweb. Then she walked upon the surface of the water just as she does today.

When Spider arrived on the island where the fire was, she had a problem. How was she to get the fire without getting burned? She was a resourceful being. She took some rags, threw these into the fire, and pulled the fire toward her in the bowl.

With the fire in the bowl and the bowl attached by gossamer webs to Spider, she returned back to the land of the birds and animals. Spider brought fire to us all. And that is how fire was obtained.

—Cherokee folktale[27]

Wise Spiders and Attentive Dogs: Divine Animals

In the Serbian countryside a peasant family has grown and flourished. It is clear that with this growth has come the need for a new dwelling. Finding a site to build a new house is no simple task, for some locations are auspicious and some are not. How to find the right place?

First, the family finds a spot that is appealing. Then they place four stones on the spots where the four corners of the building will be located. The family leaves the stones overnight and returns to their home. The next day they return. Carefully the father turns over each of the four stones. If there is a live insect under at least one of the stones, the site will be a good one. If not, the family will have to search for another site and repeat the process. If, after several attempts, they found no insect under the stones, they might have to give up the project completely.

The father is impatient. He tries another method of finding a site. With the help of his sons he builds a large enclosure surrounding the area where he might build his house. After finishing the fence, he drives his sheep into the enclosure. The next morning the sheep are all lying in one area of the enclosed field. It is in that area that the Serbian farmer builds his house.[28]

People have used animals, birds, and insects for food, for clothing, for companionship, and for ornamentation. They have also used them as tools of divination and as instruments of guidance.

Perhaps no creature has been more used as a divinatory tool than the spider. Among the Native American cultures of the American Southwest, the spider has been revered as a beneficent character. It is Spider that brings fire to humans in the Cherokee story. The Toba Indians of South America believe that the spider was the first weaver. The Tahitians regard spiders as shadows of the gods and never harm them. The Chippewas hang spiderwebs on the hoop of cradleboards to catch the harm in the air. These have been refined and marketed as "dreamcatchers." In England people protect small spiders, calling them "moneymakers."[29]

Probably the most famous spider-reading story in the West comes from Scotland. There, in 1305, the Scottish leader Robert the Bruce was imprisoned for leading a rebellion against England. Languishing and discouraged in his prison cell, Bruce watched a spider try to spin its web. Each time the spider tried, it failed. Finally, after seven tries, the spider succeeded. Bruce was impressed by the perseverance of the spider and regained his spirit. He had read the message of the spider.[30]

Spiders are used by diviners from South America to southern Africa. In central and northern Peru, to find the answer to a question, the Peruvian reader would uncover a large spider that had been contained overnight in a covered jar. If any of its legs were bent, it was a bad augury.[31]

It is in Africa that spider reading became most complex. In the northern grasslands of what was formerly the Cameroons a giant, hairy, bird-eating earth spider is the main tool of divining the daily will of the gods. Both the practice and the spider are called *ngám*. Every family head among the Tikar and Kaka people owned at least one divining spider. The method is straightforward. The Tikar reader creates a stack of cards from leaves. Designs are painted on these leaves, and the resulting decks have numbered as many as three hundred cards. The *ngám* spider is kept in an enclosure near the family's hut. It is used for cases of great importance. The diviner approaches the spider's enclosure in the evening, scatters the divinatory cards, and leaves a freshly killed or crippled insect on top of the cards to attract the *ngám*. The diviner then reads the cards, as moved by the spider, the next morning. Some diviners will do the spider reading in broad daylight and will call the spider by name. The spider will respond, perform its function of scattering the cards, and be fed as a reward.[32]

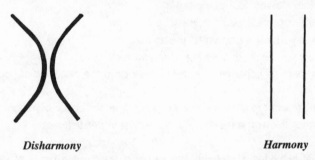

Disharmony   Harmony

Two examples of designs on cards used by Tikar diviners in consulting the ngám spider. In a marital question, for example, the design on the left can be seen to represent a couple sleeping back-to-back, a sure sign of disharmony. The card on the right, two lines going in the same direction, would indicate harmony.

Shapes have meaning all over the world. For example, the triangle has been a symbol of unity in many cultures. In the leaf cards of the Tikar people the card with two triangles represents a positive answer to the question proposed.[33]

Talking Turkey to Rex (or Muffy or Spot)

For most of us, the only animals that we regularly interact with are our pets. They are companions, friends, and associates. As with all relationships, we sometimes take them for granted. And, as with all relationships, we are known by the other party better than we think we are.

We relate to our pets and they relate to us. In this game we consciously speak to our animals and see how they respond.

I. Is there something that has been bothering you about your pet? Is there something that has been pleasing you about your pet?

II. Find a time where the two of you can be undisturbed.

III. Speak clearly to your animal and state what you need to say as pre-
cisely as possible.
IV. How do you feel doing this?
V. Are you really being honest?
VI. Are you talking down to the animal?
VII. Are you really expressing what you feel?
VIII. Is there any change in your behavior or in the behavior of your pet?

*You might want to try this over a period of time and notice any changes that
occur in either the way you behave or the way your pet behaves.*

Animal behavior is probably one of the oldest human fields of study. It
makes sense that our most ancient ancestors, having spent so much time
watching and tracking animals, would find ways to read them—to use animals
as instruments of divination.

It is deep in the forests of the Central African Republic. A man in the village is concerned. His wife has not conceived and they have been married for
over a year. He and his wife want to find out if she will conceive. The choices
for this man are clear. He can ask a diviner to use the rubbing board. There are
many in the village that know how to use this instrument. The reader takes his
special board and reads answers based on the resistance or lack of resistance
he feels as he rubs it. The man has used this for simpler questions like the best
time to visit a relative. But he is aware that such a method can be manipulated,
even unconsciously, by the reader.

This man has two other choices: the poison oracle and the termite oracle.
In the first, a special poisonous powder is forced down the throats of small
fowls. Usually they go into spasms. Sometimes they recover. No matter what,
the motions of the poisoned birds are read to answer the question at hand. This
is a potent method of divination. His people firmly believe that the poison oracle does not err. Its authority is backed by the political power of the princes
and by tradition.

The termite oracle is the man's third choice. In this, the branches of two
separate trees are cut and placed near a termite mound. The reader pokes the
mound and disturbs the termites. If the insects go to one group of branches,
a specific answer is given. If they go to the other, the opposite answer is
given.

The man is an Azande. The Azande people of Zaire, Central African Republic, and Sudan are a subsistence farming folk. They grow grain and ba-
nanas and they fish. They also gather plants and insects. For the Azandes both

animals and insects are tools for understanding their world. Every Azande household has its fowl for divination purposes.[34]

The use of animals and insects, birds and fish, as divinatory instruments is as widespread and varied as divination itself. The Naskapis of Labrador use animal and fish parts as divination tools. They toss the mandible of a codfish in the air and call out a question. If the mandible falls with teeth upward, the answer is affirmative. If it falls with teeth downward, the answer is negative. They also use the paws of an otter.[35] On the Truk Islands, in the South Pacific, the islanders use a complex technique of knots and turtle eggs to determine when the turtle will return.[36] Among the pagan Slavs, horses were used to step over a certain pattern of lances. The deftness of the horses and the pattern they described would give answers to the questions posed.[37]

The Dogon people of the African republic of Mali trace diagrams in the sand. They make patterns that correspond to the question being asked. The basic pattern is a rectangle divided into sections for the sky, the earth, and the underworld. The diviner adds marks to represent specific elements of the question. The drawing is left overnight and groundnuts are laid around to attract animals. The following morning the footprints of the animal give the solution to the question.[38]

The ancient Druids of Britain used chicken eggs and the way in which chickens scratched as a tool for divination.[39] Oklahoma Cherokees turn loose seven crayfish in the middle of a field to determine the weather. If the first crayfish heads east, there will be rain soon. If it crawls west, there will be no rain.[40] The Miao people of western Hunan, China, put two snails in a dish before taking any important action. They then watch the pattern of the snails' escape.[41]

People have always looked to nature for assistance. From eggs to snails, from otters to horses, the creatures of nature help us to read the world.

That Which Hath Wings: Birds as Augury

How Lokabrahma Eavesdropped on the Eagle

Long ago, before they found a home, the Thai people traveled to the south. At that time the world was governed by two gods. The first was the sky god, Devabrahma. He was a force of forces. He was a supreme deity, lord of all the heavens.

The second god was Lokabrahma. He resided on earth and was, in fact, quite human.

Now, Lokabrahma was a somewhat casual fellow. He was a god but not one of your fire and brimstone, lightning and thunder gods. After all, his home territory was the earth.

Devabrahma had given Lokabrahma the task of mastering the eight precepts of Buddhism. However, Lokabrahma was simply not the scholarly type. When Devabrahma made a surprise visit to earth, he was dismayed to find that Lokabrahma had forgotten all the sacred precepts.

The supreme deity of the sky was enraged. He gave Lokabrahma eight days to remember these precepts or else he, Devabrahma, would cut off Lokabrahma's head.

Even a god needs his head. Frightened at the deadline, Lokabrahma traveled far and wide to find the sacred precepts. He even made an extensive journey to heaven to ask the divine spirits for the answer. But no one could help him.

Exhausted from his search, Lokabrahma returned to earth as ignorant as he had left. There was only one day left before the Lord of the Skies would cut off his head.

Back on earth, Lokabrahma lay down to rest under a tree where there was an eagle's nest. He heard, high above, a hungry eaglet complaining to its mother. There had been no meat for quite some time, whined the eaglet.

The mother eagle told her child that she would get some meat the next day. The eaglet wanted to know from where the meat would come. The mother bird responded that Lokabrahma's head would be available in the morning.

Terrified, Lokabrahma listened to the conversation in the treetop. He was well aware of the approaching deadline.

The eaglet was curious. It wanted to know why Lokabrahma's head would be available. "Because he has not learned the eight precepts," responded the mother bird.

"But what are these precepts?" asked the ever-curious eaglet.

The mother eagle resisted her child's questions. However, like all children, the eaglet was persistent. Finally, unable to sustain the nagging of her child, the eagle told her eaglet the eight precepts.

Listening far below, Lokabrahma heard each of the eight precepts as recited by the mother bird to her child. Listening far below, Lokabrahma saved his head by eavesdropping on the eagle.

From that time on the Thai people have listened carefully to the wisdom of the birds.[42]

—Ancient Thai story

Throughout time, birds have been seen as the messengers of the gods and the carriers of the soul to heaven. The ancient Egyptians saw birds as the soul, with the hawk representing the soul of Horus and the pharaoh. Aztecs thought the dead were reborn as birds of their patron god. Among many Native Americans, birds are the embodiment of the wind and rain.

In disparate cultures throughout the world, people have felt that birds were carriers of news and signs. "Orthomancy" and "augury" were the terms eventually used to describe the practice of using birds as divination tools. In the deserts of Arabia at the time of the Prophet Mohammed, diviners looked to the birds for signs. Today the northern Arabian Rwala tribe still looks to the creatures of the sky. The ancient Germans and Japanese watched the flight of birds to understand their own paths. The Valkyries were said to understand the speech of the birds.[43]

In Samoa, in the South Pacific, birds were considered to be the incarnation of gods. The Samoans felt that their gods appeared in the form of animals. Where an animal is native, there the god resides. In several Samoan cultures the war god was incarnated in a bird. And where the bird flew, so flew the fate of the people. For these people the gods resided in herons, kingfishers, pigeons, and rail birds. In Indonesia, among the Kantu people, the deities express themselves through seven species of forest birds.[44]

It is through their sounds and their flight that birds announce themselves. It is through their sound and their flight that they have been seen as instruments of the divine. Flying across the sky, birds provide a living alphabet. The Roman writer Hyginus went so far as to claim that the invention of writing was suggested by the flight of cranes.[45] The ancient Celtic mystics had their own alphabets, called *ogam*. One of these was based on the form and movements of the birds. The study of the form of flight of birds is common from the South American Aymara Indians to the ancient Slavs; from the Philippines to the ancient Middle East and central Asia.[46]

Reading the Alphabet of the Birds

This game is best played when there are large numbers of birds in the sky. The migratory periods of autumn are the best. However, anytime there are more than a couple of birds in the sky is fine.

    I. Find a comfortable position outside, either sitting or lying on your back.

    II. Watch the birds.

    III. Watch their direction and the shape of their flock.

IV. Watch their motion. Is it fluid? Jerky? Do the birds move from right to left? Left to right?

V. Close your eyes.

VI. Ask yourself, "Where am I at this point in my life?" or any other question that is important for you at this time.

VII. Open your eyes.

VIII. Squint your eyes so that the sky and the birds are slightly blurred. (If you wear strong glasses, take them off and you won't need to squint.)

IX. Find letters in the formation of the birds and the individual birds.

X. Look at them as if you are reading a road sign where many of the letters have worn away or changed.

XI. Put all the letters together and compose the message.

XII. What does it tell you?

The General Wasn't Chicken Enough

Roman General Publius Clodius was a brave and blustery man. It was three centuries before the birth of Christ and he was in the midst of the First Punic War.

General Clodius led his ships against the naval power of Carthage. It was a campaign, he was sure, that would bring victory and glory. But tradition had to be observed.

Roman tradition held that chickens be brought along on every naval or land campaign. Tradition further dictated that the chickens be fed immediately before an attack. If the chickens ate, it was a good sign. The battle would be joined. If they refused to eat, it was a bad sign. The battle would be avoided for the time being.

Not one to buck authority unnecessarily, General Publius Clodius had his collection of chickens on board. They would serve their purpose.

Just before the battle, the general had the chickens brought out on deck. Food was laid before the fowl there assembled. But the chickens refused to eat. After much coaxing, they still refused to eat.

The crew stirred uneasily. This was not a good sign. The chickens were not eating. There should be no battle. But the general had other ideas.

General Publius Clodius was not one to wait his glory on the whims of hens. General Publius Clodius was not one to wait at all. He was eager to engage the enemy and impatient with what he felt were the superstitions of his time.

"Throw them into the water," he demanded. The chickens were thrown into the sea. "If they won't eat, let them drink," he shouted, and ordered the battle to be joined.

The battle was a disaster for the Romans. General Publius Clodius was roundly defeated and brought home to face charges of treason for refusing to listen to the chickens.[47]

—Roman story

Birds speak. They have voices and create a variety of sounds. Of course, they do not speak in human voices. They do not use words as we use words.

Many peoples have listened to the voices of birds. The ancient Incas listened carefully to the prophetic sounds of the birds.[48] Missionary priest Father du Perron visited the Huron people of the Iroquois Nation in the 1600s and found the Indians basing their actions on the words from a crow or some other bird.[49] The Yakut Indians listen to the messages of bullfinches, cuckoos, grebes, and grouse.[50]

Forty years ago Lama Chime Radha, a Tibetan mystic, was fleeing his country. The Chinese were in close pursuit and the Lama was in grave danger. Fortunately Radha was trained in the ancient Tibetan practice of *bya-rog-kyi-kad-tag-pa,* or, simply, bird divination. Fleeing with a group, Radha listened to the crows and, particularly, one crow. This crow told him of the danger nearby before it reached him and thus enabled the Lama to reach India safely.[51]

Sometimes the ability to understand the "words" of birds permeates the entire society. Sometimes it is a specialized occupation, as among the Alfoer people of the East Indies, who see the flight and singing of birds as a way of learning the will of spirits. While there are some birds that everybody can understand, there are others that require the services of a specialist.[52]

The Iban people of Borneo revere birds. Each tribe has its omen birds. Before a new piece of land is cultivated, the omen bird is consulted. The Ibans will not cultivate the land unless they hear a voice of encouragement from their bird.[53]

Listening to the Birds Talk

I. Find a place outside where there are at least two birds making sounds.

II. Get comfortable.

III. Close your eyes.

IV. Single out one of the birds.

     V. Listen to its song. Pretend that the bird is speaking to you but you can't quite make out the words. Let words come.

    VI. What feelings arise for you in listening to the song?

   VII. What thoughts pass through your mind at this moment? Just let them pass and don't hold on to them.

  VIII. Ask the bird a question that is important to you.

    IX. What answer do you get? It may come in feelings, thoughts, or words.

     X. What thoughts and feelings go through you?

    XI. Make the bird's song into a phrase or even a sentence.

   XII. Repeat the same procedure with a different bird.

You might try to listen to different birds over a period of several days and see what kinds of answers you get to your questions.

The Roman playwright Terence once said, "I consider nothing human alien to me." He could have said, "I consider nothing living alien to me." For all life is connected. Even the most humble amoeba breathes, eats, excretes, reproduces, and, in its own way, feels. It is an accepted fact that houseplants respond positively to love and Mozart.

We humans have always been dependent upon our fellow living species for food and clothing and companionship. Similarly have we depended upon plants, fish, birds, and animals to give us reflections of ourselves.

Humankind's use of nature as a divinatory tool is just another way of expressing our oneness with all forms of life. It is another way of finding a mirror around us.

CHAPTER 7

Psychic Alphabets:
The Numbers and Letters of Time

*In the beginning was the Word, and the Word was with God,
and the Word was God.*

—John 1:1

*None gave me bread,
None gave me drink,
Down to deepest depths I peered
Until I spied the Runes.
With a roaring cry I seized them up,
Then dizzy and fainting, I fell.*
—Odin, the Poetic Eddas

W<small>E</small> communicate with magical symbols. Language is magic. Words are symbols. We take for granted that *C-A-T* is the same thing as that furry little thing that rubs up against us and makes purring sounds. Yet there is an ocean of time and experience that joins the placement of these distinct letters (*C-A-T*) with that fastidious creature scratching in a litter box.

There is something magical about both letters and words. Utter the combination of *C* and *A* and *T* and nearly a billion people will see, in their mind's eye, a little furry creature. It is magic to put shapes together to make words.

Today we take this magic for granted. It has not always been thus. People have recognized the magical quality of words and letters from the time that they could see a cat represented in a block of stone or thunder in a piece of papyrus.

Letters are symbols. Words, therefore, are made up of symbols. *The American Heritage Dictionary* defines "symbol" as "something that represents something else by association, resemblance, or convention, especially a material object used to represent something invisible," and "a printed or written sign used to represent an operation, an element, a quantity, a quality, or a relation."

Symbols stir us. They touch us in deep places often without our understanding or knowledge. The ancient Indian symbol of unity and friendship, the *swastik,* was turned backward to become a symbol of might, terror, and destruction.

Alphabets have their psychic roots. We can look at the roots of alphabets. We can create our own. And we can bring the unconscious into the light of awareness.

The Word: Reading Beyond Letters

By names and images are all powers awakened and reawakened.
—G. I. Gurdjieff

In the beginning was the word—uttered, growled, spoken. Words were spoken then forgotten. They were brief flashes of communication. Then, about twenty-five thousand years ago, our ancestors made the leap from vocal to written communication. At first, people tried to represent their ideas as pictures. They scratched pictures of animals and patterns on the walls of caves to summon the spirits of the animals. The symbol contained the essence of that which it represented.[1]

Picture symbols are the earliest form of written language. In California there is an ancient rock painting. It is quite simply the picture of an eye with tears dropping from it. The message is sorrow.[2]

The alphabet was developed much later, after abstract pictographic symbols. Its origins are shrouded in mystery. The ancient Egyptians, Babylonians, Chinese, and Indians all felt that the written script was divinely created. In China today, many hold that no scrap of paper with a single character on it can be trampled underfoot. Among observant Jews, any scrap of paper or other material written in Hebrew that contains the Divine Name or any loose page or fragment of Hebrew writing is kept and not destroyed. The word and the reality are one. The letters and what they represent are connected.[3]

For some people the symbols of the alphabet were celestial. Some of the actual heavenly constellations are reproduced in Chinese characters. For example, the character for "north" is depicted by a representation of the Big Dipper.[4]

The magic and power of the alphabet travels across cultures. For example, the first letter of the Greek alphabet, *alpha,* corresponds to the first letter of the Hebrew alphabet, *alef.* The second letter of the Greek alphabet, *beta,* corresponds to *beth* in Hebrew.

The first letter in the Greek alphabet has a pictorial feel. This is *alpha:* α. If you turn it on its side, it bears a striking resemblance to the symbol for Taurus, the bull. In fact, some researchers have felt that the first letter of Greek (and Hebrew and English and a host of other Indo-European languages) does indeed represent a bull. It represents the male principle and is connected with the view of the heavens. The alphabet, for these scholars, is born from ancient reading of the skies. The letters of the various alphabets do correspond to the lunar signs and other zodiac signs.[5]

Common to many cultures is the ritual of slaughtering the bull. From Mesopotamia to China to South America the sacrifice of the bull in the spring marks the beginning of the year of fertility. It is the alpha, the α, which, turned sideways, becomes the bull, the Taurus, the sign that heralds the spring.[6]

In Egypt, hieroglyphic writing was in existence three thousand years before the birth of Christ. For the Egyptians, writing was the invention of the moon god, Thoth. The hieroglyphs were thought to have magical value and were the sole property of the priests and temple scribes. For the Egyptians of the Middle Kingdom, writing was of, by, and for the gods.[7]

Several millennia later, in 1821, a Cherokee Indian named Sequoya invented an alphabet for his people. Originally he created an ideographic, or symbolic, script. However, he realized that this system would be cumbersome and so he created the script of syllables that became the basis of the Cherokee alphabet.

Half a century after Sequoya an alphabet was created in Africa. The Sultan Njoya, of the Bamum tribe of the Cameroons, saw an alphabet in a dream. A small tribe of about 75,000 people, the Bamum had no written alphabet. According to Bamum lore, the gods' request for an alphabet came to the Sultan Njoya in a dream. It was out of that dream that the sultan created one of the most recent alphabets.[8]

Alphabets and words—how they represent power! For the Bambara people of Mali, divination and the written word are inseparable. The Bambaras believe that the written word was created by divine powers and is considered a path to the divine. Bambara seers read their world through contemplation of the written word.

My Word

Back to the cat. Everybody knows the word. It's one of the first words we learn as kids, together with "dog," "run," "good," and all those basic words that start us on the road to literacy.

Clearly, if we thought about the origins of every letter in every word, we wouldn't get much talking or writing done. But, once in a while, it's a good idea to try to reinvent the wheel. In this game we reinvent some words for ourselves.

NEEDED: paper and a writing implement.

I. Pick a noun. (For those of us who have forgotten, a noun is a person, place, or thing.)

II. Think about the word and what it means to you.

III. What are the qualities of the word? (A cat, for example, is fuzzy, affectionate, swift, slinky, fastidious, etc.)

IV. Create a picture letter, an ideogram, that expresses this word to you. This does not mean you draw the word but create a simple line drawing or image that expresses the word for you. Try to use one continuous line to create the image. You are making a simple line drawing of what the word represents. Here are some doodle ideograms that I tried with the noun "cat."

V. Do the same thing with a verb—an action word. (Think of verbs that express vivid actions like "run," "jump," "grab," and so on.)

VI. Do the same thing with a feeling.

This is the kind of game that you can play while you are waiting on the telephone or procrastinating before working or studying. It's a great doodle exercise.

The Word That Killed 42,000

The men of the tribe of Ephraim gathered and went northward. These were the descendants of Ephraim of renown. Theirs was one of the most powerful of the twelve tribes of Israel.

The men of Ephraim went north to be confronted by Jephthah, of those that were called Gileadites. Jephthah had been sorely deceived by the Ephraimites.

War and land were coupled in those days of old. War and land and the bitter heat of the desert. Jephthah and his people had been involved in a war with the neighboring people of Ammon. He had called upon his allies, the Ephraimites. But they had not come to his aid. He had been deceived and betrayed.

Now the Ephraimites came to Gilead to confront Jephthah. The battle lines were drawn. The armies were arrayed against each other on the barren fields. There, with much blood and suffering, the forces of Jephthah and Gilead defeated the Ephraimites.

The armies of Ephraim were in flight. They had to cross the Jordan River to return home. But the Gileadites blocked the way and posted throngs of armed guards to intercept all fugitives.

The Ephraimites tried to cross the river. But the guards would ask, "Art thou an Ephraimite?" If the soldier responded no, to save his life, the Gileadite would command him to say "shibboleth."

Of a different tongue and manner of speech, the Ephraimites could not pronounce "shibboleth." They would pronounce it as "sibboleth" and thus betray themselves and be slain.

There, at the passage of the Jordan River, the men of Gilead slew forty-two thousand Ephraimites because they could not pronounce a word.[9]

—Judges 12:1–6, The Holy Bible

Poetry has always been linked with the magic of words. Poetry was originally sung and the magic of music and words was joined. Nowhere is this clearer than in the Gaelic tradition of England, Scotland, Ireland, and Wales. One of the words for poet in Gaelic is *fili,* which is derived from the Gaelic root of the verb "to see." *Fili* originally meant a seer. Poetry, prophecy, and divination are closely linked in Gaelic tradition.[10]

The words we use have power to create and transform. They also have power to dull and oppress. We have seen how omens have always been alive. We have also seen how omens can become dead and routine—no longer signs, but superstitions. Then they are substitutes for experience.

So it is with words. Words are, in their origin, alive and infused with divinity. The vitality and power of words exists within each of us, just as living signs are all around us. With words, as with omens, the meanings lie within us.

With words, as with omens, we have often become oblivious to the power of the word in our everyday use of language. We can rediscover the magic of words and letters and see language in a new light. One way of doing this is to see how far we have strayed from the words within us.

For example, once upon a time a person was searching for the right way to express an idea. He was a simple man, a tinker, perhaps, or a carpenter. He was one who worked with his hands and saw the world through touch and material. A friend of his had just made a point. It was a very clear and precise point. Our carpenter wanted to tell his friend just how accurate his statement was. "You have hit the nail on the head," he told his friend.

His friend was also a man who worked with his hands and saw the world in solid and practical terms. "Hit the nail on the head!" That really expressed it—couldn't say it better.

Since that time, the expression has been used billions of times. Perhaps the first time we heard the phrase, we were able to feel it, to visualize it, to understand it in the same way that the first person heard it. But, over time, it became worn and overused. We no longer saw the nail. We no longer saw the head. It became shorthand, a cliché. Clichés are expressions that once were vibrant and alive but have become worn and weary. They are unoriginal and bloodless. Clichés are verbal vampires. They suck the life force from verbal expression.

The media is one of the greatest cliché mills. Sound bites and per-second costs contribute mightily to this. Journalists and reporters like to steal each other's phrases until a homogeneous (and cliché) form of expression results. For example, the United Nations helped to bring about an unstable peace agreement among the belligerents in Bosnia. Reporters began to refer to it as the "U.N.-brokered" peace plan. Hearing that the first time brought visions of a real estate broker or a stockbroker pulling together a deal for his clients. After the thousandth time, the phrase had become a cliché.

We all use clichés. We don't all have the time to find an original way to express everything. So we use shorthand. But we pay the price not only in lifeless language but in less conscious thought. Our words do indeed express our thoughts.

Cliché Your Way

What we say reflects what we think. If we are relying on old and tired phrases, our minds are not fully awake. Clichés are old and tired.

With clichés as with other routines, we operate on automatic pilot. In this game we consciously search out the clichés with which we are most familiar. And

we turn them around. So put your shoulder to the wheel, take the bull by the
horns, and hit the mark.

NEEDED: paper and a writing implement.

I. Make a list of fifteen cliché phrases such as "hit the nail on the head,"
"level playing field," "wake-up call," and so on. The key indicator is
whether the expression has been used over and over again and was
once a statement that people could actually visualize.
II. Put together one statement that combines six or seven of these
clichés.
III. How does it sound?
IV. Take the list that you have made and create a new way of saying the
same thing. For example, instead of saying you "hit the nail on the
head," you might say you "really switched that light on." Your goal is
to create a phrase that is visual and conveys the same meaning as
that of the original statement.
V. Spend some time, say a day or two or three, watching for clichés in
your own everyday conversations and in other people's.

A funny thing happens when we watch our speech. For one thing, we see
more clearly what it is we are trying to say and we start to see things in new
ways. As most of you might have guessed by now, this is one of the main goals
of this book: to see our world in new ways.

Word Magic Game

> *'Twas brillig, and the slithy toves*
> *Did gyre and gimble in the wabe:*
> *All mimsy were the borogoves*
> *And the mome raths outgrabe.*
> —*Lewis Carroll, "Jabberwocky"*

One multicolored autumn late afternoon I was weaving my way down the
road. With me was a beloved young friend, Premda. The countryside was filled
with all kinds of colors—yellow, red, green, and orange. Yet these names are
shorthand. The grass was more than green and the trees were more than yellow
and red. The words simply did not express the vivid quality of the colors that
Premda and I saw as we drove through that autumn afternoon.

We needed new words. On that trip we developed a new vocabulary that meant something. We passed yellow leaves lit up by the setting sun. They glowed. I told Premda they were "glowyell." The sun on green mowed grass became "preen."

Premda laughed and then took her turn. The brown bare round bushes and leaves became "brow round." She named the light yellow leaves that were not lit by the sun, "low yell." (As the sun sets, glowyell can change to low yell.) The red leaves that did not reflect the sun were "bled." But the bled leaves lit up by the sun became "bree-bled." Plain brown leaves, dull and unlit, were "rund." And as the leaves changed from glowyell to low yell, they became, for a brief instant, "glow low." There was a new world surrounding this twilight of early fall. A mystic road unfolded with glowyell leaves on trees surrounded by preen mowed grass.

We were seeing things with new eyes. We were giving the moment new words to express its uniqueness. Such is the world of poets. Such is the world of psychics.

This game can be played either by oneself or in a group. Here we create our own words to explain our own realities.

NEEDED: paper and a writing implement.

I. Find several objects of the same color. For example, you might find five or six trees and plants that are green. Or you might find different kinds of brown in the wood of a house.
II. Gaze into one of these objects. Look into the object and then pretend to be the object looking out at you.
III. Close your eyes for a moment and let the object fill you up. Become aware of whatever feelings come to you while you are doing this.
IV. Open your eyes and write down all the different words that describe its color/texture/essence. Try to keep to single words rather than phrases. The only rule is that the words cannot be found in any respectable dictionary.

While playing the game, I realized, once more, the power of language to describe, to clarify, and to express a very unique reality that is my own. Each of us has our own unique reality and we can each find our own verbal way of expressing it.

A Mad Tea Party: Mean What You Don't Say

"Then you should say what you mean," the March Hare went on.

"I do," Alice hastily replied; "at least—at least I mean what I say—that's the same thing, you know."

> *"Not the same thing a bit!" said the Hatter. "You might just as well say that 'I see what I eat' is the same thing as 'I eat what I see!' "*
>
> *"You might just as well say," added the March Hare, "that 'I like what I get' is the same thing as 'I get what I like!' "*
>
> *"You might just as well say," added the Dormouse, who seemed to be talking in his sleep, "that 'I breathe when I sleep' is the same thing as 'I sleep when I breathe!' "*
>
> —*Lewis Carroll,* Alice's Adventures in Wonderland

The way we say things is as important as the words we say. I recently heard a lawyer speak of truth while his eyes shifted all over the courtroom and his mouth formed a nervous smile. Somehow it didn't ring true. Sometimes words even come to mean their opposite. For example, when a salesman says "trust me," it is usually an alarm signal to be wary.

To see beyond appearance into reality is a basic aspect of divination. In this game we consciously separate what we say from how we say it.¹¹ Maybe then we will be able to be clearer when we say what we do mean, if you know what I mean. This is best played with one or two other people.

NEEDED: paper and a writing implement.

I. Spend a minute or two thinking of different feelings that you might want to express at various times (love, anger, hate, suspicion, gratitude, etc.).

II. Make a list of at least ten of these feelings. Include their opposites.

III. Start by expressing some feelings to the other person.

IV. First make the statements so that the feelings and the way in which you express them are the same. For example, express "I am angry" in an angry way.

V. Then make the statements but express feelings that are the opposite of what you are saying. For example, say "I'm angry" in a sweet, loving tone.

VI. Then try to carry on a conversation with the other person, making sure that your statements carry the opposite feeling.

VII. How does this make you feel?

VIII. Do you notice anything about the way words feel?

IX. Spend some time watching how other people express their words and their feelings. What differences are there between the two?

X. Spend some time watching yourself.

   a. How are your feelings expressed?

   b. How close are your words to your feelings?

Onomonowhat?

There are hundreds of words that sound like what they mean—words such as "chuckle," "clink," "swish," "crack." In this game we play with words that mean what they sound like. It is best played with a group of three or more people.

NEEDED: paper and writing implements.

I. Make a list of all the words that you can think of that sound like what they mean. (Give the group a limited period of time, say five minutes, to come up with their list.) One way of doing this is to think of words that describe sounds—"crack," "rumble," and so forth. Another way is to skim through a dictionary looking for words that sound like what they mean.

II. Pool the lists and take a few minutes to compile a single joint list.

III. Write several sentences incorporating at least two words from the list per sentence.

IV. One person starts a story using some of the words. This should take no longer than one minute.

V. A second person continues the story.

VI. Do this for two or three rotations of the group.

VII. Take about five minutes for everybody to *make up* a list of words that sound like what they mean. (These are not "real" words; that is, they cannot be words that could be found in a dictionary.)

VIII. Compile once again a joint list of the made-up words.

IX. Once again write several sentences using the made-up words.

X. Again, begin a story, this time using the made-up words. You may also use new ones as you go along if they pop into your head.

There is an old connection between poetry, music, and divination. In ancient Ireland poets would sing their poems, and their poems were often indications of the divine. Sounds and meaning were connected.

As we play with the sounds and meanings of words, we open ourselves to new ways of expression. As we come up with new ways of expression, we come up with new ways of seeing.

Words on Wood: The Power of the Rune

In about A.D. 98 the Roman historian Tacitus described a scene among the Germans in which the head of the family threw some chips from fruit or nut-bearing trees. The chips were marked with certain signs. The German patriarch threw the wooden pieces onto a white cloth. Then, after prayers to the gods and while looking up to the sky, he took three slips of wood one at a time and interpreted them according to their signs. This is one of the first written observations of the use of runes.[12]

It is fitting that the origins of the runes lie cloaked in mystery. The term "rune" can be traced to a Latin word meaning "rumor," "murmur," or "hearsay." Or it can be traced to Old English and German words that mean "to whisper or tell secretly."[13]

There are some six thousand runic inscriptions known to man. The oldest date back to the first century A.D. It seems clear that they are a native response of Germanic tribes to contact with the Roman Empire. The runes are all created on the pattern of the Latin alphabet. However, they became a code, a way in which people could communicate in ways that the uninitiated (perhaps Roman military authorities) could not understand.

In the runes the message and the symbol are one. Each rune stands by itself, as a letter of an alphabet does. At the same time, each rune is a symbol that has its own meaning separate from the other runes. With the runes, the alphabet becomes the word and the word the alphabet.

The runes became a kind of magical and symbolic alphabet that spread from the ancient Etruscans to Scotland.[14] With the advent of the Middle Ages, runes increased in usage. While the clergy and laity used the Latin alphabet, the common people continued to write with runes. Soon the clergy had to understand the runes if they wanted to communicate with the common people.[15] The runes were an underground form of communication that existed side by side with the official forms of writing.

In Scandinavia, runes became firmly established as a means of divination. According to Norse mythology, the Norns were three female deities whose spinning and weaving determined the fates of humans and gods alike. These were the guardians of Urda's well, which watered the root of the great tree Yggdrasil—the tree that extended throughout the world and from which the god Odin hung. An ancient Germanic tale tells of how these fierce goddesses scored symbols on wood upon which they laid laws, chose lives, and spoke the fates. The wood symbols were, in fact, the runes.[16] While many of the runes survived on rocks and large stones, the original runes were carved onto wood.

For thousands of years wood was the essential substance. Trees were everywhere; they were the oldest living things. In villages that kept track of ancestry some trees had been there for generation after generation. The sacred and all-powerful great tree, Yggdrasil, was the centerpiece of Norse legend. The ash groves of the Druids were holy places. For the medieval Jewish Kabbalists, the tree became a symbol for life itself. It was no accident that the runes were carved into wood.

Also carved into wood was the *ogam* alphabet of the Celts. For the ancient Celts the forests and woods are described as *eochra ecsi,* or "keys of knowledge." Judgment was called *crannchur,* or "casting the woods." Unlike the runes, the *ogam* alphabet was devised to be read by the Druid noble class and not by the common people. Like the runes, the *ogam* alphabet was symbolic, originally carved on wood and used for purposes of divination.[17]

Each letter of the *ogam* alphabet was originally connected with a tree. Some of the alphabets are connected with other natural objects. The twigs of wood from the various trees were inscribed by the diviners with the appropriate letters and these were then thrown. The diviner would then read the positions in which they fell and the relationships of the sticks to each other.

The number of mystic *ogam* alphabets increased through time. Soon there were sow *ogam,* bird *ogam,* river *ogam,* color *ogam,* and food *ogam.* There was even a finger *ogam* that was used as a secret code. In finger *ogam* the mystic could use one finger as a vertical or horizontal pole against which the combination of other fingers could be laid out to create *ogam* letters. *Ogam* letters were carved into dice and thrown to find the answers to questions.[18]

The magic of the alphabet is contained in both the runes and *ogam.* Both alphabets were not only a means of communication but a way of discovering the divine.

Finding Rune Shapes

Runes are symbols. They are shapes that have assumed meaning in the course of time. Somebody, thousands of years ago, saw a shape. The shape had meaning for him. He carved it into a piece of wood. Over time, the shape became more abstract. The meaning changed a little and the origins became dim and forgotten.

There are shapes all around us. We can find those shapes that appeal to us and create our own symbols. We can make our own runes—and we can read them.

This is not an art exercise. No artistic "talent" is necessary. The game can be played over the course of several days.[19]

NEEDED: paper and a writing implement.

I. Spend a day looking for shapes that are interesting to you.

II. As you see a shape, sketch it roughly. Jot down a couple of words about where you saw it and what it was. *Note: Try to use no more than six or seven lines to create your sketch. This is not a drawing exercise.*

III. Also jot down a word or two about what you felt when you were seeing the shape.

IV. Continue sketching, using a fresh sheet of paper for each shape.

V. At the end of the day look through the different shapes. Pick the ones that you like the best. You can pick them all if you wish. It's best to wind up with twenty to twenty-five shapes.

VI. Hang out with these shapes for a day or so.

VII. Slowly go through your collection of shapes a couple of times a day and let your thoughts wander freely.

VIII. Think of a name for each of the shapes. Write the name of each on the bottom of the sheet of paper.

IX. Write down at least two qualities that each symbol represents to you.

X. You have now created your own rune deck.

XI. Keep checking on the shapes around you and revise your deck of runes as you will. You can even spend a day with a shape, visualizing and feeling it.

After using the deck for a while, you might feel like putting the shapes on pieces of wood or painting them on smooth sea stones.

As I look around the room in which I am sitting, I notice a door open to the balcony. I am no artist but I find that the lines are simple. Thus:

The open door is an obvious symbol and can be used again and again. We go through open doors. They are opportunities to pass from one place to another. They are the opposite of obstacles. And so on. This particular open door was an opening to this chapter. I had to try out my own game, of course, and found that it opened all kinds of doors as I began looking for symbols around me.

A day or two later, I felt a bit blocked. It's the same old story—high energy one day, low energy the next. I was in the same room and looked out of the win-

dow and realized that there was another form—another rune—right in front of my nose. There were bars on the window and the lines looked like this:

What kind of thoughts come to you when you see this image? I started thinking of bars. They are associated with imprisonment. If I concentrated on the bars, I would not see the view beyond them. So the bars reminded me that I can create my own imprisonment simply by focusing on my limitations. In that sense this picture can be a tool for "looking beyond the bars." So I named this rune "beyond the bars." Get the picture?

Rune-Play

If you played the previous game, you now have your own runes. Since you have created your own set of symbolic alphabets, let's use them.

NEEDED: your own set of runes (see previous game).

    I. Start by asking simple questions, such as "What is today all about for me?" or "What do I need to look at in myself at this time?"

    II. Shuffle or shake your runes (depending on whether they are paper or something more solid).

    III. Put them in a sack or basket where you can mix them up.

    IV. Close your eyes and pick one.

    V. Which rune have you chosen?

    VI. Spend just a second seeing how this rune applies to the question you asked.

    VII. Spend the rest of this day and the next day watching to see where the runic shape appears and reappears.

    VIII. You might want to pick another rune later to see what has changed.

There are no right and wrong ways to do this. The idea is to see ourselves and our world in new ways. It is amazing to see just what we already know. That's what the runes help us to do.

I'll Sing You One, Ho: Finding Signs in Numbers

I'll sing you one, ho
Green grow the rushes ho.
What is your one ho?
One is one and all alone
And ever more shall be so.
—Traditional English folk song

On December 29, 1989, the stock market in Tokyo seemed stable enough. Trading was high and the market seemed healthy and bullish. But the market closed that day with a combination of numbers that was disastrous according to numerologists. Numbers? Disastrous? The traders who heard the rumors about the numerologists laughed and shrugged their shoulders. Shortly afterward, a crash occurred. The numerologists had been correct.[20]

When did the first person start to count? It probably happened around the same time that the first humans began to write. Maybe earlier. Our numerical system was probably an extension of the body itself. There are ten fingers and our counting system is on the base 10.

Even arithmetic has a certain mystery to it. After all, what is the significance of such random numbers as 3 or 16? Numbers are very abstract ideas. Probably no other creatures on earth other than humans are able to count.

In the fifth century before the birth of Christ, a Greek mathematician, philosopher, musician, astronomer, and philosopher named Pythagoras of Samos established a school for the study of music and astronomy. Pythagoras and his disciples analyzed mathematics and philosophy. Among the many conclusions that they drew, the most general was the statement that "all things are numbers." For the Pythagoreans numbers were the basis of art, of music, of science—of knowledge itself.[21]

Numbers are mysterious. Across the world and across time people have tried to figure out the meaning of their lives through the understanding of numbers. Among the Bambara people of Sudan, numbers are the key divinatory tool. Each number has one or several meanings. The sum of several numbers also expresses a particular idea. Finally a value is given to the succession of numbers.[22]

For the Bambara the first twenty-two numbers represent the sum total of their mystical knowledge, and each number has its own place in the mystical mirror of the people. For example, 1, or *kele,* is the word. It signifies their god, Faro. It is the powerful, the chief, the right of eldest, the right of the first. The number 2, *fla,* is the original duality, twins, love and friendship, union of beings. The number 3, or *saba,* is the sexual symbol of man and his soul. The number 4, *nani,* is the sexual symbol of woman. And so it goes. The symbolism of everyday life occurs in numbers for the Bambaras and occurs all the time.[23]

In the West there is "lucky" 7 and "lucky" 11. It's hard to know whether the game of craps created these lucky numbers or whether these lucky numbers created the game of craps. Then there's the number 13. We are all taught from the time that we are little that 13 is unlucky. Countless apartment houses and office buildings mysteriously ascend from the twelfth to the fourteenth floor. Where does this "unlucky" 13 come from? Thousands of years ago, most of the people of the world worshiped goddesses rather than gods or a god. The female was seen as the representation of the goddess upon the earth. The goddess, Mother Earth, the mother—all were seen as sacred. After all, it was the woman who gave birth to the race. Knowledge of the male's role in that most basic process of reproduction was vague, if understood at all.

In those days the moon was the sacred planet, and the moon and the goddess were interconnected. The menstrual cycle of the woman was closely connected, in time, to the cycle of the moon. Both were twenty-eight-day cycles. The year was measured in lunar time. The moon goes through its cycle thirteen times a year. There are thirteen lunar months in a lunar year. The lunar year was the sacred year. Thirteen was a holy and sacred number.

So why did 13 move from being a sacred and holy number to an unlucky number? Apparently because people began to worship gods instead of goddesses. With the victory of the new male-oriented religions of Judaism and Christianity over the older religions of the goddess, the sacred number of the old religion was cast down into the pit of evil. And 13 became "unlucky."

Numbers are the alphabet of quantity. Like letters, they are abstract and symbolic. Numbers are also seen to be divine in origin. Like letters, numbers have no existence outside of us. Numbers can be manipulated, but they can do more than help us balance our checkbooks or take arithmetic tests. We can use numbers to see signs and we can see signs in numbers.

One Is One and All Alone

We identify with numbers. Numbers are used in our language for more than a means of simply counting things. In this game we discover some of the ways we identify with numbers and find new ways of using them. You can play this game alone or with a group.

NEEDED: paper and writing implements.

I. Write down all your associations with the number 1. A few examples might be: alone, oneness, unity, indivisible, together.
   a. Can you recollect any sayings or proverbs about the number? Write these down on a piece of paper.
II. Write down all of your associations with the number 2. Again, jot down all variations on "twoness" and let it come without a great deal of thought.
III. Do the same exercise with the number 3.
IV. For 4 through 9, consider them as sums of the first three numbers. For example, 5 would be 3 and 2; 6 would be 3 and 3, etc.
V. Make a list of the different characteristics of the first three numbers.
   a. How does combining them change them? What are the characteristics of a 3 and a 2 (5)? A 6 (3 and 3)? A 7 (3 and 3 and 1, or 2 and 3 and 2)?

When we play with numbers, we see them in new ways. The more playful that we can become with them, the more we can use them as tools for understanding ourselves.

In the beginning was the word. And all was one. Letters, numbers, and words are ways in which we define the universe. In turn, they define us. How we speak is how we think is how we act. Once the spoken word was expressed in abstract writing, human beings made yet another bid for immortality. Letters, numbers, and words are the signs that we use to create order in the world around us.

CHAPTER 8

Pendulums, Hickory Sticks, Dowsing, and Daisies: Computers of the Psychic World

As I watched the patterns grow on the paper, I suddenly realized that I was looking at a binary system. The 1 and the 0 the bablawo used were the same digits used by computers, which can be easily seen on the back of any computer card. . . . Here was a man who had never used a computer card, let alone program a computer, using a system handed down to him through countless years of African religious tradition.

—A scholar watching a Santeria diviner[1]

And the Lord spake unto Moses saying
Speak unto the children of Israel, and take of every one of them a rod according to the house of their fathers, of all their princes according to the house of their fathers twelve rods: write thou every man's name upon his rod.
And thou shalt write Aaron's name upon the rod of Levi: for one rod shall be for the head of the house of their fathers.

—Numbers 17:1–3

THERE is a buzz of excitement. It is 1959. The room is filled with naval officers. The highest ranking officer is a vice-admiral of the United States Navy.

A civilian stands in front of a large table. On the table are maps of the oceans of the world. The man pulls out a small metal object at the end of a string and lets it fall just above the surface of the table. The object swings back and forth as the

naval officials watch with amusement. Some ask themselves why they are here. This just seems to be another fruitless exercise.

After several minutes, the civilian steps back. He calls the vice-admiral to the table and proceeds to identify the location of the entire U.S. submarine fleet by means of his little object on a string. He then follows this up by locating every Soviet submarine in the world.[2]

Deep in the jungles of northern Nigeria a man takes out a shell of a tortoise. The shell has been dried and hollowed out. Another man sits before him and asks whether his daughter will bear children. She has been having difficulty and the man has no other children. The diviner takes the tortoiseshell and puts a string through it. He then closes his eyes and lets the shell slide down the taut string. The diviner turns to the man and gives him the happy news: It appears that his daughter will indeed have children.[3]

It is 1931 in the more remote parts of British Columbia, Canada. There is homestead land for sale. It is government land and it is cheap. However, the presence of water is crucial. It would be a folly to build a home in the wilderness without an adequate and accessible supply of water. The British Columbian provincial government and the potential homesteaders need assistance. They call in men with forked sticks. These men travel over the homestead lands with their sticks. A water source would be indicated when the sticks point downward. The men with the sticks do their job: The sticks point down and a source is indicated.

Cut to the late 1940s, high in the Himalayas. The Dalai Lama, spiritual leader of Tibetan Buddhism, is forced to flee from his homeland with the advance of the Chinese. His advisers have told him that the best plan is to head for the state of Bhutan, only two miles away. The other choice is to go to India by way of the Chumbi Valley and then a rough climb. The Tibetan spiritual leader closes his eyes and puts his hands at the level of his shut eyes. He then puts the tips of his forefingers together. The tips of the fingers meet and the Dalai Lama decides, against the advice of his ministers, to face the forty-mile climb to India.[4]

Near the Arctic Circle a Kaska Indian hunter prepares to go to sleep. He has set out traps for the fur-bearing animals that he hunts. But, as always, in this rigorous and fierce wilderness, the results are never certain. He winds a string around a smooth round stick. The method has been handed down from one generation to the next. The hunter then places the stick and the string under his pillow.

The next morning the hunter takes the stick out. Instead of falling free, the string is looped around the stick four times. The hunter now knows that he will find four animals in his traps.[5]

Tortoiseshells, string on a stick, swinging objects, the forefingers of the hand, and forked sticks—how disparate these objects seem. Yet they all have one thing in common. They are techniques of dowsing.

Traditionally, dowsing has been associated with the use of hickory sticks to find water. And, indeed, this method has been around for a long time. In the Tassili-n-Ajjer caves on the plateau of the Sahara in southeastern Algeria researchers found pictographs showing a group of people watching someone hold a Y-rod. The purpose: finding water. The painting is at least eight thousand years old.

Then there was the Emperor Yu of China. He began as an adventurer in the latter part of the third millennium B.C. He rose to become emperor and founder of the Hsia dynasty. There is a bas-relief from that time of the Emperor Yu that describes him: "Yu of the Hsia dynasty was a master of the science of the earth and in those matters concerning water veins and springs." The Emperor Yu was one of the first dowsers known to history.[6]

The Bible has many stories of dowsing. There is the tale of Jacob, who wandered with his herd of cattle through the parched and arid lands of Canaan. His lips swollen from the heat, his cattle groaning with thirst, Jacob spots an area of green. Water!

In the ancient Middle East the appearance of water in the midst of the desert was a mixed blessing. Wells and oases were poisoned in those days either by man or by the combination of elements around them. Jacob cut down branches of poplar, chestnut, and hazel trees. He then stripped off their bark. Using the rods to point at the water, he determined it to be clean and clear, and the cattle and their master slaked their thirst.[7]

Later in time Moses led the children of Israel out of Egyptian slavery and into the desert. Wandering for years with his people, Moses is finally confronted by a sorely discontented crowd. They complain to him, and his brother Aaron, that the people are dying for lack of water. Surely, God would not have wanted it so.

Moses and Aaron leave the crowd and enter into prayer. The Lord appears to Moses and instructs him to take Aaron's rod and go outside to the people. Moses, instructed by the vision of the Lord, stood in front of a large rock with his people watching, raised the rod, and a rush of water came forth. "And Moses lifted up his hand, and with his rod he smote the rock twice: and the water came out abundantly, and the congregation drank, and their beasts also." It is probable that Moses discovered the source of water through dowsing.[8]

Dowsing involves much more than sticks and the search for water. Broadly speaking, it is the use of any instrument such as a pendulum, stick, fingers, tortoiseshell, and the like to find an answer to a question. More often than not, the question asked is one that involves two choices. The realm of the dowser is the realm of "yes/no," "here/there," "up/down." In short, the world of the dowser is the world of either/or.

Dowsing is very much all around us today. To be sure, it is practiced in remote reaches, but it is also part of the life of people in the United States. It is found in Tibet in the 1940s, in the biblical Middle East, and in China of three thousand years ago. It is also found in Warrensburg, New York, in 1977.

Have Pickup and Hickory Stick: Will Travel

It is the summer of 1977. Place: Warrensburg, New York. Warrensburg is a large small town not too far from Lake George in the lower Adirondacks. We had rented a house there for the summer months.

It was a large house in a very rural locality. Our main source of amusement, when we weren't accidentally burning things on the wood stove, was to wander into Lake George to play the pinball machines.

Then one day we got a call from the landlord. They were going to drill a new well, and a dowser would be over to check for the best place to drill.

A dowser?! I conjured up images of all the old mountain men types I had read about in westerns or seen in movies. I expected some deteriorating rural mystic with wild eyes to show up muttering gibberish under his breath, which I expected would be quite foul.

A shiny recent model Ford pickup drove into the driveway about a day after the landlord had called. Out jumped a very fit-looking young man about twenty-five or so dressed in jeans and a T-shirt that adequately displayed his muscles. With his brush-cut hair he had the bronzed good-health look of someone who spent a great deal of time outdoors.

This was the dowser. He did it for a living. He was also a generally talented handyman, but the dowsing kept him very busy. His success rate, he told me, was extremely high and the folks in the area knew that. Now, it's important to understand that upstate New York farmers are not interested in mysticism. They are interested in results. Water is something that is too important to leave in the hands of the unskilled or fuzzy-headed.

This pickup-driving, crew-cut, muscular outdoorsy dowser threw me for a loop. I bombarded him with questions: Do you have to use a hickory stick? No, any forked thing will do, including a coat hanger. Is it a gentle kind of pull that you need to learn to identify? No, sometimes the pull is so great that it can skin the palms of your hands if you hold it back. Can anybody do it? Sure, you just have to learn how to hold the stick.

I had to try. The first time, the dowser held one end of the stick, put his arm around me, and I held the other. The two of us walked along the yard, each holding an end of the stick. Suddenly the stick pulled down sharply, really sharply. It was as if someone had tied a loop around it and was pulling it down. There was no subtlety here. There definitely was a force pulling down the stick.

Still the skeptic, I asked if I could do it by myself. He showed me how to hold the stick and I went, eyes closed, along the grass. Suddenly the stick was pulled down and almost out of my hand. It was the same spot.

The spot where the stick had pulled down was not a site for a well. It was, as it turned out, the location of a cistern filled with water. The dowsing stick was indeed responding to water. After this experience, dowsing was no longer a question of belief or disbelief for me. It had happened. Some force had taken hold of me and pointed me in the direction I wanted to go.

The dowser had given me a simple kind of dowsing stick. I can't remember whether it was a clothes hanger or a jointed piece of wood. In any event it had worked. I went back to Long Island after the summer was over and stuck the dowsing stick in my closet, where it was gobbled up by the gremlins of time and motion.

Dowsing with a Body (Somebody)

This game requires the participation of two people. One is the human pendulum. The other is the "pendler."

NEEDED: playing cards.

I. The pendler places three playing cards on a table.

II. The pendler then picks one and makes a mental note of it. He does not, of course, inform the human pendulum of his choice.

III. The human pendulum stands next to the pendler with her arm outstretched. She has taken on the role of the pendulum and will simply move in accordance with the communicated thoughts of the pendler.

IV. The pendler then gives the signal to begin. He tells the pendulum that he will fill up her body with his thoughts and will direct her arm to the card he selected.

V. The pendler then fills up the pendulum with his thoughts and directs her arm without any words. The signals need to be very simple— such as "move right," "move left," "go back," etc.—but these signals are not to be spoken.

VI. When the pendulum has arrived at the right card, the pendler withdraws his thoughts from the pendulum.

It is important for both the pendler and the pendulum to move slowly rather than rush through this. Don't get discouraged if it doesn't work out just the way you wanted it to. Keep on playing. Finally, be sure to change roles.

The Eye of the Needle

Among the Cherokees, the divining of illness has an unusual component. At daybreak the diviner goes to a creekside pothole. He places two needles in the palm of his hand and then recites a prayer and blows on the needles. This is done four times. One of the needles, balanced on the middle finger of the diviner's right hand, is set afloat. The other needle, resting on the middle finger of the left hand, is placed in the water at a distance of about one foot from the first needle. If the first needle drifts over headfirst and touches its companion, there is a poor prognosis for the patient. If the first needle strikes the other one causing it to founder, only the most extraordinary efforts can save the patient. However, if the needles keep their distance, the outcome is hopeful.[9]

How does all of this work? How can a hickory stick tell you where there is water? How can a stick with string indicate anything at all? How can a needle do anything but sew? Unfortunately, at the moment, there are no clear scientific explanations. There are, however, some possible theories. For one thing we are all made of energy. That's a scientific truth. Everything is composed of different forms of energy: lightning, a glacier, a rushing train, an overflowing volcano, Mt. Everest, and Shirley MacLaine.

We can be a bit rigid about how different we are from, say, a rushing train, but we and the train represent forms of energy. In this game we try to move things with our energy. Sound crazy? Maybe it is, but it's worth a try. If it doesn't work the first time, don't give up. Just concentrate.[10]

NEEDED: a couple of small sewing needles or pins, a teacup or similar size container, water, salad oil, and a quiet place where there are no rattles, shakes, or obvious movement.

I. Put the water in the cup, leaving a little space at the top.

II. Place one of the pins on the surface of the water.

III. If it doesn't float, pour in a little salad oil. Add the oil in small droplets until the pin does float.

IV. Place the cup with the floating pin on a table.

V. Sit near the cup.

VI. Decide which direction you want the pin to move.

VII. Keep thinking of that direction and relay your thoughts to the pin. (Think of sending little pushes out to the pin so that it will move the way you want it to go.)

VIII. Close your eyes and visualize that direction in your imagination.

IX. Open your eyes and continue to send out moving energy to the pin.

X. Watch what happens. Give yourself time. (If nothing happens, don't get disillusioned. After all, it's only a game.)

XI. Change the direction that you want the pin to go.

This can also be done with more than one person. In that case everybody agrees to a direction and sends out the same signal.[11]

In Sudan a father asks an old man about where his pregnant young wife ought to give birth. The place of birth of the first child is not fixed. The oracle, or *iwa,* must be consulted. In this case, the oracle is a board, a rubbing board.

The old man takes the board and closes his eyes. He rubs his hand up and down the board. To himself, he asks questions such as, "Shall the child be born in the house of the mother?" His hand slides easily down the board—a negative response. "Shall the child be born in the house of the mother's brother?" His hand sticks on the board. The answer is positive. The midwife is chosen in the same way.[12]

The rubbing board is a common dowsing tool throughout Africa. The Azande tribe uses it as one of the main methods of obtaining answers to common questions.[13] In Zimbabwe the Bemba diviner rubs an ax over the skin until it sticks in answer to a question.[14]

The Apagibetis are hunters and horticulturists who live in the rain forests of north-central Zaire. The most frequently used oracle of the Apagibetis is the rubbing stick. The diviner addresses the oracle with questions. At the same time he rubs two flat, palm-sized, smooth-bottomed boards together. Between the boards are water and a special mixture of herbs. If the boards stick or seize while he addresses them, he knows that he has identified the answer to his question.[15]

Rubbing the Right Way

Who knows where the Apagibeti, Bemba, or Azande diviners get their information? How can a board tell us anything? The board is, indeed, mute. Perhaps the board is just helping us to contact something that we already know. Maybe we are touching a higher form of our own consciousness.

Try rubbing this one.

NEEDED: two small thin boards about the size of Ping-Pong paddles. You may actually use Ping-Pong paddles if they are sandpaper or smooth but not rubber.

I. Rub the boards together. They need to be smooth enough so that they will not automatically stick.
II. Think of a question that has a yes or no answer to it. At first a question that is not terribly significant is preferable to a vitally important question.
III. Decide whether sticking signifies yes or no.
IV. Close your eyes.
V. Rub the boards together.
VI. Do this four or five times.
VII. What answer do you receive?

With any method of dowsing, we need to be able to suspend our wishes while asking questions. Otherwise we may unconsciously manipulate the results. So this is a game to be played over time. Soon you will find that you can answer questions without influencing the results.

The Body as a Dowsing Tool

When you are going to do hand-trembling, first you close your eyes, you hold your hand out and start thinking. You say a few words in prayer. When you close your eyes you feel something like lightning or sunbeams coming from Heaven, strike down inside the house. Everything is white and bright. Nobody could see that but you. You don't see that yourself, but you are having thoughts like that. That light doesn't stay long, then your hand starts shaking. You start thinking about Singers' names, taking them one at a time. As you go along the hand-trembling kind of pushes the Singers off. Then you come to one

and the hand-trembling will push him right into the house. That
is the way I did and when I came to Ricardo it pushed him in.
— *Gregorio, Navajo hand trembler* [16]

We may not always have a needle handy. Or a string or a hickory stick. But we always have our bodies. People have probably been using the body to dowse since the beginning of time. Even in the industrialized world we find remnants of body dowsing in our lore. Ever shudder when it wasn't cold? They say that means that somebody is walking over your grave. How about the expression "My ears are burning"? Somebody must be talking about you. Itchy feet are considered a sign that we are anxious to get moving.

Our bodies can tell us things that our conscious minds conceal. Even commonly used verbal expressions tell us this. "I had a feeling in the pit of my stomach" or "I had a gut feeling" indicates an intuitive sense of something. "My heart was in my throat" indicates fear. Our feelings, our intuition, and our bodies are all one. When we "feel" things, we feel them physically as well as emotionally and intuitively.

Many peoples have utilized their bodies as instruments of divination. The Bedouin people of the Siwah and Garah cultures live in the Libyan desert. There, in the vast sandy wastes, journeys are a matter of life and death. One does not embark upon a trip across the desert without taking every precaution. One precaution was to dowse before a journey. The Bedouin man would shut his eyes. He then held his hands out in front of him, palms toward him. The two center fingers of the two hands pointed toward each other. Then, slowly, with eyes shut, he tried to bring the fingers together. The point was to make the tip of the two center fingers meet exactly. If the two fingers did meet, then the undertaking would be attended with good luck. If the exact contact did not take place, then on no account would the trip be made. This would occur three times and the answer would be strictly observed. [17]

Among the natives of New Guinea, the men of the tribe were able to consult with their own spirit guardians through body dowsing. The man would ask a question and then hang a bone over his shoulder. If the back itched on one side, the answer would be positive or yes. If the man's back itched on the other side, the answer would be no. [18]

Hand trembling is a body dowsing technique that is native to America. A highly developed practice among Navajo diviners, hand trembling is used primarily to diagnose illness and find lost articles. In this, the diviner receives his message by means of vibrations that enter his arm. [19]

The trembling of the hand is often quite extreme. As the hickory stick can almost leap out of a dowser's fist, the trembling of the hand in a sensitive diviner is unmistakable. Gregorio, the Navajo hand trembler, told of his experience: "'This isn't like a man [a doctor] comes and asks questions. This is thinking hard. We must go by this trembling-hand. Whenever your hand starts trembling, do not try to hold it back, let it go and see what it will do. Just follow your arm. . . .' " [20]

Today, body dowsing is used in the practice of kinesiology. In this, the diagnostician tests the patient by pressing down on the arms or hands. At the same time, she will give the patient a remedy or vitamin. If the remedy is appropriate, the resistance of the arm will be strong. If it is not appropriate, there will be very little if any resistance.

The Body Knows

When I first experienced kinesiology, I couldn't believe that it was working. My body was actually getting weaker or stronger depending on what I was holding in my hand. It was so simple and yet profound. In this game, which must be played with one other person, we ask our body what it knows.

NEEDED: an aspirin, vitamin pill, lump of sugar, lump of salt, black-tea bag, herbal-tea bag.

    I. Close your eyes.
    II. Have partner place one of the objects in your right hand.
    III. Close your fist around it and raise your fist, palm facing you as if you are making a muscle.
    IV. Have partner pull down on your fist, trying to straighten it out.
    V. Offer resistance but just a little bit—this is not a variety of arm wrestling.
    VI. Go through each of the items this way.
    VII. Note which ones you are holding when there is resistance and which ones you are holding when there is not.
    VIII. Change places and do the same for your partner.

After you have tried this, see what kind of pattern emerges. As you do this more and more, you might experiment with other items. Then you might experiment with actual questions. Resistance would mean a "yes" and nonresistance a "no."

That Ain't Hay: Dowsing with Grass

Hickory sticks are just one of many forked items that can be used in dowsing. Here we use dried grass or hay. This game should be played outside.

I. Find two pieces of dried grass or hay about twelve inches or longer.
II. Bend them at right angles, as illustrated below.
III. Hold the small part loosely and gently in each hand with palms up.
IV. Hold so that the two long parts cross each other:

V. Start to walk slowly.
VI. When the two pieces of grass start to move and rotate, you have walked over a place where people have lived before. This could be a former civilization, an old burial site, sacred ground, or the like.

When you play this game, experiment with different localities and different kinds of places. You might find some interesting things about the very place in which you live.[21]

Getting in the Swing: Pendulum Dowsing

> *Listen! Ha! now you have drawn near to harken, O Brown Rock; you never lie about anything. Ha! Now I am about to seek for it. I have lost a hog and now tell me about where I shall find it. For is it not mine?*
> —Cherokee diviner's chant before using the pendulum[22]

> *Pendulum. A body suspended from a fixed support so that it swings freely back and forth under the influence of gravity, commonly used to regulate various devices, especially clocks. Also called simple pendulum.*
> —The American Heritage Dictionary

In the northernmost part of what was once the Russian empire, a woman stands over a loaf of bread. Over the bread lies an upside-down sieve. Around the sieve, on the frame, is a list of diseases. In the other room a little girl is coughing. She has been sick for a week and her condition seems to be getting worse. Nobody knows what the cause of the disease is or even what it is.

The woman takes a small crucifix hung by a thread and suspends it over the sieve. Slowly the crucifix begins to move. It continues to move toward one area of the sieve. On that area is inscribed the name of a particular disease. Diagnosis has occurred.[23]

The woman is "pendling." She is using a device that hangs, as a pendulum, and reading the results based on the way in which the pendulum moves. Pendulums are among the most common divinatory tools used around the world. They have been used to find thieves. They have been used to diagnose illness. They have been used to answer important questions.

In Haiti the pendulum is used as a means of establishing whether a person is innocent or guilty. This practice is called *passage d'alliance*. The reader takes a ring and suspends it on a string above the suspect's head. If it moves back and forth in a regular pendulous way, the person is innocent. But if it swings in a circle, his guilt is established.[24]

In Finland the diviner reads the source and progress of illness through a pendulum. As the Finnish reader closes her eyes, she chants, "If the illness is mortal, then move clockwise; if it is caused by a curse, then move counterclockwise; if it comes from the water, then go to the lake; if it comes from the earth, then go northward."[25]

In America the Cherokees are among the most versatile users of pendulums. When searching for a lost article, the Cherokee shaman fasts before the search. A small rounded water-worn reddish-brown pebble suspended by a string constitutes the pendulum. The shaman holds the string between his thumb and forefinger. The pebble will swing farther in the direction of the lost article.

Beginning early in the morning, the diviner makes his first trial at the house of the owner of the lost article. He follows the direction of the pendulum and makes a second trial. He then follows up about another half mile when the stone may veer around toward the starting point. A fourth attempt creates a complete circuit. The diviner, through the use of the pendulum, has thus circumscribed the area where the article may be found. This is a form of triangulation. The diviner then goes to the center of this space and marks out on the ground a small circle that encloses a cross with its arms pointing toward the four cardinal points. He holds the stone over the center of the cross and repeats the process and notes which direction the pebble swings this time. This is the last trial and the diviner now goes slowly over the whole surface in that direction, from the center of the circle to the outside of the enclosed area, until the article is found.[26]

The Cherokee people have utilized pendulums for centuries. Their pendulum of choice is often a gold or silver coin. Sometimes it is a lump of lead. But always it is something derived from the ground.[27]

Pendulum variations are almost limitless. In Africa, among the Azande people, the fruit of the *doma* is attached to a string to form a pendulum. Here the answer is simple: If the fruit does not swing, it is a bad augury. If it swings, it is a good augury.[28]

Among the peoples of southeastern Siberia, the shaman has a special wooden figure called *pal'pang*. The Siberian diviner will ask the question and then suspend the wooden figure from a string. If the figure waves, the answer to the question is affirmative. The Siberian shaman also uses a stone kettle as a strange kind of pendulum. The kettle is hit. If it swings straight, one has an affirmative answer. If it swings to one side, the answer is negative.[29]

Farther to the north, Chukchi and Eskimo diviners use a wide variety of pendulums. Any pebble with a string around it might serve as a pendulum, although the diviner might also use the skull of an animal, a carved wooden image of a "guardian" spirit, or a piece of wood. Sometimes the pendulum is made of a boot or cap of the person asking the question. And sometimes even the body of the person himself is used.

When the body of a living person is used in pendulum divination, the diviner will bind the head of the questioner with a string. The other end of the string is tied to a stick. The questioner then lies on the ground. His questions are asked and the stick is lifted. If the answers are positive, the head will feel so light that it will be lifted by itself. On the other hand, if the answer is negative, the diviner will be unable to lift the head from the ground. The questioner, lying on the ground, does not need to ask his questions aloud. He may simply say them to himself mentally.[30]

In the Philippines diviners use a stone or piece of iron or firebrand as a pendulum.[31] In the Tonkin Delta women would suspend a ring by hair over a map to determine the location of a lost person.[32] The people of Surinam use a piece of tubing suspended from a string to answer yes or no to questions. The questions are asked when the air is not stirring. If the pendulum remains motionless, the answer is yes. If it moves, the answer is no.[33]

The Khasi people of northern India use a *shanam*. This is simply a lime case suspended by a chain. Once again, a question is asked, and if the chain swings, it is supposed to be an affirmative answer. If it does not move, it is a negative.[34] For the people of the Upper Maroni in French Guiana, a ring of fibers is suspended at the end of a string. Here the answer is affirmative if the pendulum moves from right to left and negative if it describes a circle.[35]

More often than not, pendulums are used to find the source of illness and its cure. In the province of Assam, India, the Garo people use a peculiar form of pendulum. The Garo diviner takes a thin slip of bamboo about a foot long and ties it into a bow with a piece of cotton thread. A small piece of string is allowed to hang down. The shaman then takes the loose piece of thread and rubs it on the body of the ill person. He then lifts up the bow by the tight string, holding it lightly between the forefinger and thumb of his right hand. With his left hand he supports his right wrist. The shaman then calls upon the gods one by one. The bow will oscillate when he reaches the name of the spirit to whom sacrifice must be made.[36]

If the Shoe Swings, Don't Wear It

The mistress of the house was furious. This was Kabul. This was Afghanistan. Servants were bound by their faith in the religion of their fathers and by their loyalty to their master and mistress. Obedience was expected in all things. Yet there was a silver goblet that was missing.

There was no question that the goblet was not lost. It had been there recently during a small dinner party served for some of the more important people of the town. It was gone. It was stolen!

There was no point in questioning the servants. Those who didn't take it wouldn't know who did. And the person that did take it would certainly never confess.

The mistress had all the servants assembled in the great room. With much nervousness, the maids, cooks, butlers, valets, and footmen all appeared in the room where many luxurious banquets had taken place. News had spread about the stolen goblet, so everyone knew what this was about.

The mistress came into the room with her sister. This itself was cause for alarm among the staff. For the mistress's sister was both wealthier and of worse temperament than the mistress.

Everybody watched as the mistress took out an old slipper from her gold brocade handbag. The first chambermaid knew that slipper. It was the mistress's for as long as she could remember.

There were several gasps as the mistress took a large nail and, with a small hammer, pounded the nail through the center of the slipper. She then drew a circle on the ground with a piece of charcoal.

A murmur spread among the crowd as the mistress took the companion slipper to that one she had pierced with a nail. She struck the circle with the companion slipper and then took the other. She and her sister held the slipper suspended between them, each balancing the nail on an index finger.

"Come forth, Aqbal," she ordered to the chief valet. The oldest of the servants is first as a matter of respect. He stood in front of the mistress while she said, addressing the slipper, "Oh, Nona, I take the name of your husband and ask you who is the thief. Is it Aqbal?" The slipper did not move. Aqbal was innocent. He was told he could leave.

The servants were then lined up to stand in front of the mistress, her sister, and the suspended slipper. "Is it Jasmine?" the mistress asked as a fifteen-year-old chambermaid stood nervously in front of her. The slipper remained immobile and Jasmine was free to go.

After about half an hour the mistress reached Lily, one of the newer servants. "Is it Lily?" she asked the slipper. It moved upward in a perfect right angle. Lily was guilty of the theft and broke down in tears. The slipper pendulum had once again found a thief.

—Eyewitness accounts of the Afghans[37]

Preparing to Pendle

The pendulum is both universal and difficult. Its difficulty lies in allowing ourselves really to see the answers we get. It is a practice in which our minds can really get in the way.

To be sure, it is easy to influence the results when using a pendulum. After all, if we just move our fingers a little this way or that way, we can make the pendulum do what we want it to do. But to do this consciously is definitely not the point. However, when the conscious mind steps out of the way, a higher consciousness takes over and moves the pendulum. In a sense, "we" are still moving it, but the "we" is someone we need to learn to trust, an inner and higher "we." The pendulum demands that we get out of our own way and that we do not become attached to whatever answer comes. It demands that we remain open to whatever answer we get. That can be difficult. This is assuming, of course, that we are searching for the truth.

Sig Lonegren is one of the leading practitioners of, and writers on, dowsing. He has proposed some simple and effective ways of preparing yourself for pendling. To get your personal wishes for a particular outcome out of the way, Lonegren suggests that, after asking the question, you go into the mode of a child seeing, for the first time, a lot of beautifully wrapped presents. The child asks, "I wonder what's in them."

It is the sense of childlike wonderment that makes for successful pendling. Instead of asking "I wonder what's in them," the pendler says, "I wonder what the answer is going to be." That shifts the focus from our own wishes to the pendulum and what it provides.[38]

To begin, you need to get a pendulum. All you need to do is to get something that hangs from a string. (If you want to spend five hundred dollars, you can buy a very fancy pendulum made by New Age craftspeople.) The basic principle is that you need about six inches of string and an object that can hang straight down from that piece of string. The less elaborate the better. The point is simply to create a hanging object that can swing about with very little effort.

Once you have your pendulum, you hold the end of the string and let the weight dangle. It is easiest to rest your elbow on a solid surface and let the pendulum dangle freely without the added disruption of your arm moving about.

Pendulum Consciousness

The pendulum is one of the most difficult of all psychic tools. The reason is simple. Our thoughts influence how the pendulum will move. So if we are attached to a particular answer, we will influence it. For example, if you are asking whether somebody you have a crush on cares about you, there is a good chance that you will influence the answer of the pendulum.

It is not easy to get rid of thoughts. One way is to repeat again and again, "I wonder what the answer will be." In this exercise we try another method to clear away thoughts that get in the way.

    I. Find a comfortable place to sit. Plant your feet firmly on the ground.
    II. Close your eyes.
    III. Take ten deep breaths. Breathe in through the nose and out through the mouth.
    IV. Sit quietly for a few moments just counting your breaths.
    V. Again, take ten deep breaths.
    VI. Focus all of your attention on the top of your head. Let all of your energy go to it just as if you were a human fountain.
    VII. Let all thoughts that come to you pass as if they are frames in a movie.
    VIII. Now you are ready to start playing with a pendulum.

This is a good exercise to repeat each time you start to play with a pendulum.

Deciding on Your Yes and Your No

NEEDED: your own elegant or humble pendulum and a piece of paper.

I. Find a comfortable spot where you will have little disturbance. A chair at a table is probably the best. Find a place where you won't be disturbed.

II. Sit facing the table with feet firmly on the floor and back straight.

III. Have a piece of paper on the table with a small circle drawn on it. The circle should be approximately the size of a quarter.

IV. Close your eyes. (Yes, once again we close our eyes to help us see.)

V. Feel whatever tension there is in your body.

VI. Begin with your feet and tense them as much as possible for about ten seconds. Then relax.

VII. Do the same thing with your calves, thighs, buttocks, stomach, arms, hands, chest, neck, mouth, face, and every other body part.

VIII. Put your elbow on the table and hold the pendulum so that it is slightly above the center of the circle.

IX. Decide how you want the pendulum to move for a "yes." A common way is a clockwise circle, but you can choose your own—for example, an up-and-down, vertical motion, like a nod, can signify "yes."

X. Decide what movement you want for a "no." Counterclockwise is also common, but a lateral motion from left to right is another possibility.

XI. Without consciously moving your fingers tell the pendulum to describe a "yes."

XII. Give it time.

XIII. Do the same thing for a "no."

XIV. Repeat this several times.

XV. You now have the basic ingredients to be able to pendle.

Find the Pea

It is easier to use a pendulum when the answer is not that important. For example, we are much less attached to playing a hide-and-seek game than we are to finding out whether the object of our desire loves us.

Hiding the pea under one of three cups is a legendary con game. It can be done with a pendulum. So if you ever encounter a circus con man with three cups and a pea, just whip out your pendulum and you're set.

Two people play this game.

NEEDED: three identical cups, a pea (or something small and round), and a pendulum.

I. One person is the pea hider and the other the pea finder.
II. Pea finder leaves the room (or turns his back).
III. Pea hider turns the three cups upside down and places the pea under one of them.
IV. Pea finder returns and takes out his pendulum.
V. Pea finder closes eyes (of course) and takes a few deep breaths.
VI. Pea finder holds pendulum and moves it slowly over the cups. He asks the pendulum to give him a "yes" motion when it finds the cup with the pea. Again, approach the question like a child asking himself what is inside a beautifully wrapped present.
VII. Pea finder must take his time. Go over the cups a few times before you get the answer.
VIII. Repeat this about ten times and then give the other person a chance.

You might want to keep a record of this just to judge the accuracy of your answers. Remember, if you become attached to finding out where the pea is rather than just enjoying the search, you will mess up the results.

Find the Hidden . . .

This is a game that has unlimited possibilities. After all, you can hide just about anything just about anywhere. It's a variation of the old "hot or cold" game that most of us played as kids. You'll need a partner for this one.

NEEDED: pendulum and something to hide.

I. One person is the hider and the other the finder.
II. Finder leaves the room.
III. Hider places object somewhere in the room.
IV. Finder returns.
V. Finder takes pendulum and slowly walks across the room. (I suggest that the finder use "yes" as the indicator of "warm" or "hot" and "no" as "cold.")
VI. After several passes finder decides on where the object is hidden.

In this game you might find that the pendulum will move more and more decisively one way or the other. That is why this game is similar to the old "hot *or cold" game; the pendulum might tell you that you are getting warmer by the growing intensity of its "yes" motion, or colder by the growing intensity of its "no" motion.*

Do-It-Yourself Dowsing

We can create for ourselves the dowsing charts that serve our needs. All we need is the basic form, which looks something like this:

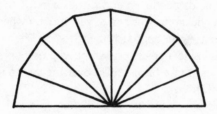

The form is very simple to draw. It's half a pie cut into eight slices. (With a big enough half-pie you might want to create sixteen slices.) It needs to be big enough so that each slice has enough space for the pendulum to stop clearly. It has enough segments so that you can pick and choose the categories that you want to include. There is no one chart that everyone can use. The best chart is one that fits your needs. You are the only person who can figure that out.

In this game you create a chart that provides answers for questions you might want to ask. You can also use it as a meditative tool. For example, each day for a week or so (or a year or two if you really get into it) you start by letting the pendulum swing over the little pie to find out what category is present for you on that day.

NEEDED: piece of standard 8 1/2 by 11 paper, a dark pen, and a pendulum.

    I. Using a protractor, a computer, or simply tracing the drawing provided here, draw a shape like the pie illustration. (I suggest making a photocopy of your blank pie so that you may make other charts.)

    II. Close your eyes and take a couple of deep breaths.

    III. Make a list of about fifteen one-word categories (love, work, health, etc.).

    IV. Choose eight of these.

    V. Write down each category in a slice of the pie.

    VI. Put the pie chart on a flat surface.

VII. Hold your pendulum so that the point is hanging over the place where all the lines come together.

VIII. Ask the pendulum to bring you to the area most important for the day.

IX. Watch where the pendulum swings.

Finding the Categories

The only limit to the number of categories and questions that we can ask is the limit that we impose upon ourselves. In this exercise we create categories and questions that are important to us. This is not an effort to create the universal chart. Efforts at universality make for bad poetry and rotten pendulum charts. These charts are for your use. So make them useful for you.

NEEDED: paper and a writing implement.

I. Using whatever means you wish, create a circle or semicircle with sixteen or eight slices in it.

II. On a separate piece of paper, pick a category that is important to you. (Writing, for example, is important to me.)

III. Write eight or sixteen subcategories within the main category that would come up as issues. (Again in my case, the subcategories of writing could be: focusing; getting stuck; meditating; brainstorming; rereading; taking a rest; getting another opinion; organizing schedule. These are eight subjects that I could list under my main topic of writing.)

IV. Write the subcategories on the slices.

V. Place the pendulum on the point where the lines converge.

VI. Let it carry you to the information for that day.

You can use this to assess all kinds of things, from automobiles to relationships. For example, Anne Williams, a very talented dowser, has created many packets of dowsing charts. One of them features the various parts of an automobile. The purpose is to find out (with the pendulum) just what is wrong with the car. I found that it was amazingly accurate the several times that I used it. Another chart involves lists of vitamins and supplements. The purpose is to find which supplements you might need. The possibilities are endless. It is important to include in each list the category "none of the above." Sometimes there is nothing wrong with the car, we don't need any supplements, and so forth.

To See the World in a Grain of Rice: Psychic Computers

At the heart of dowsing is the same principle that governs the most complex computer: a binary system. To put it more simply: yes or no. There are only two answers to most questions asked of a pendulum. Yet, despite the simplicity of this method, there are infinite varieties of binary divination.

Most of us have experienced binary divination techniques when we have flipped a coin to make a choice or taken a daisy and pulled out the petals intoning, "she loves me, she loves me not."

It is easy to dismiss these forms of divination as childish. After all, how can something that is so "random" have any kind of connection to reality? We can look at the hologram as a model. Any piece of the hologram can generate the entire picture. If we can see the world in a grain of sand, as the mystic poet William Blake stated, then perhaps we can see it in other grains as well.

Among the Miao people of Hunan province in China, chickens and rice are used to determine the fate of a family. At the grave of a family member rice is thrown into the bottom of the pit and a cock is let down. If the cock eats the rice on the left side, then the male members of the family will have good luck. If it eats on the right side, then the female members will have peace. If it eats in the center, then both men and women will have luck.[39]

If an article is stolen among the Ainu people of Japan, a skull will point the way. The questioner holds the skull while speaking a prayer. Then, placing the underjaw on his head, the person bows forward until it falls. The direction toward which the skull falls indicates where the lost or stolen article might be found. If it falls on its side or with teeth down, the answer is indecisive and must be repeated.[40]

The diviners among the Baganda people of Africa would place ground herbs on a stone. The person seeking the answer to a question would then urinate in a jug which the priest would then pour on the stone. If the herbs scattered evenly, it was a good sign. If they scattered in odd directions, it was an inauspicious sign.[41]

The Naskapi hunters of Labrador use the paws of an otter for their binary divination. The questioner first combs his hair with the claws of one paw. He then tosses both paws in the air. If both paws fall palms-up, the answer is positive. If they both fall palms-down, it is negative. And if one is up and the other down, the answer is so-so.[42]

For the Yakutat Tlingit people of Alaska the humerus of a seal is used. A question is asked by speaking into the hole of the bone and the humerus is then flipped with a quick jerk of the wrist. If the bone falls on either of the two flatter sides, the answer is no. If it balances on the edge, this means yes. But if, by some miracle, it stands upright on the smaller end, this means not only a yes but God's truth.[43]

People have used the face of coconuts to determine the answers to their questions. In Fiji the people would want to know whether they would have a fair wind for sailing to the southern islands. The questioner would take a mature coconut with the husk and hold it while addressing the god Tutumatua, "If it is your wish that we may go tomorrow, let the coconut arise and face me." The man would then twirl the coconut. If it faced him, it would be said to face right. If it did not face him, then it faced wrong. A right answer would have to be repeated again, since two right answers were required before the boats would sail. The coconut was also used to diagnose sickness and find thieves.[44]

Tuareg hunters of North Africa press their thumbs into the sand to make two rows of holes close to each other. The hunter does it so swiftly that he loses track of how many holes he has made. He then counts the total number of holes in each row and makes count of which are odd and which are even. After doing this six times, he finds the answer to his question.[45]

Perhaps the most famous and widespread form of binary divination is the casting of lots. The ancient Vikings, Romans, and Germans all cast lots to determine the answer to questions.[46] In this, the questioner simply throws out sticks or pieces of paper, and the results are determined by either odd or even placements. For example, if you throw out a bundle of corn kernels and divide them willy-nilly into two piles, odd will mean one thing and even another.

She Loves Me, She Loves Me Not

In ancient Hawaii pebbles were used to find the answers to questions. One person chooses between two piles of odd and even numbered stones. Even would signify luck and odd would not.[47] Borrowed from ancient Hawaii, this game allows for any kind of yes/no question.

NEEDED: any odd number of small objects (thirty-one thumbtacks, seventy-five small marbles, ninety-nine dry lentils, etc.).

I. Think of a yes/no question that you are interested in pursuing.

II. Take the objects and divide them into two roughly equal groups. (Don't count them at this point or that will defeat the purpose of the whole game.)

III. Decide whether odd signifies yes or no. Common practice usually recognizes odd as no/masculine/negative and even as yes/feminine/positive.

IV. Focusing on the question, pick a pile.

V. Count the objects and you have your answer.

Most of us have taken daisies and plucked the petals to find out if our true love loves us. This is one of the most basic of binary devices. While this may seem totally random, we are, once again, gaining access to our inner sight. The daisy doesn't hold the answer. We do.

Daisies and pendulums challenge the very notion of "coincidence" and "random choice." If we trust our inner sight, we can find answers through these vehicles. Their simplicity is deceptive. If we play with them, they become yet another tool for understanding ourselves and our world. After all, we live in a world of choices.

Now, there are definitely times when choices are essential. We often have to make a decision for one thing over another. It is at those times that the binary system of divination is used. Pendulums, divining rods, pieces of corn, or thumbprints in the sand—all have helped people to make choices.

How can some piles of grain indicate a proper place to build a house? How can a rock suspended on a string diagnose an illness? Someday there will be a scientific explanation for the seeming miracle of dowsing. Until that time we must be content with the understanding that, very often, it does work. And, as always, it is the human being that is the medium of the message.

CHAPTER 9

Signs of the Times:
A Variety of Vehicles, Old and Unborn

No one can step twice into the same river, nor touch mortal substance twice in the same condition. By the speed of its change, it scatters and gathers again.

—Heraclitus, sixth century B.C.

IT was the third millennium before the birth of Christ. According to legend, the Emperor Fu Hsi of China was sitting by a river. Perhaps he was meditating. As the emperor sat quietly, an ancient tortoise climbed onto the bank of the river.

Fu Hsi watched the tortoise with increasing interest. He focused his attention on the shell of the large reptile. The emperor was seeing the tortoise as he never had before. He was neither in the future nor in the past. He was totally absorbed in that moment and saw with the eyes of a child. For an instant, everything was new.

The lines on the tortoise's shell formed patterns in the mind of the Emperor Fu Hsi. Out of these patterns came the first eight "trigrams" that came to be the basis of the ancient *I Ching,* the *Book of Changes.*[1]

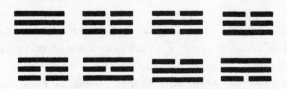

The eight original trigrams of the I Ching

For over three thousand years people have read these trigrams to interpret the world around them. Originally people tossed various stalks to find a corresponding pattern. Later people used coins. Each throw would either be even (--) or odd (-), and the trigram would be built from the bottom up. Later two trigrams were used, creating a hexagon. The original eight trigrams of the emperor Fu Hsi evolved into the sixty-four hexagons of the modern *I Ching*.

Every psychic method, whether reading the stars or divining from cracked animal bones, started with the creativity of some ancient, unsung, and long-forgotten person. Every tool of divination started with someone perceiving the world as if for the first time.

Every child, every human being, sees the world for the first time. As we get older, we often think that things are the same. We think we travel along the same road every day. We think we brush our teeth the same way every day. All of us have our ruts. We think we sit in the same seat the same way every day. Children—and diviners—know differently.

What has made kids and diviners so special is that they have been able to see the world as if they had never seen it before. They can see all kinds of things because they let themselves. All of us can do that.

For kids and diviners there is nothing strange about seeing the world in a plate of spaghetti or hearing birds talk. Diviners are artists that see the world as their palette. Just about everything can be read. And just about everything has been read from elephant dung to white horses; from ripples in the leaves to clouds; from sneezes to blinks. The entire world is our mirror.

The number of psychic vehicles is infinite. They depend only on the imagination of the person doing the reading. The Crow Indians see everything as a vehicle for divination. They see the whole world as a vehicle to be read playfully. The world, our universe, contains millions of texts available to us as long as we are willing to search and stretch.[2]

Among the Crow Indians there has never been a set system of divination. Nor has there ever been an institutionalized divination that dictated the right and wrong interpretations of signs and reality. Every Crow confronted the divinities on their own and each child grew up with a confidence in their own personal revelations.[3]

Originally people created their own methods of divination. Reading the signs was just another way that a person looked at the world each morning. Probably everyone did it. Today there are still cultures where reading the signs—divination—is a universal birthright. Among the Klamath Indians of the American Northwest, for example, the quest for the supernatural is open to everyone. Men, women, boys, and girls—all may engage in the search for the divine. They search for it in the everyday.[4]

To the Yaruro Indians of South America divination is an ordinary experience of everyday life. To be sure, there are diviners among the Yaruros, but these shamans, both male and female, are not considered authorities with special gifts. Rather are they considered to be the voice of the community. They are the spokespeople for the values of the society. Similarly, in the highlands of Burma, anybody can be a diviner. It is simple. One merely needs to spend some time orienting oneself.[5]

Among the !Kung Bushmen of Africa, oracle discs are a common vehicle of divination. These are five leather discs about two to three inches in diameter that are thrown to determine the answers to questions. Only men may throw the discs. But any man can do it and any man can interpret. There are no divining specialists among the !Kungs.[6]

People have always taken the "raw material" for divination from the world around them. This makes sense. It is natural. We are constantly creating and re-creating the vehicles of divination. Some vehicles have undergone variations and permutations through time and across cultures. There are as many variations as leaves in the trees. While we're on the subject let's take leaves as an example.

The residents of the Marshall Islands consult leaves for all kinds of questions. For instance, to find out whether a specific medical treatment will be successful, the Marshall Islanders will try to fold a pandanus leaf in equal sections. If the last section is longer than the others, the patient is taken to another house to be cured. This practice is called *bubu,* which means "to read that which is to come by folding leaves."[7]

Another way of reading the leaf is to cut down a fresh leaf from the coconut tree and split it into four strips plus the middle rib. Each leaf strip is lopped over itself and tied a random number of times to form a series of knots. As knots in the leaf strips are completed, the strips are inserted in the spaces between the fingers. When one hand holds four knotted leaf strips, the diviner counts the knots and comes up with an answer according to the number of knots. Each number represents the number of different answers that are possible.[8]

Among the Uru-Chipaya Indians of South America, leaves are an essential instrument of divination. The diviner takes a handful of leaves and, after appropriate prayer, determines the answer to the question by the position of the leaves.[9]

In the East the reading of tea leaves has been a tool of divination for several millennia. Bodhidharma was the Indian who introduced Buddhism to China. He was a fiercely dedicated individual. The story goes that one day he found himself dozing off while he was meditating. To keep himself from falling asleep, Bodhidharma cut off his eyelids and threw them on the ground. From these eyelids sprang the first tea plants.

The reading of tea leaves, or tasseomancy, was introduced into the West as late as the eighteenth century. It quite naturally followed the tracks of trade. As the drinking of tea became established, so did the reading of tea leaves, which has been done, in the West, almost exclusively by women.

In China, where the tea is more twiggy, the symbols are closer to the ideograms of the *I Ching*. In India, where a leafier form of tea is used, the patterns are both symbolic and in letter form.[10]

Tea is more than just a drink. It has been a symbol of awareness. So is coffee. Both can be used to "read."

Leaf Well Enough Alone

Scene: a dark and musty room with windows shaded and a candle burning on a table.

Sitting at the table is an old lady—so old that no one could guess her age. Her hair is bound into a tight knot, and an old kerchief covers the knot. She gazes intently into a cup that she holds in both of her hands. In the bottom of the cup are tea leaves. This is a tea reading. It is an image that most of us hold dear.

But you don't have to be old and gray in a musty room to read tea leaves.

NEEDED: loose tea (preferably black), water, a teacup, and a saucer.

   I. Boil the water.

   II. Put a teaspoonful of loose tea in the bottom of the teacup.

  III. Fill the cup so that you leave a little room on the top (unless, of course, you enjoy hot wet substances sloshing all over the place).

  IV. Focus all of your attention on the water as it begins to turn a new color. How does it feel? (Not how does it feel on your skin or fingers, but how does the color affect your senses?)

   V. Gently swirl the tea around in the cup.

  VI. Watch the shapes as the tea leaves fall to the bottom.

 VII. How are they moving? Swiftly? Smoothly? Slowly?

VIII. Look at the shapes that are formed by the tea in the bottom of the cup.

  IX. Make a list of at least three different things that you can see in the shapes. (Even a lump looks like something. And three lumps look like three different somethings. Just use your imagination.)

X. When you have finished looking at the shapes in the cup, pour off the water, then turn the cup over onto the saucer, letting the tea spill onto it. Lift it and see what shapes are formed.

Tea for Two

Reading tea leaves can be fun when it's done with two people. In this game each person reads the other's tea leaves.

NEEDED: loose tea, two teacups, water, and two white paper napkins.

I. Boil the water.

II. Put a teaspoonful of loose tea in the bottom of each teacup.

III. Each person pours the boiling water into his or her cup.

IV. Slowly drink and enjoy the tea.

V. In the process of drinking it visualize taking in and "sipping" the other person. This is best done in silence or with a minimum of conversation.

VI. Spend time smelling and tasting the tea.

VII. Take a moment with eyes closed to take in the presence of the other person.

VIII. When the tea is finished, the first person to be read turns his cup upside down on a white paper napkin, letting the tea leaves spill onto it.

IX. The person reading looks at the tea leaves first as the shape of the other person's life.

X. What shapes are evident? What feelings are associated with the shapes?

XI. If there is more than one shape, the reader then sees how the shapes relate to each other.

XII. The person reading then closes her eyes and lets whatever images come in.

XIII. The person reading then turns over her teacup and lets the other read her leaves.

In this, as with so much, simplicity is best. A single, clear image is preferable to a number of vague ones.

Fingerprints, Hands, and Palms

> *He sealeth up the hand of every man; that all men may know*
> *his work.*
>
> —*Job 37:7*

It is the hand that separates the human from the beast. Even the most advanced chimpanzee cannot begin to use his hands the way people can. For the hand is the extension of the human mind, and the human mind is an extension of the divine.

One social philosopher put it succinctly when he stated the difference between humans and animals. What distinguishes the worst of architects from the best of bees, said this scholar, is that the architect *sees* his product before he begins to build, whereas the bee constructs the complex hive with a complexity of instincts that are ingrained.

The architect transfers his concepts from his mind to the blueprint. It is the hand that transfers them. The seamstress transforms the cloth into garment. The instruments of that transformation are her mind and her hands. The writer moves his ideas from the narrow confines of his skull into the world. His words form on a page in a magical pattern and mystical process that ultimately communicates to millions of the literate world. What are the instruments of that transformation? The vehicle through which the words leap into life? The hands.

The hand is the instrument through which we touch the world. It is the part of the body that caresses and kills. The hand is synonymous with touch, and touch is synonymous with feeling. We communicate with our hands and, if we are deaf, we speak primarily with our hands. We build bridges with our hands and play the violin. We borrow rides with our thumb. We express rejection with our middle finger and place the ring of marriage next to it. We accuse with our index finger and slap our hands together in approval.

Look at the palm of your hand. The complexity of lines is unique. No other creature has such a network of lines and creases as we do. It is little wonder that the fingers and the hands have been used by countless cultures as instruments of divination. Among the shamans of the highlands of Colombia the hand is a map of health.[11] The Navajos, as we have seen, use the trembling of the hand to answer questions.[12] Among the Fiji islanders the two hands "speak" to each other. The diviner will feel a sting in his hand as an answer to a question.[13] In Chinese body divination the hand is used much the way a pendulum is used.[14]

Palmistry, which is the main survivor of hand reading in the contemporary

West, is a practice that goes back at least three thousand years. Old Indian texts discuss the connection between the lines of the hands and the potential of a person, a system that derives from the ancient Indian divinatory practice of Lakshana, which originally involved the reading of all parts of the body.[15]

Holding Hands as a Psychic Game

Hands transmit energy. Something happens when you hold somebody's hand. It's quite a bit different than if you held a person's ear or nose. When we hold our mother's or father's hand as children, we are doing more than just hanging on. We are, in some greater way, connected to them at that point. They are connected to us. When lovers hold hands, the love goes through the hands. It is an exchange of energy. Remember that awkward first moment when you held another's hand as a teenager? The thrill, the anxiety, the chill, the warmth?

Here we hold someone's hand and see what we feel and feel what we see. This game requires the participation of two or more people (preferably an even number).

   I. Pick a partner.
   II. One person is the hand feeler. The other is the hand giver.
   III. Both people get comfortable.
   IV. Hand feeler takes the other person's hand.
   V. Hold it in a relaxed way with both hands.
   VI. Close your eyes.
   VII. What feelings and thoughts are passing through your mind at this moment?
   VIII. Gently let go of the hand and spend a moment just letting whatever comes to you.
   IX. Take up the hand again.
   X. What different feelings do you experience when holding the hand and not holding the hand?
   XI. What images, if any, come to you?
   XII. Take the other person's hand in your other hand and repeat the exercise.
   XIII. Switch roles and allow the hand feeler to become the hand giver.

Handspeak Plainspeak

Sometimes we can get so caught up in looking that we don't see what is in front of our nose (or in our hands). This is true especially when we get involved in "predicting" and "interpreting." All we have to do is just look. In this game, which we play with a partner, we look at hands.[16]

I. Pick a partner.

II. One person provides the hands. The other is the observer.

III. The observer takes the partner's hand in hers.

IV. She describes exactly what she sees. (This means no interpretation, no judgment—just description.)

V. She examines the back of the hand as well as the front.

VI. She describes the shape, quality, age, flexibility, symmetry, and so forth.

VII. Switch roles and have the other person repeat the process.

Talk with Your Hands

Hands have always provided a universal language. Native American cultures boasted as many languages as there were tribes. Verbal communication was often difficult among members of different nations. Thus hand language became a major form of communication among the early nations of the North American continent. In this game we talk only with our hands but hear a great deal.

NEEDED: blindfolds for everyone. This is a game for groups of four or more people. It is helpful to have someone act as the coordinator of the game.

I. Divide into two groups of equal numbers.

II. Make inner and outer circles, both facing inward.

III. Everybody puts on a blindfold.

IV. Those in the outer circle join hands and take three steps to the right. Those in the inner circle do the same.

V. Inner circle turns and faces outer circle.

VI. Each person reaches out to a partner.

The purpose from here on is to communicate unconditionally with your partner, using only your hands.

VII. Say hello to each other.

VIII. The outer person expresses playfulness.

IX. The inner person goes along with it.

X. Then the inner person expresses a feeling. (There are lots of possibilities, like anger, love, fear, resentment, anxiety, and quite a few more.)

XI. The outer person responds and the hand-to-hand communication begins.

XII. Say goodbye.

The coordinator will decide when enough time has passed and then everybody can move to a new partner and begin the exercise again.

Thumbspeak and Palmtalk

Some of us just have to talk with our hands. It helps to get the point across. If you watch political candidates on television, you can see how they have been coached to use their hands. In this game we just do it. You can play this game all day long.

I. Focus on your hands.

II. Whenever you speak to anybody (whether on the phone or in person), use your hands as an active part of the communication.

III. Watch how you communicate with your hands.

IV. Which fingers are important?

V. Do you find it easy or difficult?

VI. Are you relaxed or self-conscious?

VII. Experiment with gestures that you have never used before.

Picture a scene several hundred years ago. High in the rugged mountains of Wales, two men encounter each other. The two men are diviners, poets, and readers. Neither has met the other but each "knows" the other is a like-minded soul. They can communicate verbally, but the older man raises his right hand and makes a sign with his fingers. The other man responds with his own fingers. Soon the two men are conversing warmly as brothers who have not seen each other for a long time. The two Welshmen are practicing the ancient art of finger *ogam*. This utilizes the fingers of the initiate as a way of signing the mystical alphabet of *ogam*.[17]

Fingers are the agents of the hands. And the curious designs on the inside of our fingers have long pointed to the uniqueness of the human being. Today fingerprints are mostly used to track down criminals. But long before the FBI, the CIA, Interpol, John Dillinger, or James Bond, the Chinese recognized that fingerprints were unique to each person. As long as thirteen hundred years ago Chinese diviners used fingerprints as a map of the person they were reading.[18]

Fingerprint Game: Picture a Print

This game should be played with two or more people.

NEEDED: a pile of scrap paper, an ink pad (adult supervision is recommended if this is to be played by people younger than ten), paper, paper towel (to wipe off the ink), and colored pencils or felt-tip pens.

I. Everybody takes a print of each of the fingers on one hand, including the thumb. (No need to press hard—just roll the finger onto the ink pad and then onto a piece of paper, just like they do in the police movies.) Use a separate piece of paper for each print.

II. For identification, each person makes up a symbol or letter, preferably not a name or initial, and writes this on the back of each of her fingerprints.

III. With each print, each person draws a simple picture using her own fingerprint as the main substance of the picture.

IV. Each person creates five pictures out of five prints.

V. Each person composes a story made up of the five pictures.

VI. Everyone relates her story to the group, holding up each picture to illustrate different episodes.

VII. Everybody exchanges prints and tells stories using other people's prints and pictures.

From Soup to Nuts: Food for Divination

Signs are all around us. Everything that we touch is a source of divination. Everything that touches us is an instrument for understanding. In this sense, there is no limit to the possible tools that we can use.

Even dung has had its place among the tools of divination. Inca diviners used pellets of llama dung to seek the answers to basic questions.[19] The Shona diviners of Africa collect special fruit seeds from elephant turds to conduct their inquiries.[20]

Diviners have read the spit on their hands, the fingernails of young boys, the rustling of the leaves in the trees. They have looked into mirrors, crystal balls, and the play of the wind upon still waters. They have listened to the sounds of birds and the rumbling of thunder.

The possibilities for signs and tools of divination spring from the everyday, and there is nothing more everyday than food. Of food, perhaps grains are the most widely used tools of divination.

The development of agriculture is one of the greatest leaps in the history of human beings. Planting and growing food crops allowed humans to know where their next meal was coming from. Unlike their hunting and gathering ancestors, the first farmers were able to stay in the same place and plan for the future. Farming allowed people to produce more than they needed—to create a surplus. This surplus allowed them to survive dry spells and store food during good spells.

Grains are among the first crops planted by the first farmers. They are the earliest cultivated crop. Descended from the wild grasses, grains have always been a mainstay of the human diet. It is little wonder that grains, and, in particular, corn, have been used for a long time as instruments of divination.

The casting of corn is one of the most widespread practices of diviners throughout the world. Among the Zapotec people of Oaxaca, Mexico, the practice is called *tirar mais,* or "throwing corn." The grains are blackened on one side and the diviner throws them onto a mat. Some diviners read the numbers of black (positive) as opposed to white (negative). Other diviners look at the shape.[21]

Across the world, on the Celebes island, east of Borneo, a diviner takes grains of corn in his fist and blows into his fist. He then pours them from one hand to another and throws them to the floor. Using an elaborate system of counting, the diviner will determine the signs by the number of pairs that are presented.[22]

In the remote regions of Russia an old woman takes a handful of grain. On a table is a piece of paper ruled carefully into squares. Within each square is an aphorism or a figure representing an aphorism much like a Chinese fortune cookie. The woman casts the grain along the paper and reads the results.[23]

The Iroquois have a complex way of using grain to divine remedies for illness. The Iroquois diviner will take a few grains of corn and place them inside a weasel skin, which is put in water overnight and then planted. When the corn grows and forms ears, the most abnormally shaped ear is picked. The Iroquois healer will then take some article of clothing belonging to the sick person and wrap it about the ear of corn. All of this is then placed under the healer's pillow and his dreams provide the answers.[24]

In Java the reader creates a pattern, like the one below, that represents the days of the week. He takes a handful of corn kernels and places one at each point of the pattern that represents a day until he is finished. The day on which the greatest number of kernels has fallen is the most propitious. The one with the least kernels is the most unwise for action.[25]

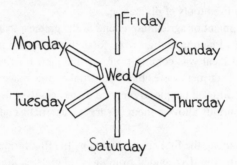

Playing with Your Food: A Game Even Grandma Would Like

Once I was doing readings at a party. At that time I only used the tarot cards. However, after an hour or so I tired of being the wandering card minstrel. When a rather strong and independent-looking woman asked me for a reading, I looked around for another vehicle.

Since the party was being catered by a Chinese restaurant, there was a bowl of dried noodles nearby. I had the woman stick her hands into the bowl, grab some noodles, and drop them on the tablecloth. When I looked at the noodles she had scattered, I got an entirely different impression of her. They formed a pattern like this:

It was a primitive representation of a house. When I told her that the most

important thing in her life was house and home, her friends agreed. The noodles had spoken.

As has been mentioned, the world around us is a vehicle to be read playfully. It contains millions of texts to be accessed by us as long as we are willing to look and stretch.

Since all of us spend so much time eating, it is appropriate that we use food as one of the vehicles for psychic play. Just think of the many variations of color, texture, associations, taste. The consumption of food uses all of the five senses. Even hearing comes into play when you think of things like bacon sizzling, corn popping, and Rice Krispies crackling.

This game allows us to free-associate from somebody's plate.

  I. Wait until the person to be read has finished his meal.
  II. Ask for his plate.
  III. Is there any immediate feeling that you get from looking at the plate?
  IV. Without changing a single crumb, observe the plate.
  V. What is left on the plate?
  VI. What colors strike you about what is on the plate?
  VII. Are there any patterns in the remains on the plate?
  VIII. Look at the plate as if you are a detective trying to break a code. What are some of the things that the plate is telling you about the person who left it?
  IX. Use the patterns and the colors to "read" the person using the plate.

What's in a Voice?

How we express ourselves is a factor not only of the words that we use but of how we sound. Our voices tell infinite amounts about who we are. The problem is that usually others don't listen and we don't listen ourselves. In this game we don't listen to the words, we listen to the voice behind the words. We listen to what the voice tells us.

This is best played in a group where people don't know a great deal about each other.[26]

NEEDED: blindfolds for everyone.

  I. Divide into two groups of equal numbers.
  II. One group puts on blindfolds and spreads out.
  III. Each nonblindfolded person stands before a blindfolded person.

IV. Nonblindfolded person starts talking to the blindfolded partner. The subject is unimportant. In fact, the subject of the talk should be light and trivial. Could be the weather, telling a story. It is the voice itself that is important. (Don't listen to the words. Listen to the voice.)

V. Nonblindfolded person must continue talking.

VI. Blindfolded person pays attention to his feelings, images, and thoughts.

VII. After three or four minutes, nonblindfolded person stops talking.

VIII. After a moment of silence, what arises in the blindfolded person?

IX. The blindfolded person tells his partner what he has experienced and what he makes of it. He describes the images that have come to him.

X. Blindfolded person removes blindfold.

XI. Persons without blindfolds put them on.

XII. Everyone finds new partners and begins again.

You can play variations of this game by yourself. Listening to a politician on television or the radio, close your eyes and try to listen just to the sounds and not the words. Or, in a group when someone is talking, do the same thing. You will hear much more than the message that the words convey.

Becoming an Ear

Since the number of psychic vehicles is almost infinite, it would be foolhardy to attempt to list them. In fact, no such list is possible. The list of possibilities grows within each of us.

The intuitive or psychic sense is often called the sixth sense. But our psychic sense really uses the other five. After all, how could we tune in to anything without using our five senses?

While our five senses are part of our birthright, they can be refined, conditioned, sharpened, or dulled. They can also be developed as we tune in to the world around us.

It is a well-known fact that blind people develop other senses more acutely than sighted folks. This includes the intuitive sense. If we let ourselves be "blind" for a little while, we will tune in to things that we otherwise would have overlooked.

This game is a solitaire. It does not matter how many people are around you or how noisy or quiet it is. To play, all you need is a few minutes to yourself.

I. Close your eyes and become a giant ear. As the ear does nothing, so you do nothing. Just as the ear takes in sounds, so you take in sounds.

II. First take in all the sounds immediately around you. Just let them go through you. Make a mental note. Do not judge.

III. Extend outward, taking in all the sounds in a larger and larger area like the ripples in a pond when the pebble is thrown. Become a giant antenna receiving sounds from as far as you possibly can. Travel to the farthest edge of the sounds. Stay there for a moment. Then travel to the sounds closest.

IV. What thoughts go through your mind?

V. What memories?

VI. What feelings?

VII. Now differentiate between the sounds that come from a living creature (animal, human, insect, or bird) and those that are lifeless (car horns, doorbells, etc.).

VIII. Concentrate on one life sound. Let yourself travel toward the living sound. Travel into the sound. Be the sound.

This is something that you can do just about anyplace where you can close your eyes for a few moments. It is amazing how many sounds there are around us that we simply do not hear. We hear so much more when we pay attention to our ears.

For variety you might try to become a giant nose. Extend your sense of smell the same way you extended your sense of hearing. It's amazing how many smells we can pick up when we pay attention to that sense.

From the back of a tortoise to the sound of the wind, signs present themselves in ways that are always original. The shape of a puffy cloud on a clear summer's day can provide us with a mirror. And then, like the cloud itself, the mirror disappears, never to reappear in exactly the same way.

Every real omen is seen only the first time. After that it becomes a part of the past. Signs are part of the moment. And how we see them is part of the moment as well. As the ancient Greeks said, we cannot step into the same river twice. We cannot stare into the same salad plate or pile of noodles twice. It is also true that you cannot look with the same eyes twice. Each time we look for a sign we are looking at a new moment in time. Everything is different even though it may look the same as before. We are different as well. Psychic vehicles help us see the world with innocent eyes. And we can create and re-create them to help us do that.

CHAPTER 10

Mirror to Mirror:
Reading Another Person as an Act of Love

For now we see through a glass, darkly;
But then face to face:
Now I know in part;
But then shall I know even as also I am known.
> *—1 Corinthians 13:12*

Let us remember that when we meet others, we should consider them as mirrors and whatever we see in them we should first of all search in ourselves. In this way, in the mirror of day-to-day relations, a person becomes busy in searching his own self. Running away from the world and its relations is not only cowardice, it is also useless. What is right is that we should use those relations for a search of the self. In their absence, it is as impossible to find out oneself as it is to see one's own face without a mirror. In the form of others, we constantly keep meeting our own selves. Heart, which is full of love, sees love in all others.
> *—Osho Rajneesh,* The Earthen Lamps

He who sees the entire world
of animate and inanimate objects
in himself
and also sees himself
in all animate and inanimate objects,
because of this
does not hate anyone.
> *—Ishavasya Upanishad*

THERE are signs around us all the time. We have found maps in the thunder and lightning. We have heard angels in the voices of birds. We have listened to the whispers of the fire and read the wind in the sand and the leaves.

The world is our mirror. We have reflected, in the most basic sense of the word, that which is around us. We have seen our reflections in the stars and the stones. We have seen our paths in the shape of trees.

People have read just about everything. From bones to stones to the call of a goose, we have read the world. However, the deepest readings are those in which we read each other.

Renowned archaeologist Dr. Richard Leakey has found many skeletons of humans from hundreds of thousands of years ago. This is part of his work. Among these skeletons are bones that had been broken and healed.

Times were hard for our ancestors. They hunted, they gathered, and they lived by their wits. Even today a broken leg or arm can put us out of commission for weeks. For our cave-dwelling ancestors a broken limb was a matter of life or death. They could not have survived alone. People are ill equipped physically compared with the rest of the animal world. Any fish swims faster. Any four-legged creature can run faster. The bear is stronger. Even the fox is warmer. People found that they needed each other.

The broken bones that Dr. Leakey examined had been set and healed. They were injuries that took place before the death of the individual. The conclusion was clear: Since a person with a broken leg could not have survived alone in the Neolithic wilderness, he or she had to be taken care of. People were taking care of the wounded and the ill. People were taking care of each other.

It was in that same Neolithic wilderness that our ancestors gathered together to get food. These human beings took their torches, formed a circle, and surrounded the giant woolly mammoths and drove them off the cliffs. Individually our ancient relatives were small and weak. Together they were a powerful force that could intimidate even the largest beast of the land. Cooperation, nurturing, and sharing are the qualities that define the human species. They are also aspects of love. Love is a very refined and human quality. Although other animals may share that quality, only humans can communicate it through language. We are a cooperative and sharing species. People need each other. We take care of each other through sharing.

It is always easier to see someone else clearly than it is to see ourselves. For that reason we need each other to help us see ourselves. So seeing someone else can be an act of sharing.

Reading another person can be an act of love. Rarely do we have the opportunity to look at another person without judgment and say what we see. Rarely do others give us an honest and loving look at ourselves. Yet we have the opportunity, in giving and receiving a reading, to do just that, to see ourselves as others see us. When we do a psychic reading, it's hard to know just who is giving and who is receiving. What is really happening, at best, is an exchange of energy.

The bottom line: It feels good to share our perceptions honestly and lovingly. It feels good to receive other people's perceptions in the same way. To be a mirror for another is an act of friendship. It is an act of trust and caring. And trust and caring is the essence of true psychic reading.

The Algonquin Indian diviner was wise to call the instrument of divination "my mirror."[1] We are mirrors all the time. We reflect our friends and lovers. And they reflect us. We see them. They see us. We share. That's what it's all about.

With all of the vehicles that we have explored, people have read each other. The *arahati,* or seer, of Honduras used the mirror to answer questions that a client brought to her. The diviner herself became the mirror for the client. The Cherokee diviner used stones to answer questions that were posed by someone else. Among the Amazulu of southern Africa the reading of bones involved the reading of the person. There, too, the diviner was counselor. And diviners, whether they were astrologers or Navajo stargazers, used the stars as a way of answering questions and gaining insight into another person.[2]

Tuning in to the life force, or *qi,* was something that a person had to do for himself. But, when applied to a village or community, tuning in to the *qi* was cooperative. Diviners used the psychic alphabets of the runes to read themselves and to read others. And the Celtic mystical alphabet of *ogam* was a form of communication that, by definition, required another person.

Dowsing is also a vehicle for sharing. Aside from the obvious uses of finding water sources, dowsing has been used for centuries to answer a multitude of questions. Whether it be the body of a living person held as a pendulum among the Chukchi Eskimos or the divining rod of the Ila people of Rhodesia, reading is a cooperative venture. One person reads another. Or a group of people try to make sense out of their lives.[3]

From mirrors to pendulums, from bones to runes, the techniques of divination have been about seeing our world and each other in new ways. We can draw upon the tools of ten thousand years. We can utilize omens, bones, stones, mirrors, runes, and the wind to better see ourselves and each other.

The Eyes Have It

Many cultures consider the eyes to be the window to the soul. Recently I found that there is an ancient Eastern meditation, called Tratak, that involves staring into and through the eyes of another.

In this game we simply look into the eyes of another person while that person is looking into ours. Nothing more. Nothing less.

    I. Find a place that is relatively quiet and sit facing each other. You need to be no more than two feet away from each other.
    II. Look straight into the eyes of the person opposite you. Try not to blink.
    III. How do your eyes feel? Relaxed? Tense?
    IV. How do you feel about looking into the eyes of the other person?
    V. See your reflection in the eyes of the other.
    VI. Now close your eyes for a few moments.
    VII. How do you feel now?

If at first you feel a bit nervous, just continue. Play this game for at least five minutes and then see how you feel at the end.

Staring for Fun (Discreetly)

We must overcome our fear of staring. As children we were all told that it is impolite, if not bad, to stare. Yet every child wants to stare. Watch a little kid when she sees someone new and interesting. Her mouth will drop open, her eyes will widen, and she will stare. When we tell a child not to stare, we are telling her not to look. For the child, staring is a way of seeing.

As grown-ups we have learned not to stare and, often, not to look. Yet we need to look at another closely if we are going to read him. It is easier to stare when nobody knows that you are staring. In this game we begin staring (and looking) again, but we do it in safe places. You can play this in a crowded bus, theater lobby, train station, from the window of a car in a city, or just about anyplace where there are lots of people and you have a chance to be still and look.

    I. Find a place where there are lots of people.
    II. Pick one and check out what that person is doing.
    III. Study everything about the person: clothes, face, posture, activity.
    IV. What can you say about the person at this time?
    V. What kind of work do you think the person does?
    VI. Is the person happy?
    VII. Use your imagination and create a life for the person. Describe his family. What are his problems? What are his favorite things to do? What is he doing at this moment? Where is he going?

The point here is to learn how to look at people playfully and let your imagination roam. Imagination is a key ingredient in all divination.

There is a card in the traditional tarot deck called the Star. It portrays a young woman kneeling at a stream. She has a cup in each hand. One cup is lifted to the moonlit sky, receiving the energy from above. The other is turned down, pouring its contents into the stream. For me the card has always represented the two inseparable aspects of love: giving and receiving.

It is difficult to know just where giving ends and receiving begins. Is a mother breast-feeding her newborn child giving or receiving? Clearly she is giving both her body and her love *and* she is receiving the unconditional love of her child. The baby is both receiving the milk of his mother and giving his love. What is happening between mother and child is an exchange of energy. Love and nurturing are flowing back and forth.

Reading another person is an exchange of energy. Through time, the reader, whether it be an Ifugao chicken egg diviner of the Philippines, a Mayan crystal seer, or an Irishman looking at the shapes of hot lead as it hits the water, must remain open. The reader, after all, is allowing himself to experience new perceptions. Similarly the person being read must be open. It's a two-way street.

We are a naturally receptive species. We come into the world trusting and receptive. And, no matter what happens as we grow older, that open part of us is still within. In a reading we contact that openness. At a certain point in any reading it is difficult to tell who is giving and who is receiving.

Heart to Heart

In countless cultures the heart has been the symbol of love and caring. It is also the symbol of the soul itself. Any decent intuitive reading is done from the heart. But we all can use some help in contacting our hearts.

This game can be played in a group with people breaking into couples, or it can be played with just two people.

I. Sit opposite your partner.

II. Close your eyes.

III. In your mind's eye focus on the area of your chest where your heart is.

IV. Pretend that you are now feeling the entire world through your heart. Let your heart become the sensory organ of your body.

V. Imagine your heart opening.

VI. Let out your heart energy to your partner.

   VII. Let your partner's energy in.

  VIII. Be aware of any thoughts, feelings, or sensations.

    IX. Let yourself imagine shapes.

     X. What colors come to mind?

    XI. What pictures come to mind?

   XII. Animals? Plants? Flowers? Minerals? People? Scenes?

  XIII. Open your eyes and look at your partner.

  XIV. Close your eyes and do it again.

No need to force this game. Just let it happen.

That Certain *Je ne sais quoi*

> *It doesn't mean a thing if it ain't got that certain je ne sais quoi.*
> —Peter Schickele

It is weird how difficult it is for most of us to compliment someone directly without any motive. This is strange because human beings are naturally innocent and loving. It is true that love has become just another four-letter word. Yet without a loving and caring attitude there can be no decent kind of reading.

Like many other things, the more we start verbalizing what we see, the more we see. When we say what we see, we are forced to see things differently. Words are strange that way. Once they are out of our mouths, they have an unusual way of having an effect on both the other person and ourselves. When we blurt out something in anger—a statement that is hurtful—it has impact on the other person. It also has impact on us. We may feel guilty or remorseful. Our fury subsiding, we may see the whole situation differently, but the words have already had their effect.

On the other hand, if we say something that is caring to another, there is also an impact. There is the impact of the words on the other person. There is also the impact of our words upon us. It is a warm feeling that all of us have experienced. And when we consciously approach others with caring statements, we begin to see the world in a different way.

Reading as a Warm Fuzzy[4]

Many years ago, Dr. Claude Steiner wrote a tale for children and adults about warm fuzzies. Warm fuzzies were food for the heart. They were compliments, stated sincerely. They were unconditional expressions of love and caring.

In the story everybody was used to receiving these warm fuzzies until an evil witch came around. She peddled plastic fuzzies. These were conditional statements like "You're a good person when you aren't complaining" or "Sometimes you are really nice." Soon the plastic fuzzies glutted the world and people were starving for the original warm fuzzies.

A couple of years ago, I was working at an arts camp for kids. The staff was unusually loving, but by the sixth week of camp everybody was exhausted. Small things irritated people. And even the most dedicated counselor occasionally thought of running away.

It was during this sixth week of camp that I offered a "warm fuzzy" workshop. Few of the kids had any idea of what it would be about, but about twenty kids and staff showed up. In this workshop everybody wrote something loving and sincere to somebody else in camp. I encouraged everybody to be specific. The letters had to be anonymous.

At first, people were hesitant—saying something that is caring and warm to another person is not that common—but then the words started to flow.

The workshop lasted for a little over an hour. The group had produced at least 150 letters. A stream of anonymous loving letters flooded the camp mail. For a brief period, the mood in the camp grew lighter. For a day or two, people were less exhausted and less annoyed.

The people who enjoyed it the most were the ones who wrote the letters. In this game we give warm fuzzies, which are a basic aspect of reading. This game gives us some practice. It is best played with three or more people.

NEEDED: paper and writing implements.

I. Everybody takes a few minutes to concentrate on the others in the group.
   a. Try to pick up some characteristics about each person, the way he carries himself, the way in which he speaks, anything.
II. Write one paragraph to each person in the group. Without judgment write something about the person that has to do with who that person is. It is not at all necessary to know the person you are writing about.
III. Put the name of the person you are writing about on the paper, but do not include your name.
IV. One person collects the papers and distributes to the others the warm fuzzies that were written about them.
V. Each person reads some or all of his aloud.
VI. No comments are allowed.

Reading Yourself with Fuzzies

It's not easy to verbalize positive things about ourselves. We are told to be modest. We are conditioned not to be conceited. We end up thinking that to say something nice about ourselves is taboo. In this game we break the taboo—and begin to read ourselves.

I. Take two or three minutes with eyes closed.
II. Focus on yourself as if you are focusing on another person.
III. What qualities do you like about yourself?
IV. What qualities bother you?
V. Write a caring, nonjudgmental letter to yourself as if you were writing to another person.
VI. How different was this than writing to others?

Maybe Yes. Maybe No.

There was an old man who lived in the village with his only son. He was a feeble old man. The boy's mother had died giving birth to him.

When the mother died leaving the old man with his infant son, the villagers took pity. Some of them came to the old man and told him, "You are most unlucky."

"Maybe yes. Maybe no," answered the old man. "Who knows?"

Many of the villagers thought the old man a little dotty. They explained it as being the result of his wife's death or his age.

But his son, born in the twilight of the old man's life, was a vital boy. He would cut the wood, build the fires, feed and care for the few animals. He would even make the meals, for he and his father lived alone together.

The old man's love for the boy was unbounded. On his thirteenth birthday the boy received what he had always wanted: a white stallion, as young and vital as he was himself. The old man had scrimped and saved and bartered, and the boy had his horse.

"How lucky your son is," said many of the villagers to the old man.

"Maybe yes. Maybe no," answered the old man. "I love him more than my heart itself, but who knows?"

The boy could not be separated from his horse. He and the horse galloped like the wind. They became one. They both rushed forward with the recklessness of youth.

It was a recklessness that led both boy and horse to ignore a ditch in the field. Both boy and horse broke a leg. The horse had to be shot. The boy could only move about with great effort and pain.

"How unlucky are you and your son," said the villagers to the old man.

"Maybe yes. Maybe no," answered the old man. "Who knows?"

Once again the villagers thought the old man foolish or senile.

While the boy was still recovering, war broke out. For the people of the village, the land they tilled was the only country they knew. But soldiers came with guns and swords and took all of the able-bodied men and boys of the village to fight and die far from the land of their mothers and fathers.

Of the young men, only the boy was saved. He could not fight. He could not even walk without crutches. No army wanted him.

A few of the old men and women left in the village came to the old man. "We were wrong, old man," said one. "How lucky are you and your son."

"Maybe yes. Maybe no," answered the old man. "Who knows?"

The boy recovered from his injuries. With all of the young men of the town gone to war and all the young girls left behind, the boy had his pick.

He was a brash boy. And, even though he loved his father much, he took his own counsel in matters of the heart. The boy fell in love with the blacksmith's daughter. Both of them had the hearts of eagles and longed to see the rest of the world together.

So it was that the boy and his beloved girl eloped together. In the dark hours of the early morning they left the village to see the world together.

With his son gone, the old man had lost his right arm.

Several of the villagers came to console the old man. "How unlucky you are," they said.

"Maybe yes. Maybe no," answered the old man. "Who knows?"

—Adapted from a Sufi tale

Judge Not Lest . . .

We are taught to judge from a very early age—good from bad, right from wrong. It is definitely a tradition that is more of the West than the East.

In the East the notions of *yin* and *yang* permeate the work of the diviners.

Where there is dark there is light. Where there is cold there is heat. Everything is contained within the whole. For example, the Chinese word for crisis is *wei-chi*. It is composed of two words meaning "danger" and "opportunity." Danger and opportunity linked together create a crisis. Out of crisis comes change.

In the West we have the sayings "Every cloud has a silver lining" and "When one door shuts, new doors open." These sayings recognize that things shift. Out of hardship comes ease. Out of disaster comes opportunity.

All judgments are taught, they are not inborn. When we do a reading, it is important to be aware of our own judgments. We all have them—views of what is moral and what is immoral, ideas of what people *"should"* be doing. If all we do in a reading is project these judgments upon another, then we are simply reinforcing our old ideas.

Since ancient times, divination has been a technique of seeing the world in new ways. Judgments simply preserve the old ways that we have of seeing the world. They prevent us from seeing signs and reading people. That's why they are out of place in a reading.

Disaster or Gift?—Judgment Game

I once did a reading for a man who had a severe limp. This, I later learned, was the result of a near-fatal car crash suffered by him and his wife seven years earlier. His wife had a speech impediment as a result of brain damage due to the crash. Both had nearly been killed.

Most of us would see this experience as a hardship and a disaster. That would be a judgment. The reality was quite different. To be sure, a life-threatening car accident is, on the one hand, a disaster. It's the other hand that we so often ignore.

This man was one of the most life-affirming and joyous individuals I had met in a long time. He had the spontaneity and innocence of a child. He lived every day for itself and had very little worry in his life. He was not always like that, he said. He became that way after the crash. Before the crash, he said, he was a workaholic.

His brush with death was a gift. He himself realized that the experience was an opportunity. It was an opportunity to learn how beautiful living in the moment could be; how rich life is.

Often the gifts we get are not the ones we expect. But gifts abound, and illness, brushes with death, and separations can be as much gifts as winning a prize or achieving a goal.

In this game, which we play alone, we search for gifts in the face of disaster. In that way, we come to terms with judgments.

NEEDED: paper and a writing implement.

I. Close your eyes and take ten slow deep breaths. (Or any other method that you may have developed to clear your mind and calm yourself down.)

II. Think of three or four major mishaps that have occurred in your life.

III. Open your eyes and write them down.

IV. Write briefly how you felt about each event when it occurred.

V. Write briefly how you feel about each event now.

VI. How have your feelings changed?

VII. In a few words write down how the mishap led you to the point that you are now at.

VIII. Try to find a positive aspect in each event. Force yourself if necessary. (If you can't do it with each one, that's fine. The point is really just to begin thinking in that way.)

As an additional exercise, watch your judgments for a couple of days. Try to see how each negative occurrence has a positive aspect. The more we are aware of our judgments, the less likely we are to place them upon others either in daily life or in readings.

Reading Faces (and Flowers)

In the short story "The Lost Boy," by Thomas Wolfe, the author speaks of the way a boy's clothes "uttered him." Once we start looking closely at each other, we notice that all kinds of things "utter" us. Our clothes "utter" us. So do the expressions on our face and the timbre of our voice. There are many ways that we speak.

In the 1970s people began to pay more attention to body language. This was not a new pursuit. Diviners in ancient cultures looked at the way people stood and watched the expressions on their faces. Just about anything could be utilized as a means of seeing a person more clearly.

In our daily life we don't notice a lot about other people. We often see the same people day after day at work or even at home. More often than not, we see the same people in the same way. This is only habit. Just as we cannot step into the same river twice, so we cannot look at the same person twice. We are always changing. Yet we think that we are seeing the same people with the same eyes.

It is different when we read another person. Then we put ourselves in the position of seeing with "new" eyes. We need to pretend that we know nothing about the person we are reading. We need to imagine that we are meeting this person for the first time. Then, and only then, will we be able to see things we have never seen before. Then looking at a person becomes an adventure. And that's part of what reading is all about.

Seeing a Person for the First Time

We do see people for the first time. In this game we see people for the first time even if we have seen them before. All that means is that we pay attention to details, to aspects that we ordinarily would not be conscious of.

The ancient Indian text the Parisista shows how the reader can interpret the gestures of men, women, and children. Yawns, sneezes, and the blinking of eyes are all part of the repertoire of the ancient reader.[5] In this game we focus on everything we can in the other person's face.

    I. Sit opposite your partner.

    II. Close your eyes and take a few deep breaths just to relax and clear yourself.

    III. Stare at the other person. You may blink.

    IV. Take in every part of the person, the wrinkles in the skin, the shape of the eyes, the shape of the mouth.

    V. After about five minutes of staring, close your eyes.

    VI. What thoughts come into your head?

    VII. What images?

    VIII. What feelings? (Do not worry if the thoughts, images, or feelings don't specifically relate to the person sitting across from you.)

    IX. See if you can put these thoughts, images, and feelings together in some way that says something about the person sitting in front of you.

When we see new things about a person, we are, in a sense, reading her.

My Fine Flowered Friends

> *Consider the lilies how they grow: they toil not, they spin not; and yet I say unto you, that Solomon in all his glory was not arrayed like one of these.*
>
> *—Luke 12:27*

I was in New Orleans for our annual family reunion. My aunt Charlotte, a great plant person, had a small garden in front of her house. It was a riot of colors, blooming in early April. As I looked at these flowers, I started to see each one individually. Each had its own personality. Each was its own being and, at the same time, in concert with the others. Suddenly I saw my family in this reunion of flowers. There was a shy pink flower with clear, firm lines that seemed to be related to my aunt Charlotte. There was a splashing yellow bloom that had to be my aunt Ev. My mother was represented by a deep red flower with shocks of purple that got more and more complex the more I looked at it.

It was a family of flowers. Ever since then I have looked at flowers differently.

Like the flowers, we are all unique. When we read another person, it is important to focus on that individuality. This game helps us to see the uniqueness of another—as a flower.

I. Sit opposite a partner.

II. Close your eyes and take some deep breaths. Or you might try imagining that your head is a fountain out of which is pouring a rainbow of colors. This helps getting into colors.

III. Open your eyes and look at your partner.

IV. First focus on every feature of the person in sharp detail.

V. Then let your eyes go blurry and fuzzy while looking at the other person.

VI. Close your eyes again.

VII. Let your imagination run with colors and shapes.

VIII. Open your eyes.

IX. Describe a flower that would best fit the person opposite you. If you don't know much about flowers or can't think of one that is specific to the person opposite you, make up a fantasy flower that describes the person.

A variation of this game is to consider the person as an animal or bird. Or, if you find yourself in a garden with lots of flowers, you might play this in reverse. That is, you would find the flower to suit the person that you were with or any other person you might want to characterize.

In the movie Wayne's World one of the characters compares another to a flavor of ice cream. Are you chocolate? Raspberry? Or orange sherbet? If we can read people as flowers or animals or birds, we can read them as flavors of ice cream.

Photographs and Frozen Time

Photographs are strange things. From the time that photography developed in the last century, photographs have held a certain mystical quality. They are frozen moments of time, instants when a person is caught on a piece of paper in picture format.

People show each other snapshots and sometimes bore each other doing so. But snapshots don't have to be boring. And, while you might think that it is impolite to stare, it is perfectly fine to stare and glare at a photograph.

Photographs are an opportunity to practice the skills of reading another. We can learn a lot by examining the faces in photographs. A petrified moment of time can give us all kinds of ideas. It is a fascinating exercise to take down a family photo album and look with new ways at the faces of familiar people. Look at the pictures of aunts and uncles and even of yourself as if you had never seen them before. See what you can tell about the people in the pictures. If you want to read other people, looking at photographs is a good place to begin.

Reading by Kodak

In this game, which should be played with at least two people, we use photographs of people that we know. These can be photos of friends or family or even ourselves. It must be people with whom we have some personal connection.

NEEDED: Each person should come with photographs—at least five different photographs are satisfactory, but the more the better.

 I. Exchange photographs with each other.
 II. Look at the person in the photo as if to take in everything about them.
 III. Close your eyes for a moment.
 IV. What color would you associate with the person in the picture?
 V. What animal would you associate with the person in the picture?
 VI. What melody would you associate with the person in the picture?
 VII. What was this person like as a child?
 VIII. If the person is an adult, what kind of adolescence did she or he have?
 IX. Start saying all that comes to mind about this person.
   a. What weaknesses does this person have?

b. What strengths?
c. What loves?
d. What hates?

Each person take turns going through the photos. While one person is speaking, the other person remains quiet. The idea is not to be "right" but to let our sight wander into new alleys and byways. If we worry about accuracy, we will bog ourselves down. It's all meant to be playful. It's not a test.

Reading as an Act of Trust

A reading is a process of discovery. If you already know the answers, why bother reading at all? Every reader—a Chinese *feng-shui* master seeking the ideal location to build a house or a Naskapi diviner observing the cracks on a piece of burned bone—approaches his reading with a fresh perspective. So it is when we read another person.

The temptation for any reader is to attempt to be all-knowing. The reality is that the best any reader can be is a very well polished mirror. Each person has, within himself, the most complete knowledge of his being. No reader can tell others anything about themselves that they don't, on some level, already know. At the very most a reader is contacting the higher awareness of the person who is being read. That's a relief. Since we are not telling others anything about themselves that they don't already know, a reading becomes much less scary. Even if we are frightened about what we already know, we are not likely to become more frightened by a reading.

This makes the task of the reader a bit easier. A reader is simply a reflector of the truths that each person has. She is as neutral, unbiased, and honest as she can be. Neutral and unbiased—those are qualities that are difficult to find in ourselves.

We all have judgments. We all have feelings about what is right and what is wrong—for ourselves and others. When we read another person, we must be conscious of those biases. We must be as aware of them as we can be. And then we must try to suspend them. Reading another person is about reflecting and describing that person. It is not about prescribing.

A wag once said that advice is the only thing in the world that is given away free and yet taken by nobody. This is true. On the other hand, whoever heard of a mirror with a point of view? And mirror is what we become when we read.

When we read another person, we have an opportunity to suspend our old biases and judgments. We have a chance to look with new eyes. It is an opportunity to see another with a clarity that we don't normally have.

When we read another person, we have an obligation to be as clear of our prejudices as we possibly can be. The reader can get a great deal out of that. We don't normally have a situation where we are mandated to drop our projections, our righteousness, our judgments.

Giving a reading is a two-way act of trust. The person being read is agreeing to be seen. That may sound trivial, but it means that the other person is agreeing, for a period of time, to be open. This is an act of trust. The person doing the reading is agreeing to see the other person and to say what she sees in a clear and unbiased way. That, too, involves a risk. That, too, is an act of trust.

What Old Problem?

As soon as we stop judging things as "good" or "bad" we can start being more honest about ourselves and others. It is the judgment that creates guilt. No judgment, no guilt.

All of us have old problems that we still make for ourselves. They get in our way. These problems are usually rooted in self-defeating judgments. We can point out to the person we are reading their problems or self-defeating patterns. This can be done with cards, crystals, or just about anything. You'll need a partner, but this can also be played in a group where the individuals divide into groups of two.

    I. Sit facing a partner.
    II. Close eyes for about two minutes.
    III. Focus on the person.
    IV. Let whatever thoughts and feelings come in.
    V. Tell your partner how you perceive her making an old problem for herself.

The key in this is to be completely nonjudgmental and caring.

Signs in Each Other: Reading as an Act of Love

When all is said and done, we read each other all the time. From the time we were little, we looked at other people and analyzed how they acted and what they said. And, as little children, we were very clear. The story of the emperor's new clothes is a story about all children. As we get older we learn that there are some things that just "shouldn't be said." We learn to push aside our intuitive observations of others, even the positive ones. Yet it is impossible for us to push away our very sensibilities. We continue to feel. We continue to observe others, even if we pay little attention to these perceptions.

Diviners and children allow themselves to use all their senses. Within us there is both the diviner and the child. To use our intuitive senses to see another person is one of the most gratifying experiences. It can be playful and loving, and involves both giving and receiving.

We have looked at many of the variations of intuitive vehicles that have been used for thousands of years. We can adapt many of the games in this book to read each other.

Throwing a Stoned Reading[6]

As human beings we have a rich heritage of divination tools. As we have used everything from bones to birds to read our world, so we can use them to read ourselves and each other. Some of these vehicles—notably stones and crystals—lend themselves more easily to reading another person than do others.

People have cast stones to find answers to their questions throughout the world. In southern Cameroon diviners use pebbles and shells. The ancient Celts used patterns of stones as indications of otherworldly information.[7] Among modern Turkish diviners stones, together with beans, cards, and coffee grounds, are an important part of the divinitory repertoire. The Masai medicine men of Africa place stones in a buffalo or ox horn, then shake the horn and find out what is going to happen by the number of stones that fall out.

This is a game that you can carry with you in a little pouch and play wherever and whenever you choose. In this game we use stones, as many or as few as you wish, and of an endless variety of shapes and colors.

NEEDED: stones and a pouch for holding them.

I. Make a list of ten to fifteen things that are important to you—for example, work, health, love, children (this can be the child inside of you as well as offspring), etc.[8]

II. Go to a stone source. Unless you live in Madagascar, it is unlikely that you'll find a wide variety of stones lying about on the ground. So a crystal or rock shop would be your best bet. The stones do not have to be fancy or expensive.

III. Collect as many stones as you have items on your list, picking them to correspond with each of the categories. (Keep in mind that all of the stones together should be able to fit in the palm of your hand. Boulders simply will not do.) There is no "right" way to pick a stone. Just pick the ones that feel right. You can either look for a stone to match the category, or you can find a stone and then see what category it would fit. Sometimes you might even find that the stone you have picked generates a new category. Just remember that there are no guidelines other than the ones you set for yourself. But you might try to match the stones—their colors and their shapes—with the quality that they will represent. For example, humor, for me, is represented by a bright yellow bead because of its lightness and roundness. Brilliance is expressed in my collection by a tiny but very brilliant Herkimer diamond. As always, use your imagination.

IV. Put the stones in the pouch. Shake up the pouch and pour them on the table. Another way is to take them all in your hands and shake them up and throw them on the table. (To read others, you may ask them to place the stones on the table in whatever fashion they choose, deliberately or randomly, since they do not know what each of the stones means.)

V. Look at the pattern of the stones. See how they lie in relation to each other. Describe these patterns and relationships with reference to the qualities that the stones represent.

Above is an imaginary spread with five stones. They represent the following: s=sadness; h=humor; w=work or the material world; L=love; and c=children. By simply describing the way the stones are laid out we can interpret some basic things. For example, work is bracketed by humor and sadness. One could easily say that, for this person, work is a mixed bag and that humor probably plays a very important role in keeping the person's equilibrium. Children and love are directly connected to each other. This is obvious. A little less obvious, but right there in front of us, is the separation of love and child from the workplace. It is clear in this that work and love are in two separate fields. Unlike many folks, this person is most comfortable with children and has a definite ambivalence about the work scene. And so on and so on. The more stones that you use, the more variation.

This is a very simple kind of game. It is one that can easily be done with friends and loved ones. Or even total strangers. All you are doing is describing the patterns and the relationships of the stones and their meanings. Of course, as always, you are doing it without judgments. You will be amazed at the results.

If you wish, you can substitute just about anything for the stones. The person being read can gather a handful of any small object. Either you or he can give these objects definition. I have seen people use small flowers, twigs, earrings, and much more.

What's in a Word: Using Anagrams as Psychic Tools

An anagram is a play with words. We just take a word and use the letters in the word to make other words. For example, anagrams from the word anagram might result in the sentence "Nag a ram."

We can find meaning in words beyond the meanings that we learn. That is the fun of anagrams. In this game the idea is to let your mind play with letters and come up with new words from familiar things.

This can be played either with one partner being read or with a group.

NEEDED: paper and a writing implement.

I. Sit opposite your partner.
II. Write down the full name of your partner.
III. Derive as many different words from that name as you can. (You do not have to use all the letters, but the letters you use must be from the name.)
IV. See which words apply to the person.
V. Try to create a sentence using those words.
VI. Then create a paragraph describing your partner with the words created from her name.

Crystal-Clear Reading

It was the last day of a month-long class on intuitive games that I had given for a group of teenagers at an arts camp. The class was given on a dance platform under a canopy of trees and next to a running brook and cool woods. Naturally the kids were distracted, not only by the external surrounding but by their internal hormones. The class had gone as well as could be expected.

For the remainder of this last session I had brought small quartz crystals to be held by the kids. The class broke into groups of two and I told them to hold the crystal in the middle of their forehead and to let them experience whatever they could about their partners. Within seconds, they were alive with chatter.

Each kid had seen something about his partner. In this game we do the same thing.

NEEDED: one clear crystal for each person.

   I. Sit opposite your partner.
   II. Close your eyes and take several deep breaths.
   III. Hold the crystal up to your forehead.
   IV. Let whatever pictures come into your inner eye.
   V. Let whatever feelings flood your senses.
   VI. Describe the images and/or feelings to your partner.
   VII. Describe how you think your insight reflects your partner.

Don't Worry, Be Honest:
Seven Guidelines and Ten Commandments

Lightness is perhaps the most important ingredient of any reading. We have a tendency to think that the more serious something is, the closer to the truth it becomes. This neglects the fact that the people throughout history who have always been identified with the truth have been the court jesters and the comedians. The lighter we are in a reading, the easier it is to be heard and the easier it is to speak what we see.

A lot of the games in this book can be adapted to read another person. However, we can create as many different vehicles as we wish. We can use people's salad remains and see what kind of pictures come to us. We can use fingerprints. There is no end to the possibilities. There is no end to the enjoyment of being seen and seeing as a mirror.

A false mystique about psychic reading has developed in the West. People are fascinated by the "magic" of someone else knowing things about them, and rightfully so. However, in our showbiz world the real magic becomes more of a magic trick. For example, if a psychic tells someone that her youngest uncle has a wart on his left cheek, that is supposed to be the ultimate in psychic ability. Somehow that kind of useless information is considered the test of a "real" psychic.

We don't hear about the psychic who tells someone that she is sabotaging herself with her own self-doubt. Or the reader who tells another person that she is standing at a crossroads in her life and is fully capable of making the right decisions. To sight the wart on an uncle's cheek is glitzy and showy but insignificant. To tell people about what is going on in their lives at this moment is significant.

Professional psychics, like any other professional group, like to make themselves different and special. Isn't being a psychic somewhat like being a brain surgeon or architect? Don't you need training and a special gift? No, you don't need special training. And we all have the gift.

To be sure, it is daunting to consider reading another person. Most of us have never done anything like that. What if we are wrong? What if we don't see anything? What if we don't have the ability to do a reading? What if? Don't worry. Be honest. You simply cannot fail.

SEVEN GUIDELINES TO READING ANOTHER

1. *Don't worry. Be honest.* You have been doing readings of other people for your whole life. From the time that we are little we are picking up information from others. It is not something that we learn. It is something that we have. A reading, after all, is simply picking up and trusting what we see and feel.

2. *It's not a test.* In school we learn all kinds of knowledge. In the realm of the psychic we uncover what we already know. In school we learn that there are right answers and wrong answers. The realm of the psychic is different. It requires being openhearted. If we try to be showy and find out if somebody's uncle has a wart, then we can make mistakes. If we are sincerely trying to see another person, we really can't go wrong.

3. *The more you work, the worse it is.* Doing a reading is definitely a lazy person's occupation. In the left-brain world of work we have to do a great deal in order to achieve. The right-brain world of reading is very different. Here, the less you do, the better it is. What we really are doing is *letting* things come in. We are letting things happen. The more we get out of our own way with our training of doing and our notions of what is right and wrong, the better the reading. And the easier it is.

4. *A reading is a two-way street.* A reading is a process involving two people, not just the reader. Both the reader and the person being read need to remain open. Both the reader and the person being read need to take responsibility for what is happening. When I give a reading, I make the person getting a reading responsible for understanding what is happening. I want to be able to chatter away and not worry about whether the person is following me. So at the beginning of every reading I tell the person, "I have only one rule and that is if I say anything that doesn't make sense or sounds wrong, you must interrupt."

5. *The more you do, the easier it gets.* It's simply a matter of trusting your-

self. The more you say what you see, the easier it becomes. The more you say what you see, the more you see. It's the opposite of a vicious cycle. It's a benevolent cycle.

6. *Leave fortune-telling to the gypsies.* We have seen how omens are rooted in the here and now. They are something that we see in the moment. Prediction is a very tricky business and one best left to the meteorologists. When you do a reading, you are seeing the person at the very moment that you are doing the reading. To be sure, time is not a line. If we really look carefully into the moment, we can see where things are headed and where they have come from. But this is very different from seeing someone bumping his head on a door three years, five months, two days, and six hours down the road.

7. *You never tell anybody anything that they don't already know.* That's the reason why a good reading isn't really scary. What we are doing is bringing up things that people already know. At most, a reading is a form of affirmation.

The Ten Commandments of Psychic Reading

Often in the stillness of the night, when all nature seems
asleep about me, there comes a gentle rapping at the door of my
heart. I open it and a voice inquires, "Pokagon, what of your
People? What will their future be?" My answer is: Mortal man
has not the power to draw aside the veil of unborn time to tell
the future of his race. That gift belongs of the Creator alone. But
it is given to him to closely judge the future by the present . . .
and the past.

—*Simon Pokagon (1830–99), Potawatomie chief*

Pharaoh: "You have a way of making it seem as though
everything is all beautifully clear whereas so far you have only
told me what I knew already."
Joseph: "Pharaoh errs . . . if he thinks he does not know.
His servant can do no more than to prophesy to him what he
already knows."

—*Thomas Mann, Joseph in Egypt*

For a long time there have been codes of ethics for diviners and readers. One of the most succinct was found in ancient Aztec civilization. For the Aztecs a diviner was one who "remembered." He was one who made things clear. An ancient Aztec text puts it quite clearly: "The good soothsayer is one who reads the day signs for one; who examines, who remembers. . . . He reads the day signs; he brings them to one's attention. The bad soothsayer is a deceiver, a mocker, a false speaker, a hypocrite—a diabolical, a scandalous speaker. He disturbs, confounds, beguiles, deceives others."⁹

In the spirit of the Aztec wise ones, I offer these commandments.

1. *Thou shalt not tell people what to do.* First of all, you are not their mother. Second, it's none of your business what they do. Third, do you want to take responsibility for their decisions? Most of us have a hard enough time taking responsibility for our own.

2. *Thou shalt not be a "should-er" or a "should notter."* A famous American psychiatrist once said we tend to "should" all over ourselves. The bottom line is this: A "should" tells us to be somewhere else other than where we are. Since we can only be where we are, a "should " asks of us the impossible. To ask of ourselves and others the impossible is to make ourselves feel powerless and/or guilty. Who needs that?

3. *Thou shalt not judge.* I mean, really, who asked you to say "this is good" or "that is bad"? The reader is neither God nor the Supreme Court.

4. *Thou shalt not predict except that thou givest six grains of salt and a light and humorous disclaimer.* This is not about fortune-telling. It is about now. If those fortune-tellers are so good, why ain't they rich?

5. *Thou shalt never predict mortality.* If you think you're God, you *really* better have your head examined.

6. *Thou shalt not be a psychic terrorist.* One of the reasons that so many people have strong hostilities to psychics is that they have experienced psychic terrorists. Psychic terrorists are those that enjoy scaring people with dire predictions. That's a power trip like the one I used to play on my kid brother. Leave the horror stories to Stephen King.

7. *Thou shalt read with open heart, compassion, and love.* There is no other way. This is what it is all about.

8. *Thou shalt be humble in thy readings.* The best readings I have ever done have very little to do with me. The worst were those where I thought I was doing something great.

9. *Thou shalt use thy eyes and ears. Neither shalt thou close thy nose.* Sometimes we get so caught up in the magic that we forget what is right in front of our noses. The more of our senses we use, the more we see.

10. *Thou shalt speak sincerely and truthfully of what thou sees.* If you are not going to say what you see, why do the reading at all?

Notes

Chapter 1. Ides and Tides or a Wind That Comes

[1] Quoted in Robert Redfield and Alfonso Villa Rojas, *Chan Kom: A Maya Village* (Chicago: University of Chicago Press, 1934), p. 171.

[2] C. D. Bijalwan, *Hindu Omens* (New Delhi: Om Prakash Jain for Sanskriti in association with Arnold-Heinnemann Publishers, 1977), p. 12.

[3] Jamie Sams, "Sacred Medicine: Native North American Divination Systems," in John Matthews, ed., *The World Atlas of Divination: The Systems, Where They Originate, How They Work* (Boston: Little, Brown, 1992), p. 110.

[4] Redfield and Rojas, *Chan Kom*, pp. 210–11.

[5] Irwin Taylor Sanders, *Balkan Village* (Lexington: University of Kentucky Press, 1949), p. 48.

[6] Jan Jakob Maria de Groot, *Religion in China: A Key to the Study of Taoism and Confucianism* (New York: Putnam, 1912), pp. 262–63.

[7] Ruth Murray Underhill, *Papago Indian Religion*, Columbia University Contributions to Anthropology, no. 33 (New York: Columbia University Press, 1946), p. 234.

[8] Diamond Jenness, *The Ojibwa Indians of Parry Island, Their Social and Religious Life*, Bulletin of the Canada Department of Mines, no. 78 (Ottawa: National Museum of Canada, 1935), p. 82.

[9] Julian Haynes Steward, "Culture Element Distributions: XIII. Nevada Shoshoni," in *University of California Anthropological Records* 4, no. 2 (Berkeley: University of California Press, 1941), p. 270.

[10] August P. Erdland, *Die Marshall-Insulaner, Leven und Sitte, Sinn und Religion eines Sudsee-Folkes* (The Marshall Islanders: Life and Customs, Thought and Religion of a South Seas People) (Munster: Anthropos Bibliothek Ethnological Monographs, 1914), vol. 2, no. 1, p. 75.

[11] Frederick Wilkerson Waugh, *Iroquois Foods and Food Preparation* (Ottawa: Government Printing Bureau, 1916), pp. 29–32.

[12] Ibid.

[13] John F. Burns, "Science Can't Eclipse a Magic Moment for Millions," *New York Times*, Oct. 25, 1995.

[14] Maria Leach, ed., *Funk & Wagnalls Standard Dictionary of Folklore, Mythology and Legend* (New York: HarperSanFrancisco, 1984), pp. 337–38.

[15] Michael Loewe, "China," in Michael Loewe and Carmen Blacker, eds., *Oracles and Divination* (Boulder, Colo.: Shambala, 1981), p. 40.

[16] Ivan Starr, *The Rituals of the Diviner* (Malibu, Calif.: Undena Publications, 1983), p. 3.

[17]Erle Leichty, *The Omen Series Summa Izbu* (Locust Valley, N.Y.: J. J. Augustin, 1970), p. 79.

[18]O. R. Gurney, "The Babylonians and Hittites," in Loewe and Blacker, *Oracles and Divination*, pp. 146–47.

[19]Quoted in Gurney, "Babylonians," p. 143.

[20]Gurney, "Babylonians," p. 147.

[21]M. N. Srinivas, *Religion and Society Among the Coorgs of South India* (Oxford: Clarendon Press, 1952), p. 88.

[22]Jacques Faublee, "Presages et Divination a Madagascar," in André Caquot and Marcel Leibovici, eds., *La Divination*, vol. 2 (Paris: Presses Universitaires de France, 1968), p. 374; J.-P. Roux and P. N. Boratav, "La Divination chez les Turcs," in Caquot and Leibovici, *La Divination*, vol. 2, p. 295.

[23]Leland Clifton Wyman, "Navaho Diagnosticians," *American Anthropologist* 38 (1936), 236.

[24]Charles G. Seligmann and Brenda Z. Seligmann, *The Vedas* (Cambridge: Cambridge University Press, 1911), p. 241.

[25]Bijalwan, *Hindu Omens*, pp. 14–15; A.-M. Esnoul, "La divination dans l'Inde," in Caquot and Leibovici, *La Divination*, vol. 1, pp. 121, 117.

[26]Brenda E. F. Beck, *Peasant Society in Konku: A Study of Right and Left Subcastes in South India* (Vancouver: University of British Columbia, 1972), App. D.

[27]Steward, "Nevada Shoshoni," p. 257.

[28]Joseph Gilbert Joregensen, *The Sun Dance Religion: Power for the Powerless* (Chicago: University of Chicago Press, 1974), p. 173.

[29]Bjorn Collinder, *The Lapps* (Princeton: Princeton University Press for The American Scandinavian Foundation, 1949), p. 146; William Kester Barnett, "An Ethnographic Description of Sanlei Ts'un, Taiwan, with Emphasis on Women's Roles: Overcoming Research Problems Caused by the Presence of a Great Tradition" (diss., Michigan State University, 1970), p. 387; Edward Evan Evans-Pritchard, *Witchcraft, Oracles and Magic Among the Azande* (Oxford: Clarendon Press, 1937), pp. 264–65.

[30]Ralph Linton, *The Tanala: A Hill Tribe of Madagascar* (Chicago: Field Museum of Natural History, 1934), p. 233.

[31]Verrier Elwin, *The Muria and Their Ghotul* (Bombay: Geoffrey Cumberlage, Oxford University Press, 1947), p. 201.

[32]John Matthews, "By Stick and Stone: Celtic Methods of Divination," in Matthews, *World Atlas of Divination*, p. 32.

[33]Ibid., p. 31.

[34]Bernardino de Sahagun, *Florentine Codex: General History of the Things of New Spain*, bk. 12, *The Conquest of Mexico*, translated from the Aztec by Arthur J. O. Anderson and Charles E. Dibble (Santa Fe: School of American Research and University of Utah, 1955), p. 1; Miguel Leon-Portilla, ed., *The Broken Spears: The Aztec Account of the Conquest of Mexico*, translated from Nahuatl into Spanish by Angel Maria Garibay K., English translation by Lysander Kemp (Boston: Beacon Press, 1962), pp. 4–6.

[35]Horst Nachtigall, *Tierradentro, Archaologie und Ethnographie einer Kolumbianischen Landschaft* (Tierradentro, Archaeology and Ethnography of a Colombian

Region), trans. Frieda Schutze, *Mainzer Studien zur Kultur und Volkerunde* 2 (Zurich: Origo Publishing House, 1955), pp. 264–65.

36 Morris E. Opler, *Chris. Apache Odyssey: A Journey Between Two Worlds* (New York: Holt, Rinehart & Winston, 1969), p. 140 n.

37 Berard Haile, *Origin Legend of the Navaho Enemy Way* (New Haven: Yale University Press, 1938), in Human Relations Area Files, p. 1.

38 Savannah Unit, Georgia Writers' Project, Work Projects Administration, *Drums and Shadows: Survival Studies Among the Georgia Coastal Negroes* (Athens: University of Georgia Press, 1986), p. 18.

39 Bijalwan, *Hindu Omens*, p. 69; Margaret Lantis, "Fanti Omens," *Africa* 13 (1940), p. 153.

40 This is not meant to substitute for the services of a qualified car-care specialist.

Chapter 2. Mirror, Mirror on the Wall

1 John Cooper, "Northern Algonkian Scrying and Scapulimancy," in *Festschrift Publication d'Hommage Offerte au P. W. Schmidt* (Austria, 1927), in University Museum Library, University of Pennsylvania, p. 206.

2 Eve Juster, introduction to Theodore Besterman, *Crystal-Gazing: A Study in the History, Distribution, Theory and Practice of Scrying* (New Hyde Park, N.Y.: University Books, 1965), p. v; Besterman, *Crystal-Gazing*, pp. 2–3.

3 Elmer Schaffner Miller, *Harmony and Dissonance in Argentine Toba Society*, HRAFlex Books, Ethnography Series, SI12-001 (New Haven: Human Relations Area Files, 1980), pp. 96–97.

4 Besterman, *Crystal-Gazing*, p. 7.

5 Frank Gouldsmith Speck, *Naskapi: The Savage Hunters of the Labrador Peninsula* (Norman: University of Oklahoma Press, 1935), p. 127.

6 Ibid., pp. 159–60.

7 Cooper, "Northern Algonkian Scrying," p. 210.

8 Barrie Reynolds, *The Material Culture of the People of the Gwembe Valley* (New York: Frederick A. Praeger, 1968), p. 186; Elliot Percival Skinner, *The Mossi of the Upper Volta: The Political Development of a Sudanese People* (Stanford: Stanford University Press, 1964), p. 41.

9 Besterman, *Crystal-Gazing*, p. 96.

10 William Harlen Gilbert, Jr., *The Eastern Cherokees* (New York: AMS Press, 1978), p. 345.

11 H. Favre, "Les Pratiques Divinatoires des Mayas," in André Caquot and Marcel Leibovici, eds., *La Divination*, vol. 2 (Paris: Presses Universitaires de France, 1968), p. 231.

12 Thomas W. Overholt, *Prophecy in Cross-Cultural Perspective: A Sourcebook for Biblical Researchers* (Atlanta: Scholars Press, 1986), p. 99; Berard Haile, *Starlore Among the Navaho* (Santa Fe: Museum of Navaho Ceremonial Art, 1947), pp. 38–42.

13 Willard Williams Hill, *The Agricultural and Hunting Methods of the Navaho Indians* (New Haven: Yale University Press, 1938), p. 165.

14 Ruth Murray Underhill, "The Autobiography of a Papago Woman," *Memoirs of the American Anthropological Assocation* 46 (Menasha, 1936), pp. 20, 25.

[15] James Mooney, *Myths of the Cherokee and Sacred Formulas of the Cherokees* (Nashville: Charles & Randy Elder, 1982), p. 460.

[16] Gilbert, *Eastern Cherokees*, p. 345.

[17] Ibid., p. 330.

[18] Mooney, *Myths of the Cherokee*, p. 460; Gilbert, *Eastern Cherokees*, pp. 332–33, 342.

[19] Alanson Skinner, "Notes on the Eastern Cree and Northern Saulteauz," *Anthropological Papers of the American Museum of Natural History* 9, pt. 1 (New York, 1912), 166.

[20] John Gregory Bourke, "The Medicine Men of the Apache," in U.S. Bureau of Ethnology, *Annual Report to the Secretary of the Smithsonian Institution* 9 (1887–88) (Washington, D.C.: Government Printing Office, 1892), p. 461.

[21] Robert Redfield and Alfonso Villa Rojas, *Chan Kom: A Maya Village* (Chicago: University of Chicago Press, 1934), pp. 170, 373.

[22] Besterman, *Crystal-Gazing*, pp. 93–95.

[23] Ibid., pp. 95–96.

[24] Retold in Geoffrey Keyte, *The Healing Crystal* (London: Blandford, 1989), pp. 19–20, and retold yet again by Sarvananda Bluestone.

[25] Cooper, "Northern Algonkian Scrying," p. 211.

[26] Andrew Lang, "Magic, Mirrors and Crystal Gazing," *Monthly Review* 127 (London, 1901).

[27] My thanks to Dorjea Funk, who suggested this game.

[28] Elsie Worthington Clews Parsons, *The Social Organization of the Tewa of New Mexico* (Menasha: American Anthropological Association, 1929), p. 257.

[29] Rev. Edwin W. Smith and Captain Andrew Murray Dale, *The Ila-Speaking Peoples of Northern Rhodesia*, vol. 1 (London: Macmillan, 1920), p. 271.

[30] Ruy Galvao de Andrade, "The Black Carib of Honduras: A Study in Acculturation" (diss., Northwestern University, 1955), p. 210.

[31] E. S. Craighill Handy, "The Native Culture in the Marquesas," Bernice P. Bishop Museum, *Bulletin* (1923), p. 278.

[32] Ralph Linton, *The Tanala: A Hill Tribe of Madagascar* (Chicago: Field Museum of Natural History, 1934), p. 203.

[33] David Wason Ames, "The Dual Function of the 'Little People' of the Forest in the Lives of the Wolof," *Journal of American Folklore* 71 (1958), 25.

[34] Sir Charles Bell, *Portrait of the Dalai Lama* (London: Collins, 1946), p. 41.

[35] O. R. Gurney, "The Babylonians and Hittites," in Michael Loewe and Carmen Blacker, eds., *Oracles and Divination* (Boulder, Colo.: Shambala, 1981), p. 152; W. R. Halliday, *Greek Divination: A Study of Its Methods and Principles* (Chicago: Argonaut, 1967), p. 147.

[36] Halliday, *Greek Divination*, p. 149.

[37] Speck, *Naskapi*, p. 160.

Chapter 3. Stars, Stones, and Bones

[1] Quoted in Thomas Moore, *The Planets Within: Marsilio Ficino's Astrological Psychology* (Lewisburg: Bucknell University Press, 1982), frontispiece.

[2] New York: Pantheon, 1984, p. 31.

[3] Origen, *Homilae in Leviticum*, 5.2. Quoted in Moore, *The Planets Within*, frontispiece.

[4] R. L. Wing, *The I Ching Workbook* (New York: Doubleday, 1989), p. 8.

[5] Jan Jakob Maria de Groot, *Religion in China: A Key to the Study of Taoism and Confucianism* (New York: Putnam, 1912), p. 250.

[6] Ernest J. Eitel, *Feng-Shui: The Science of Sacred Landscape in Old China* (Tucson: Synergetic Press, 1993), pp. 9–10.

[7] H. Favre, "Les Pratiques Divinatoires des Mayas," in André Caquot and Marcel Leibovici, eds., *La Divination*, vol. 2 (Paris: Presses Universitaires de France, 1968), p. 221.

[8] Martin Brennan, *The Stones of Time: Calendars, Sundials, and Stone Chambers of Ancient Ireland* (Rochester, Vt.: Inner Traditions, 1994), p. 64.

[9] Jan Jakob Maria de Groot, *Religion in China: A Key to the Study of Taoism and Confucianism* (New York: Putnam, 1912), p. 262.

[10] A.-M. Esnoul, "La Divination dan l'Inde," in Caquot and Leibovici, *La Divination*, vol. 2, p. 121.

[11] G. Dumoutier, "Astrologie des Annamites" (Annamese Astrology), *Revue des Traditions Populaires* 5 (Paris: Librairie de l'Art Independant, 1890), 513–24; L. Austin Waddell, *The Buddhism of Tibet or Lamaism* (London: W. H. Allen & Co., 1895), pp. 451–53; J.-P. Roux and P. N. Boratav, "Divination chez les Turcs," in Caquot and Leibovici, *La Divination*, vol. 2, p. 291; Rev. Antoine Mostaert, introduction, *Manual of Mongolian Astrology and Divination* (Cambridge: Harvard University Press, 1969). These are but a small sample of the multitude of studies that show that astrology has roots in probably every culture.

[12] I am grateful to Prem Aashti, a pioneering experiential astrologer, who came up with the ideas for many of the games that follow and has used them herself.

[13] Frank Gouldsmith Speck, Leonard Broom, and Will West Long, introduction to *Cherokee Dance and Drama* (Norman: University of Oklahoma Press, 1983). Retold by Sarvananda Bluestone.

[14] Diamond Jenness, "The Ojibwa Indians of Parry Island: Their Social and Religious Life," *Bulletin of the Canada Department of Mines* 78 (Ottawa: National Museum of Canada, 1935), 82.

[15] Esnoul, "La Divination," p. 117.

[16] C. D. Bijalwan, *Hindu Omens* (New Delhi: Om Prakash Jain for Sanskriti in association with Arnold-Heinnemann Publishers, 1977).

[17] Maria Leach, ed., *Funk & Wagnalls Standard Dictionary of Folklore, Mythology and Legend* (New York: HarperSanFrancisco, 1984), p. 243.

[18] Timothy Ferris, *The Red Limit: The Search for the Edge of the Universe* (New York: William Morrow, 1977), p. 106.

[19] William Morgan, "Navajo Treatment of Sickness: Diagnosticians," *American Anthropologist* 33 (1931), 394–95; John Adair and Kurt W. Deuschle, *The People's Health: Medicine and Anthropology in a Navajo Community* (New York: Appleton-Century Crofts, 1970), p. 6.

[20] Berard Haile, *Starlore Among the Navajo* (Santa Fe: Museum of Navajo Ceremonial Art, 1947), pp. 38–42.

[21] Berard Haile, *Origin Legend of the Navajo Enemy Way* (New Haven: Yale University Press, 1938), in Human Relations Area Files, p. 1; Willard Williams Hill, *The Agricultural and Hunting Methods of the Navajo Indians* (New Haven: Yale University Press, 1938), p. 165.

22 Thomas W. Overholt, *Prophecy in Cross-Cultural Perspective: A Sourcebook for Biblical Researchers* (Atlanta: Scholars Press, 1986), p. 99.

23 Jack Frederick Kilpatrick and Anna Gritts Kilpatrick, *Notebook of a Cherokee Shaman* (Washington: Smithsonian Institution, 1970), p. 105C.

24 Jamie Sams, "Sacred Medicine: Native North American Divination Systems," in John Matthews, ed., *The World Atlas of Divination: The Systems, Where They Originate, How They Work* (Boston: Little, Brown, 1992), p. 116.

25 Ibid.

26 Ibid.

27 Eitel, *Feng-Shui*, p. 4.

28 Henri A. Junod, *The Life of a South African Tribe*, vol. 2 (London: Macmillan, 1927), p. 548.

29 Sams, "Sacred Medicine," p. 116.

30 Jamie Sams and Twylah Nitsch, *Other Council Fires Were Here Before Ours* (New York: HarperCollins, 1991), p. 27.

31 James Mooney, *Myths of the Cherokee and Sacred Formulas of the Cherokees* (Nashville: Charles & Randy Elder, 1982), p. 460.

32 William Harlen Gilbert, Jr., *The Eastern Cherokees* (New York: AMS Press, 1978), p. 345.

33 Jack Frederick Kilpatrick and Anna Gritts Kilpatrick, *Run Toward the Nightland: Magic of the Oklahoma Cherokee* (Dallas: Southern Methodist University Press, 1967), p. 115; Kilpatrick and Kilpatrick, *Notebook of a Cherokee Shaman*, p. 105C.

34 Gonzalo Orbe Rubio, *Punyaro* (Quito, Ecuador: Editorial Casa de la Cultura Ecuatoriana, 1956), trans. Amelia I. Sherwood, p. 248.

35 James F. Downs, *The Navajo* (New York: Holt, Rinehart & Winston, 1972), p. 100.

36 Brennan, *Stones of Time*, pp. 7, 64.

37 George F. Will and Herbert J. Spinden, *The Mandans: A Study of Their Culture, Archaeology, and Language* (Cambridge: Harvard University Press, 1906), p. 138. The Minnetaree Indians had a similar stone.

38 Caitlin and John Matthews, *Encyclopedia of Celtic Wisdom: A Celtic Shaman's Sourcebook* (Rockport, Mass.: Element, 1994), p. 254.

39 William Charles White, *Bone Culture of Ancient China: An Archaeological Study of Bone Material from Northern Honan, Dating About the Twelfth Century, B.C.* (Toronto: University of Toronto Press, 1945), p. 20.

40 James Mellon Menzies, *The Oracle Records from the Waste of Yin* (Shanghai: Kelly & Walsh, 1917), pp. 1–2.

41 White, *Bone Culture*, pp. 24–25.

42 Ibid.

43 Nigel Pennick, "The Chinese Book of Changes, Ancient Wisdom from the I Ching," in Matthews, *World Atlas of Divination*, p. 138.

44 Gerald Freeman Winfield, *China: The Land and the People* (New York: Duell, Sloane, c.1948), p. 178.

45 Richard J. Smith, *Fortune-Tellers and Philosophers: Divination in Traditional Chinese Society* (Boulder, Colo.: Westview Press, 1991), p. 14.

46 Far Eastern and Russian Institute, Washington State University, *A Regional Handbook on Northwest China* (New Haven: Human Relations Area Files, 1956), p.

325; Matthias Hermanns, *Die A Mdo Pa-Grosstibeter die Social-Wirtschaftlichen Grundlagen der Hirtenkulturen Innerasiens* (The A Mdo Pa Greater Tibetans: The Socioeconomic Bases of the Pastoral Cultures of Inner Asia), trans. Frieda Schutze (Freiburg: Philosophische Fakultat der Universitat Freiburg in der Schweiz, 1948), p. 102.

[47] Roux and Boratav, "Divination chez les Turcs," pp. 302–4.

[48] John Matthews, "By Stick and Stone: Celtic Methods of Divination" in Matthews, *World Atlas of Divination*, p. 31.

[49] J. E. Campbell, *Honour, Family and Patronage: A Study of Institutions and Moral Values in a Greek Mountain Community* (Oxford: Clarendon Press, 1964), p. 352.

[50] Frank Gouldsmith Speck, *Naskapi: The Savage Hunters of the Labrador Peninsula* (Norman: University of Oklahoma Press, 1935), pp. 159, 139, 141, 151. This is one of the more amazing studies, as the author clearly got involved in the life of the Naskapi rather than remain an aloof observer.

[51] Eveline Lot-Falck, "La Divination dans l'Arctique et l'Asie Septentrionale," in Caquot and Leibovici, *La Divination*, vol. 2, p. 256.

[52] Vladimir Germanovich Bogorz-Tan, "The Chukchee: Material Culture," *Memoirs of the American Museum of Natural History* 11 (Leiden: E. J. Brill, 1907), 487–88.

[53] Frederica de Laguna, *Under Mount Saint Elias: The History and Culture of the Yakutat Tlingit*, Smithsonian Contributions to Anthropology, vol. 1 (Washington, D.C.: Smithsonian Institution, 1972), p. 521.

[54] Gosta Montell, "The Torguts of Etsin-Gol," *Royal Anthropological Institute of Great Britain and Ireland Journal* 70 (1940), 91.

[55] Claude Savary, "La Divination—un Art du Diagnostic," in Claude Savary, ed., *Afriques Magiques* (Geneva: Musée d'Ethnographie de la Ville de Genève, 1992), p. 27; Erika Bourguignon, "Divination, Transe et Possession en Afrique Transsaharienne," in Caquot and Leibovici, *La Divination*, vol. 2, p. 334; Michael F. C. Bourdillon, *The Shona Peoples: An Ethnography of the Contemporary Shona, with Special Reference to Their Religion*, Shona Heritage Series, vol. 1 (Gwelo: Mabo Press, 1976), pp. 177–79; Michael Gelfand, *Witch Doctor, Traditional Medicine Man of Rhodesia* (London: Harvill Press, 1964), p. 75; Eileen Jensen Krige, *The Social System of the Zulus* (Pietermaritzburg: Shuter & Shooter, 1965), p. 300. The Ila people of Zimbabwe call their divining bones *makakata*. See Rev. Edwin W. Smith and Captain Andrew Murray Dale, *The Ila-Speaking Peoples of Northern Rhodesia*, vol. 1 (London: Macmillan, 1920), p. 272.

[56] H. Callaway, *The Religious System of the Amazulu* (Cape Town: C. Struik, 1970), p. 333. Facsimile of edition of c. 100 years earlier.

[57] Henri A. Junod, *The Life of a South African Tribe*, vol. 2 (London: Macmillan, 1927), p. 543.

[58] Ibid., p. 552.

[59] William Howells, *The Heathens, Primitive Man and His Religions* (Garden City, N.Y.: Doubleday, 1950), p. 73.

Chapter 4. Air, Earth, Fire, and Water

[1] Quoted in Thomas Moore, *The Planets Within: Marsilio Ficino's Astrological Psychology* (Lewisburg: Bucknell University Press, 1982), p. 67.

[2] Hans Biedermann, *Dictionary of Symbolism, Cultural Icons and the Meanings Behind Them*, trans. James Hulbert (New York: Meridian, 1994), p. 6.

[3] Basil Valentine, *The Last Will and Testament of Basil Valentine, Monke of the Order of St. Bennet. Which being alone, He hid under a Table of Marble, behind the High-Altar of the Cathedral Church, in the Imperial City of Erford: Leaving it there to be found by him, whom Gods Providence should make worthy of it. To which is added Two Treatises, the First declaring his Manual Operations. The Second shewing things Natural and Supernatural* (London: Edward Brewster, 1671), p. 136. In the Edward F. Smith Collection at the University of Pennsylvania Library.

[4] See Moore, *The Planets Within*, p. 71.

[5] Derek Walters, "Dragon Lines in the Land: Feng-Shui," in John Matthews, ed., *The World Atlas of Divination: The Systems, Where They Originate, How They Work* (Boston: Little, Brown, 1992), p. 147; Ernest J. Eitel, *Feng-Shui: The Science of Sacred Landscape in Old China* (Tucson: Synergetic Press, 1993), p. 14. See Chapter 5 for a more detailed discussion of *feng-shui*.

[6] Tenney L. Davis and Lu-Ch'iang Wu, "Chinese Alchemy," *Scientific Monthly* 31 (Sept. 1930), 226.

[7] Valentine, *Last Will and Testament*, pp. 384, 405; Eitel, *Feng-Shui*, p. 9. Valentine says, "Therefore the Macrocosme and Microcosme, yea, the things which grow and are found therein, are compared to a round Circle, in whose middle there is a Center, let the Circle be turned which way it will, it keepeth round every way, and its Center stayeth unremoved. A Philosopher also must know rightly the Center of each matter, which must stand unremoved in every substance, but the substance may be turned any way he pleaseth, and make of it several forms, according as it received its power from above" (p. 405).

[8] Quoted in Emilie Savage-Smith and Marion B. Smith, *Islamic Geomancy and a Thirteenth-Century Divinatory Device* (Malibu, Calif.: Undena Publications, 1980), p. 55.

[9] Sig Lonegren, "Dowsing the Way: Divining with Pendulum and Rod," in John Matthews, ed., *The World Atlas of Divination: The Systems, Where They Originate, How They Work* (Boston: Little, Brown, 1992), p. 205.

[10] http://www.isy.liu.se/~tegen/jan95_hydroquebec.html

[11] http://www.isy.liu.se/~tegen/febost.html

[12] N. Adriani and Albert C. Kruyt, *De Bare's Sprekende Toradjas van Midden-Celebes (de Oost-Toradjas)* (The Bare'e-Speaking Toradja of Central Celebes [the East Toradja]), 2nd ed., vol. 1, Koninklijke Nederlandse Akademie van Wetenschappen, Verhandelingen, Afdeling Letterkunde, Nieuwe Reeks, Deel 54 (Amsterdam: Noord-Hollandsche Uitgevers Maatschappij, 1950), pp. 21, 172.

[13] League of Nations, Health Organization, Intergovernmental Conference of Far-Eastern Countries on Rural Hygiene, *Preparatory Papers: Report of French Indochina*, League of Nations Publications, III: Health (Geneva: League of Nations, 1937), pp. 55–56; Tran-van Trai, *La Famille Patriarcale Annamite* (The Annamite Patriarchal Family), trans. C. A. Messner (Paris: P. Lapagome, 1942), p. 25.

[14] Lonegren, "Dowsing the Way," p. 207.

[15] Germaine Dieterlen, *Essai Sur la Religion Bambara* (An Essay on the Religion of the

Bambara), trans. Katia Wolf (Paris: Presses Universitaires de France, 1951), p. 182.

16 Dim Delobsom, *L'Empire du Mogho-naba: Coutumes des Mossi de la Haute-Volta* (The Empire of the Mogho naba: Customs of the Mossi of upper Volta), trans. Kathryn A. Looney (Paris: Domat-Montchrestien, 1932), p. 22.

17 Robert Francis Murphy, *Mundurucu Religion* (Berkeley: University of California Press, 1958), p. 41.

18 Savage-Smith and Smith, *Islamic Geomancy,* pp. 4, 11.

19 Bess Allen Donaldson, *The Wild Rue: A Study of Muhammadan Magic and Folklore in Iran* (London: Luzac, 1938), p. 194.

20 Jacques Faublee, "Presages et Divination a Madagascar," in André Caquot and Marcel Lebovici, eds., *La Divination,* vol. 2 (Paris: Presses Universitaires de France, 1968), p. 386; Dieterlen, *La Religion Bambara,* pp. 274–75; Siegfried Frederick Nadel, *Nupe Religion* (London: Routledge & Paul, 1954), p. 381.

21 Barbara C. Sproul, *Primal Myths, Creation Myths Around the World* (San Francisco: HarperSanFrancisco, 1991), p. 44.

22 Wande Abimbola, *Ifa Divination Poetry* (New York: NOK Publishers, 1977), pp. 2–3.

23 Eveline Lot-Falck, "La Divination dans l'Arctique et l'Asie Septentrionale," in Caquot and Lebovici, *La Divination,* vol. 2, p. 254.

24 W. R. Halliday, *Greek Divination: A Study of Its Methods and Principles* (Chicago: Argonaut, 1967), p. 146.

25 Jamie Sams and Twylah Nitsch, *Other Council Fires Were Here Before Ours* (New York: HarperCollins, 1991), pp. 27–28. Retold by Sarvananda Bluestone.

26 Albert Tafel, *Meine Tibetreise (My Tibetan Trip),* volume 2, trans. Carol Cerf (Stuttgart: Union Deutsche Verlagsgesellschaft, 1914), p. 231.

27 J. B. Heisler and J. E. Mellon, *Czechoslovakia: Land of Dream and Enterprise* (London: Czechoslovak Ministry of Foreign Affairs, Department of Information, 1945), p. 53.

28 V. Busuttil, *Holiday Customs in Malta and Sports, Usages, Ceremonies, Omens and Superstitions of the Maltese People* (Malta: L. Busuttil, 1894), pp. 140–41, 141 n.

29 Phyllis Kemp, *Healing Ritual: Studies in the Technique and Tradition of the Southern Slavs* (London: Faber & Faber, 1935), p. 132.

30 David Friend Aberle, "The Peyote Religion Among the Navaho," *Viking Fund Publications in Anthropology* 42 (New York: Wenner-Gren Foundation for Anthropological Research, 1966).

31 Michael Sandivogius, *A New Light of Alchymy Taken out of the Fountain of Nature and Manual Experience, To Which is Added A Treatise of Sulphur* (London: A. Clark, 1674), p. 101.

32 Maria Leach, ed., *Funk and Wagnalls Standard Dictionary of Folklore, Mythology and Legend* (New York: HarperSanFrancisco, 1984), p. 665.

33 Alan Haymes, "The Frozen North: Divination Among the Peoples of the Arctic and Eurasia," in Matthews, ed., *World Atlas of Divination,* p. 22.

34 Lucy Mary Jane Garnett, "Albanian Women," in *Women of Turkey and Their Folk-Lore,* vol. 2 (London: David Nutt, 1891), p. 295.

35 Virginia Gutierrez de Pineda, "Organizacion Social en la Guajira" (Social Organization in la Guajira), *Revista del Instituto Etnologico Nacional* 3, no. 2 (Bogota, 1948), 196.

[36] Jan Jakob Maria de Groot, *Religion in China: A Key to the Study of Taoism and Confucianism* (New York: Putnam, 1912), pp. 261–63.

[37] John MacInnes, "The Seer in Gaelic Tradition," in Hilda Ellis Davidson, ed., *The Seer in Celtic and Other Traditions* (Edinburgh: John Donald Publishers, 1989), p. 18.

[38] Jackson Steward Lincoln, *The Dream in Primitive Cultures* (London: Cresset, 1935), p. 216, from Miss M. Wheelwright, unpublished manuscript, "The Myth of Sontso." See Chapter 3.

[39] Robert H. Lowie, *Ethnographic Notes on the Washo* (Berkeley: University of California Press, 1939), p. 318.

[40] André Caquot, "La Divination dans l'Ancien Israel," in Caquot and Lebovici, *La Divination*, vol. 1, pp. 90, 102.

[41] William Morgan, "Navaho Treatment of Sickness: Diagnosticians," *American Anthropologist* 33 (1931), p. 395; Berard Haile, *Origin Legend of the Navaho Enemy Way* (New Haven: Yale University Press, 1938), in Human Relations Area Files, p. 1.

Chapter 5. Tuning In to the *Qi*

[1] "No. 54. Cultivating Insight," in Stan Rosenthal, trans., Lao Tzu, *Tao te-ching*, internet http://www.ii.uib.no/~arnemo/tao_tey_ching_transl.html

[2] Max Kaltenmark and Ngo Van Xuyet, "La Divination dans la Chine Ancienne," in André Caquot and Marcel Leibovici, *La Divination*, vol. 1 (Paris: Presses Universitaires de France, 1968), pp. 333–34.

[3] Brian F. Windley, "Plate Tectonics," *The Academic American Encyclopedia* (Danbury, Conn.: Grolier, 1995).

[4] Derek Walters, "Dragon Lines in the Land: Feng Shui," in John Matthews, ed., *The World Atlas of Divination: The Systems, Where They Originate, How They Work* (Boston: Little, Brown, 1992), pp. 143–44; Ping Xu, "Feng-shui: A Model for Landscape Analysis" (Ph.D. diss., Harvard University, Graduate School of Design, May 22, 1990), p. 5.

[5] Ping Xu, "Feng-shui," pp. 22–23.

[6] Ibid., p. 24.

[7] "Opium Wars," Academic American Encyclopedia; Donald Southgate, "Victoria, Queen of England, Scotland and Ireland," ibid.; Ping Xu, "Feng-shui," p. 6. Ping Xu's dissertation is remarkable. I have relied heavily upon it. *Feng-shui* is an extremely involved practice. I have been told that it takes twenty years of work and apprenticeship to become a *feng-shui* master. This section is merely a cursory survey of *feng-shui* from a layman's perspective. The work of *feng-shui* belongs to the master.

[8] Doug Tsuruoka, "True Believers, Malaysian Stock Investors Seek Celestial Guidance," *Far Eastern Economic Review,* June 17, 1993, p. 57.

[9] Nury Vittachi, "The Old-Fashioned Way," *Far Eastern Economic Review,* Nov. 18, 1993, p. 58.

[10] Walters, "Dragon Lines," p. 144.

[11] Handler used the most advanced technology available to him at the time he wrote his book. It is a case where the ancient and modern methods arrived at the same place.

[12] Ping Xu, "Feng-shui," pp. 219, 133.

[13] I am grateful to Ed Levin for his inspiration in this game.

[14] Ping Xu, p. 26; Ernest J. Eitel, *Feng-Shui: The Science of Sacred Landscape in Old China* (Tucson: Synergetic Press, 1993), p. 43.

[15] Ibid., p. 45.

[16] Ibid.

[17] Ibid., p. 48.

[18] Story told by Osho Rajneesh and retold by Sarvananda Bluestone.

[19] Richard J. Smith, *Fortune-Tellers and Philosophers: Divination in Traditional Chinese Society* (Boulder, Colo.: Westview Press, 1991), p. 139.

[20] Tenney L. Davis and Lu-Ch'iang Wu, "Chinese Alchemy," *Scientific Monthly* 31 (Sept. 1930), 226.

[21] Translated and quoted in ibid.

[22] Smith, *Fortune-Tellers and Philosophers*, p. 23.

[23] Ibid.

[24] Quoted in Ping Xu, "Feng-Shui," p. 29.

[25] Ping Xu (ibid., p. 31) has the opposite definition of *yin* and *yang* to that of many other interpretations. While he has unquestionably utilized and translated original material, I have chosen to follow the more traditional interpretations of the two forces.

[26] Ibid., pp. 33–34.

[27] Ibid., p. 35.

Chapter 6. "That Which Hath Wings"

[1] Quoted in Peggy V. Beck, Anna Lee Walters, and Nia Francisco, *The Sacred Ways of Knowledge, Sources of Life* (Tsaile, Ariz.: Navajo Community College Press, 1992), p. 332.

[2] Arthur C. Parker, *Seneca Myths and Folk Tales* (Buffalo: Buffalo Historical Society, 1923), pp. 4, 305.

[3] Ake Hultkrantz, *Native Religions of North America* (San Francisco: HarperSanFrancisco, 1987), pp. 3, 20–21.

[4] Nevill Drury, "Seers and Healers: The Ancient Tradition of Shamanism," in John Matthews, ed., *The World Atlas of Divination: The Systems, Where They Originate, How They Work* (Boston: Little, Brown, 1992), p. 8; Willard Z. Park, *Shamanism in Western North America: A Study in Cultural Relationships* (Evanston: Northwestern University, 1938), pp. 15–16.

[5] J.-P. Roux and P. N. Boratav, "La Divination chez les Turcs," in André Caquot and Marcel Leibovici, eds., *La Divination*, vol. 2 (Paris: Presses Universitaires de France, 1968), pp. 313–14.

[6] I am indebted to Betsy Stang for her suggestion of this game and for a long and lovely talk on Native American culture that she gave me.

[7] Quoted in Park, *Shamanism*, p. 16.

[8] An excellent work on the animal guides is Jamie Sams and David Carson, *The Medicine Cards: The Discovery of Power Through the Ways of Animals* (Santa Fe: Bear & Co., 1988).

[9] Albert L. Bennett, "Ethnographic Notes on the Fang," *Anthropological Institute of Great Britain and Ireland Journal* 29 (1899), pp. 66–98; Walter McClintock, *The Old North Trail; or Life, Legends and Religion of the Blackfeet Indians* (Lincoln: University of Nebraska Press, 1968), p. 352; Robert Harry Lowie, *The Crow In-*

dians (New York: Farrar & Rinehart, 1935), p. 34; Marvin Kaufman Opler, "The Southern Ute of Colorado," in Ralph Linton, ed., *Acculturation in Seven American Indian Tribes* (Gloucester, Mass.: Peter Smith, 1963), pp. 140–41; George Turner, *Samoa, A Hundred Years Ago and Long Before. Together with Notes on the Cults and Customs of Twenty-three Other Islands in the Pacific* (London: Macmillan, 1884), pp. 48ff.

[10]Caitlin and John Matthews, *Encyclopedia of Celtic Wisdom: A Celtic Shaman's Sourcebook* (Rockport, Mass.: Element, 1994), p. 243.

[11]Jamie Sams, "Sacred Medicine: Native North-American Divination Systems," in Matthews, ed., *World Atlas of Divination*, p. 112.

[12]Erminie W. Voegelin, "Totem, Totemism," in Maria Leach, ed., *Funk and Wagnalls Standard Dictionary of Folklore, Mythology and Legend* (San Francisco: Harper-SanFrancisco, 1984), p. 1120.

[13]Sam D. Gill and Irene F. Sullivan, *Dictionary of Native American Mythology* (New York: Oxford University Press, 1992), p. 306.

[14]I am grateful to the work of Stephen Eligio Gallegos, especially his *Personal Totem Pole, Animal Imagery, the Chakras and Psychotherapy* (Santa Fe: Moon Bear Press, 1990), for inspiring this game.

[15]Erdland, "Die Marshall-Inulaner," p. 75.

[16]Julian Haynes Steward, "Culture Element Distributions: XIII. Nevada Shoshoni," *University of California Anthropological Records* 4, no. 2 (Berkeley: University of California Press, 1941), p. 270.

[17]Gill and Sullivan, *Native American Mythology*, p. 253; Katharine Luomala, "Rainbow," in Leach, *Dictionary of Folklore*, pp. 922–93.

[18]2 Samuel 5:20–25 (King James Version)

[19]Sams, "Sacred Medicine," p. 111.

[20]Ping Xu, "Feng-shui: A Model for Landscape Analysis" (Ph.D. diss., Harvard University, Graduate School of Design, May 22, 1990), p. 26.

[21]Kuo-chun Ch'en, "Kweichow an-shun miao-i ti tsung-chiao hsin yang" (Religious Beliefs of the Miao and I Tribes in An-shun Kweichow), *Pien-chen Kung-lun (Frontier Affairs)* 1, no.7/8 (1942), p. 13.

[22]John Matthews, *Taliesin, Shamanism and the Bardic Mysteries in Britain and Ireland* (London: Aquarian, 1991), p. 234.

[23]Robert Sutherland Rattray, *Religion and Art in Ashanti* (Oxford: Clarendon Press, 1927), pp. 44–45.

[24]André Caquot, "La Divination dans l'Ancien Israel," in Caquot and Lebovici, *La Divination*, vol. 1, p. 102.

[25]Alfred Metraux, "Tree of Life," in Leach, *Dictionary of Folklore*, p. 1123.

[26]My thanks to Joanne Ferdmann, astrologer, Kabbalist, and eternally youthful reader, for helping me see the beauty of the Kabbalist image of the tree of life.

[27]Jack Frederick Kilpatrick and Anna Gritts Kilpatrick, *Eastern Cherokee Folktales: Reconstructed from the Field Notes of Frans M. Olbrechts* (Washington, D.C.: U.S. Government Printing Office, 1966), p. 387; Jack Frederick Kilpatrick, ed., *The Wahnenauhi Manuscript: Historical Sketches of the Cherokees; Together with Some of their Customs, Traditions and Superstitions* (Washington, D.C.: U.S. Government Printing Office, 1966), p. 188. Retold by Sarvananda Bluestone.

[28]Chedo Mijatovich, *Servia of the Servians* (New York: Charles Scribner's Sons, 1914),

p. 52; Joel Martin Halpern, *A Serbian Village* (New York: Columbia University Press, 1958), p. 112.

[29] Erminie W. Voegelin, "Spider" and "Spider, Spider Man, Spider Woman," in Leach, *Dictionary of Folklore*, p. 1074; Kilpatrick and Kilpatrick, *Eastern Cherokee Folktales*, p. 387.

[30] Voegelin, "Spider," p. 1074. The story is also retold in the Disney classic *Song of the South.*

[31] John Howland Rowe, "Inca Culture at the Time of the Spanish Conquest," *Bureau of American Ethnology Bulletin* 143, vol. 2 (Washington, D.C.: Smithsonian Institution, 1946), p. 304.

[32] Paul Gebauer, "Spider Divination in the Cameroons," *Milwaukee Public Museum Publications in Anthropology* 10 (Milwaukee: North American Press, 1964), pp. 11–18, 28–56.

[33] Ibid., pp. 56, 49. See also David Zeitlyn, "Spiders in and out of Court, or 'The Long Legs of the Law': Styles of Spider Divination in their Sociological Context," *Africa* (Spring 1993), pp. 219–40. Zeitlyn covers other African cultures that use spiders in their divination as well.

[34] Edward Evan Evans-Pritchard, *Witchcraft, Oracles and Magic Among the Azande* (Oxford: Clarendon Press, 1937), pp. 187–88, 125, 352–54, 281–83.

[35] Frank Gouldsmith Speck, *Naskapi: The Savage Hunters of the Labrador Peninsula* (Norman: University of Oklahoma Press, 1935), pp. 163–66. Of course, humans around the world have used the bones of animals for purposes of divination. See Chapter 3.

[36] Frank M. LeBar, "The Material Culture of Truk" (unpublished manuscript on file at the Human Relations Area Files, New Haven, Conn., 1963), pp. 148–49.

[37] F. Vyncke, "La Divination chez les Slaves," in Caquot and Lebovici, *La Divination,* vol. 2, p. 313.

[38] Lucy Mair, *Witchcraft* (New York: McGraw-Hill, 1973), pp. 95, 98–99.

[39] Caitlin and Matthews, *Encyclopedia of Celtic Wisdom,* p. 244.

[40] Jack Frederick Kilpatrick and Anna Gritts Kilpatrick, *Run Toward the Nightland: Magic of the Oklahoma Cherokee* (Dallas: Southern Methodist University Press, 1967), p. 18.

[41] Ling Shun-sheng and Ruey Yih-fu, *Hsiang-hsi miao-tsu tiao-ch'a pao-kao* (A Report on an Investigation of the Miao of Western Hunan) (Shanghai: Institute of History and Philology, Academia Sinica, 1947), no. 23, p. 20.

[42] H. G. Quaritch Wales, *Divination in Thailand: The Hopes and Fears of a Southeast Asian People* (London: Curzon Press, 1983), p. 2. Retold by Sarvananda Bluestone.

[43] William Howells, *The Heathens, Primitive Man and His Religions* (Garden City, N.Y.: Doubleday, 1950), p. 71; Rosemary Ellen Guiley, *Harper's Encyclopedia of Mystical and Paranormal Experience* (San Francisco: HarperSanFrancisco, 1991), p. 60; J. S. Morrison, "The Classical World," in Michael Loewe and Carmen Blacker, eds., *Oracles and Divination* (Boulder, Colo.: Shambala, 1981), p. 87; W. R. Halliday, *Greek Divination: A Study of Its Methods and Principles* (Chicago: Argonaut, 1967), p. 264; R. B. Serjeant, "Islam," in Loewe and Blacker, *Oracles,* p. 231; Hilda Ellis Davidson, "The Germanic World," in Loewe and Blacker, *Oracles,* p. 125; Carmen Blacker, "Japan," in Loewe and Blacker, *Oracles,* p. 71.

[44] Turner, *Samoa,* pp. 32–35, 48, 54, 64, 65; Michael R. Dove, "Uncertainty, Humility,

and Adaptation in the Tropical Forest: The Agricultural Augury of the Kantu," *Ethnology* 32 (Spring 1993), p. 148.

45 Nigel Pennick, *Games of the Gods: The Origin of Board Games in Magic and Divination* (York Beach, Maine: Samuel Weiser, 1989), p. 21.

46 John Matthews, "By Stick and Stone: Celtic Methods of Divination," in Matthews, *World Atlas of Divination*, p. 30; Harry Tschopik Jr., "The Aymara," *Bureau of American Ethnology Bulletin* 143, vol. 2 (Washington, D.C.: Smithsonian Institution, 1946), 563–64; Alfred Louis Kroeber, *Peoples of the Philippines* (New York: American Museum of Natural History, 1928), p. 202; R. B. Serjeant, "Islam," in Loewe and Blacker, *Oracles*, p. 231; Washington State University, Far Eastern and Russian Institute, *A Regional Handbook on Northwest China* (New Haven: Human Relations Area Files, 1956), p. 325.

47 Retold from J. S. Morrison, "The Classical World," in Loewe and Blacker, *Oracles*, p. 87.

48 E.-J. de Durand, "Aperçu sur les Présages et la Divination de l'Ancien Perou," in Caquot and Leibovici, *La Divination*, vol. 2, pp. 22–23.

49 Ake Hultkrantz, *Native Religions of North America* (San Francisco: HarperSanFrancisco, 1987), p. 30.

50 J.-P. Roux and P. N. Boratav, "La Divination chez les Turcs," in Caquot and Leibovici, *La Divination*, vol. 2, pp. 312–14.

51 Lama Chime Radha Rinpoche, "Tibet," in Loewe and Blacker, *Oracles*, pp. 21–22.

52 G. A. Wilken, *Handleiding voor de Vergelijkende Volkenkunde van Nederlandsch-Indie* (Manual for the Comparative Ethnology of the Netherlands East Indies), ed. C. M. Pleyte, trans. S. Dumas Kaan (Leiden: E. J. Brill, 1893), p. 585.

53 H. Ling Roth, ed., "The Natives of Borneo," *Anthropological Institute of Great Britain and Ireland Journal* 22 (1893), 23–24.

Chapter 7. Psychic Alphabets

1 David Diringer, *The Alphabet: A Key to the History of Mankind*, vol. 1 (New York: Funk & Wagnalls, 1968), p. 5.

2 Ibid., pp. 11–12.

3 David Diringer, foreword to Hugh Moran and David Kelley, *The Alphabet and the Ancient Calendar Signs* (Palo Alto: Daily Press, 1989), p. xiii.

4 Hugh A. Moran, *The Alphabet and the Ancient Calendar Signs: Astrological Elements in the Origin of the Alphabet* (Palo Alto: Pacific Books, 1953), pp. 21–22.

5 Ibid., p. 31.

6 Moran and Kelley, *The Alphabet*, p. 14.

7 Ibid., pp. 30–31.

8 Ibid., pp. 107–8.

9 Judges 12:1–6.

10 John MacInnes, "The Seer in Gaelic Tradition," in Hilda Ellis Davidson, ed., *The Seer in Celtic and Other Traditions* (Edinburgh: John Donald Publishers, 1989), p. 10; Juliette Wood, "Prophecy in Middle Welsh Tradition," in Davidson, *The Seer*, p. 53.

11 My thanks to Sangi Finsrud, who helped me develop this game.

12 Stephen E. Flowers, *Runes and Magic: Magical Formulaic Elements in the Older Runic Tradition* (New York: Peter Lang, 1986), p. 154.

[13] "Draft Proposal for Runic Extension of ISO 10646," http://www.columbia.edu/kermit/futhark.html, p. 6.

[14] Michael Howard, *Understanding Runes* (London: Aquarius, 1990), p. 7; Nigel Pennick, *Rune Magic* (London: Aquarius, 1992), pp. 11–12.

[15] "Draft Proposal," p. 8.

[16] Flowers, *Runes and Magic,* p. 155.

[17] John Matthews, *Taliesin, Shamanism and the Bardic Mysteries in Britain and Ireland* (London: Aquarian, 1991), pp. 214–22.

[18] John Matthews, "By Stick and Stone: Celtic Methods of Divination," in John Matthews, ed., *The World Atlas of Divination: The Systems, Where They Originate, How They Work* (Boston: Little, Brown, 1992), pp. 28–30.

[19] My thanks to my friend Rinzai Zwerin, who suggested this whole thing.

[20] Nury Vittachi, "The Old-Fashioned Way," *Far Eastern Economic Review,* Nov. 18, 1993, p. 58.

[21] Janice A. Henderson, "Pythagoras of Samos," *The 1995 Grolier Multimedia Encyclopedia.*

[22] Germaine Dieterlen, *Essai sur la Religion Bambara* (An Essay on the Religion of the Bambara), trans. Katia Wolf (Paris: Presses Universitaires de France, 1951), p. 269.

[23] Ibid., pp. 270–71.

Chapter 8. Pendulums, Hickory Sticks, Dowsing, and Daisies

[1] Migene Gonzalez-Wippler, *The Santeria Experience* (Englewood Cliffs, N.J.: Prentice-Hall, 1982), p. 155.

[2] Greg Nielsen and Joseph Polansky, *Pendulum Power* (Rochester, Vt.: Destiny Books, 1987), p. 51.

[3] Siegfried Frederick Nadel, *Nupe Religion* (London: Routledge & Paul, 1954), p. 381.

[4] Sir Charles Bell, *Portrait of the Dalai Lama* (London: Collins, 1946), p. 84.

[5] John J. Honigmann, *Culture and Ethos of Kaska Society,* Yale University Publications in Anthropology, no. 40 (New Haven: Yale University Press, 1949), p. 220.

[6] Sig Lonegren, "Dowsing the Way: Divining with Pendulum and Rod" in John Matthews, ed., *The World Atlas of Divination: The Systems, Where They Originate, How They Work* (Boston: Little, Brown, 1992), pp. 202–4.

[7] Genesis 30:37–38.

[8] Numbers 20:1–11.

[9] Rennard Strickland, *Fire and the Spirits: Cherokee Law from Clan to Court* (Norman: University of Oklahoma Press, 1975), p. 116.

[10] My thanks to Svargo Bernard, who suggested this game to me when this book was just a gleam.

[11] Every once in a while, I am sure that there will be some wise guy who will shake the table and make nervous jokes about table rapping and séances and such. There are always kids of all ages who need to be the center of attention. My suggestion is to give them some attention briefly and then start again and tell the child either to play by the rules or get lost.

[12] Charles Gabriel Seligman and Brenda Z. Seligman, *Pagan Tribes of the Nilotic Sudan* (London: George Routledge & Sons, 1932), p. 517.

[13] Edward Evan Evans-Pritchard, *Witchcraft, Oracles and Magic Among the Azande* (Oxford: Clarendon Press, 1937), pp. 10–11.

[14] Wilfred Whiteley, *Bemba and Related Peoples of Northern Rhodesia* (London: International African Institute, 1950), p. 30.

[15] Alden Almquist, "Divination and the Hunt in Pagibeti Ideology," in Philip M. Peek, *African Divination Systems, Ways of Knowing* (Bloomington: Indiana University Press, 1991), p. 104.

[16] Alexander H. Leighton and Dorothea C. Leighton, *Gregorio, the Hand-Trembler: A Psycho-Biological Personality Study of a Navaho Indian*, Peabody Museum of American Archaeology and Ethnology, Harvard University, *Papers* 40 (1949), 20.

[17] Walter Buchanan Cline, *Notes on the People of Siwah and El Garah in the Libyan Desert* (Menasha: Banta, 1936), pp. 540–41. This was also the means by which the Dalai Lama decided on his escape route from Tibet (Sir Charles Bell, *Portrait of the Dalai Lama* [London: Collins, 1946], p. 84).

[18] Margaret Mead, *Growing up in New Guinea: A Comparative Study of Primitive Education* (New York: Morrow, 1930), p. 103.

[19] Mark Carl Bauer, "Navajo Conflict Management" (diss., Northwestern University, 1983), p. 243.

[20] Leighton and Leighton, *Gregorio,* p. 21.

[21] My thanks to Abhar Davis, who suggested this game. She has used it herself many times in various parts of the world.

[22] James Mooney, *Myths of the Cherokee and Sacred Formulas of the Cherokees* (Nashville: Charles & Randy Elder, 1982), p. 386.

[23] Bjorn Collinder, *The Lapps* (Princeton: Princeton University Press for The American Scandinavian Foundation, 1949), p. 150.

[24] Harold Courlander, *The Drum and Hoe: Life and Lore of the Haitian People* (Berkeley: University of California Press, 1960), p. 100.

[25] Collinder, *The Lapps,* p. 150.

[26] Mooney, *Myths of the Cherokee,* p. 386.

[27] Jack Frederick Kilpatrick and Anna Gritts Kilpatrick, *Run Toward the Nightland: Magic of the Oklahoma Cherokee* (Dallas: Southern Methodist University Press, 1967), p. 114.

[28] C. R. Lagae, *Les Azande ou Niam-Niam: L'Organisation Zande, Croyances Religieuses et Magique, Coutumes Familiales* (The Azande or Niam-Niam: The Zande Organization, Religious Beliefs and Magic, Family Customs), Bibliothèque-Congo, vol. 18 (Bruzelles: Vromant & Co., 1926), pp. 83–86.

[29] Lev Iaklovich Shternberg, *Giliaki, Orochi, Goldy, Negidal'tsy, Ainy: Stati i Materialy* (The Gilyak, Orochi, Goldi, Negidal, Ainu; Articles and Materials) trans. Leo Bromwich and Norbert Ward (Khabarovsk: Dal'giz, 1933).

[30] Vladimir Germanovich Bogorz-Tan, "The Chukchee: Material Culture," "Religion," "Social Organization," *Memoirs of the American Museum of Natural History* 11 (Leiden: E. J. Brill, 1907), p. 485.

[31] Alfred Louis Kroeber, *Peoples of the Philippines* (New York: American Museum of Natural History, 1928), p. 202.

[32] Pierre Gourou, "Les Paysans du Delta Tonkinois: Etude de Geographie Humaine" (The Peasants of the Tonkin Delta: A Study in Human Geography), *Ecole*

Française d'Extreme-Orient Publications 27 (Paris: Les Editions d'Art et d'Histoire, 1936), p. 296.

[33] Morton C. Kahn, *Djuka: The Bush Negroes of Dutch Guiana* (New York: Viking, 1931), p. 149.

[34] Philip Richard Thornhagh Gurdon, *The Khasis* (London: D. Nutt, 1907), p. 119.

[35] Jean Hurault, "Etude Demographique Comparée des Indiens Oayana et des Noirs Réfugiés Boni du Haut Maroni (Guyane Française)" (Comparative Demographic Study of the Oyana Indians and the Boni Refugee Blacks of the Upper Maroni [French Guiana]), trans. Richard Fort, *Population* 14 (1959) (Paris: Institut National d'Etudes Demographiques), pp. 509–34

[36] Alan Playfair, *The Garos* (London: David Nutt, 1909), p. 97.

[37] Based on material in Sirdar Ali Shah Ikbal, *Afghanistan of the Afghans* (London: Diamond Press, 1928), pp. 80–81.

[38] Correspondence between Sig Lonegren and the author in 1995, notably April 13, 1995. My great thanks to Sig Lonegren for his insightful suggestions and encouragement.

[39] Ling Shun-sheng and Ruey Yih-fu, *Hsiang-hsi miao-tsu tiao-ch'a pao-kao* (A Report on an Investigation of the Miao of Western Hunan) (Shanghai: Institute of History and Philology, Academia Sinica, 1947), No. 23 p. 102.

[40] Romyn Hitchcock, "The Ainos of Yezo, Japan," *United States National Museum Report,* 1889/1890, p. 474.

[41] Apolo Kagwa, *The Customs of the Baganda*, trans. Ernest B. Kalibala, *Columbia University Contributions to Anthropology* 22 (New York: Columbia University Press, 1934), 126.

[42] Frank Gouldsmith Speck, *Naskapi: The Savage Hunters of the Labrador Peninsula* (Norman: University of Oklahoma Press, 1935), pp. 163–66.

[43] Frederica de Laguna, *Under Mount Saint Elias: The History and Culture of the Yakutat Tlingit, Smithsonian Contributions to Anthropology* 7 (Washington, D.C.: Smithsonian Institution, 1972), 807–8.

[44] Arthur Maurice Hocart, *Lau Islands, Fiji* (Honolulu: Bernice P. Bishop Museum, 1929), p. 203.

[45] Johannes Nicolaisen, *Ecology and Culture of the Pastoral Tuareg, With Particular Reference to the Tuareg of Ahaggar and Ayr* (Copenhagen: National Museum of Copenhagen, 1963), p. 172.

[46] Scott Cunningham, *The Art of Divination* (Freedom, Calif.: Crossing Press, 1993), p. 25.

[47] Martha Beckwith, *Hawaiian Mythology* (Honolulu: University of Hawaii Press, l982), p. 89.

Chapter 9. Signs of the Times

[1] R. L. Wing, *The I Ching Workbook* (New York: Doubleday, 1989), p. 8; Nigel Pennick, "The Chinese Book of Changes: Ancient Wisdom from the I Ching," in John Matthews, ed., *The World Atlas of Divination: The Systems, Where They Originate, How They Work* (Boston: Little, Brown, 1992), p. 138.

[2] Robert Harry Lowie, *The Crow Indians* (New York: Farrar & Rinehart, 1935), p. 251.

[3] Leslie Spier, *Klamath Ethnography* (Berkeley: University of California Press, 1930), pp. 237–39.

[4] Spier, *Klamath Ethnography*, p. 94.

[5] Anthony Leeds, "The Ideology of the Yaruro Indians in Relation to Socio-Economic

Organization," *Anthropologica* 9 (1960), 7; Edmund Ronald Leach, *Political Systems of Highland Burma* (Cambridge: Harvard University Press, 1954), p. 192.

6 Lorna Marshall, "!Kung Bushmen Religious Beliefs," *Africa* 32 (1962), p. 153.

7 Augustin Kramer and Hans Nevermann, *Ralik-Ratak (Marshall-Inseln), Ergebnisse der Sudsee-Expedition 1908–1910, Ethnographie: Mikronesien,* vol. 11, trans. Charles Brant and John M. Armstrong (Hamburg: Friederichsen, De Gruyter & Co., 1938), pp. 235, 250.

8 Frank Joseph Mahoney, "A Trukese Theory of Medicine" (diss., Stanford University, 1969), p. 265; Akira Matsumura, "Contributions to the Ethnography of Micronesia," *Journal of the College of Science,* Imperial University of Tokyo, 40 (1918), 92–93.

9 Alfred Metraux, "Les Indiens Uro-Cipaya de Carangas" (The Uru-Chipaya Indians of Crangas), trans. Priscilla Reynolds, *Journal de la Société des Americanistes* 27 (1935–36), 387–88.

10 Marian Green, "Wise Women Counsellors, Popular Methods of Divination," in Matthews, *World Atlas of Divination,* p. 85.

11 Horst Nachtigall, *Tierradentro, Archaologie und Ethnographie einer Kolumbianischen Landschaft* (Tierradentro, Archaeology and Ethnography of a Colombian Region), trans. Frieda Schutze, Mainzer Studien zur Kultur und Volkerunde, vol. 2 (Zurich: Origo Publishing House, 1955), pp. 264–65.

12 Mark Carl Bauer, "Navajo Conflict Management" (diss., Northwestern University, 1983), p. 243; John Adair and Kurt W. Deuschle, *The People's Health: Medicine and Anthropology in a Navajo Community* (New York: Appleton-Century Crofts, 1970), p. 6; Leland Clifton Wyman, "Navaho Diagnosticians," *American Anthropologist* 38 (1936), 236–46.

13 Arthur Maurice Hocart, *Lau Islands, Fiji* (Honolulu: Bernice P. Bishop Museum, 1929), p. 173.

14 William A. Lessa, *Chinese Body Divination: Its Forms, Affinities and Functions* (Los Angeles: United World Academy & Fellowship, 1968), p. 112.

15 C. D. Bijalwan, *Hindu Omens* (New Delhi: Om Prakash Jain for Sanskriti in association with Arnold-Heinnemann Publishers, 1977), p. 16.

16 Thanks to my friend Prartho, an excellent palmist, who suggested this.

17 John Matthews, "By Stick and Stone: Celtic Methods of Divination," in Matthews, *World Atlas of Divination,* p. 29.

18 Keith Ellis, *Prediction and Prophecy* (London: Wayland, 1973), pp. 165–66.

19 John Howland Rowe, "Inca Culture at the Time of the Spanish Conquest," *Bureau of American Ethnology Bulletin* 143, vol. 2 (Washington, D.C.: Smithsonian Institution, 1946), p. 303.

20 Michael F. C. Bourdillon, *The Shona Peoples: An Ethnography of the Contemporary Shona, with Special Reference to Their Religion,* Shona Heritage Series, vol. 1 (Gwelo: Mabo Press, 1976), p. 177.

21 Elsie Worthington Clews Parsons, *Mitla, Town of the Souls and Other Zapoteco-Speaking Pueblos of Oaxaca, Mexico* (Chicago: University of Chicago Press, 1970), pp. 306, 315.

22 N. Adriani and Albert C. Kruyt, *De Bare's Sprekende Toradjas van Midden-Celebes (de Oost-Toradjas)* (The Bare'e-Speaking Toradja of Central Celebes [the East Toradja]), 2nd ed., vol. 2, trans. Jenni Karding Moulton, Koninklijke Nederlandse

Akademie van Wetenschappen, Verhandelingen, Afdeling Letterkunde, Nieuwe Reeks, Deel 55 (Amsterdam: Noord-Hollandsche Uitgevers Maatschappij, 1951).

[23] Yuri Matveevich Sokolov, *Russian Folklore,* trans. Catherine Ruth Smith (New York: Macmillan, 1950), p. 243.

[24] Frederick Wilkerson Waugh, *Iroquois Foods and Food Preparation* (Ottawa: Government Printing Bureau, 1916), p. 46.

[25] Clifford James Geertz, *The Religion of Java* (New York: Free Press of Glencoe, 1964), p. 33.

[26] My thanks to Pratibha de Stoppani for this suggestion. Pratibha has pioneered work with the voice and has conducted trainings in this technique, called *Voicing®,* all over the world. For further information: Osho Nuvole Bianche Institute, AP Castello, CH-6988 Ponte Tresa, Switzerland (Tel. 0041 91 71 37 52). Also, Mr. Irwin Grief, one of the most sensitive psychics I have ever encountered, uses voice almost exclusively in his readings.

Chapter 10. Mirror to Mirror

[1] John Cooper, "Northern Algonkian Scrying and Scapulimancy," in *Festschrift Publication d'Hommage Offerte au P. W. Schmidt* (Austria, 1927), in University Museum Library, University of Pennsylvania, p. 209.

[2] Douglas MacRae, *The Black Carib of British Honduras,* Viking Publications in Anthropology, 17 (New York: Wenner-Gren Foundation for Anthropological Research, 1951), p. 136; Jack Frederick Kilpatrick and Anna Gritts Kilpatrick, *Run Toward the Nightland: Magic of the Oklahoma Cherokee* (Dallas: Southern Methodist University Press, 1967), p. 115; H. Callaway, *The Religious System of the Amazulu* (Cape Town: C. Struik, 1970), pp. 323–33 (facsimile of edition of c.100 years earlier).

[3] Vladimir Germanovich Bogorz-Tan, "The Chukchee: Material Culture," "Religion," "Social Organization," *Memoirs of the American Museum of Natural History* 11 (Leiden: E. J. Brill, 1907), 483; Rev. Edwin W. Smith and Captain Andrew Murray Dale, *The Ila-Speaking Peoples of Northern Rhodesia,* vol. 1 (London: Macmillan, 1920), pp. 266–67.

[4] Thanks to Dr. Claude Steiner, for this groundbreaking tale for children and adults.

[5] A.-M. Esnoul, "La Divination dans l'Inde," in André Caquot and Marcel Leibovici, eds., *La Divination,* vol. 1 (Paris: Presses Universitaires de France, 1968), p. 128.

[6] I am indebted to my friend Prartho Sereno who introduced me to the art and magic of throwing stones. Prartho has been throwing stones for ages, and amazing people with her stone readings.

[7] Paul Gebauer, "Spider Divination in the Cameroons," *Milwaukee Public Museum Publications in Anthropology* 10 (Milwaukee: North American Press, 1964), 16; J.-P. Roux and P. N. Boratav, "La Divination chez les Turcs," in Caquot and Leibovici, *La Divination,* vol. 2, p. 324; Alfred Claud Hollis, *The Masai: Their Language and Folklore* (Oxford: Clarendon Press, 1905), p. 324; Matthews, *Encyclopedia of Celtic Wisdom: A Celtic Shaman's Sourcebook* (Rockport, Mass.: Element, 1994), p. 240.

[8] The list that I use, for example, includes the following categories: children; humor; sadness or tears; material world (which includes money and home); others (which includes friends); area of brilliance; survival; expression; the heart; consciousness.

You may use that as a base but will, undoubtedly, end up with your own list expressing your own interests and needs.

[9]Fray Bernardino de Sahagun, *General History of the Things of New Spain. Book 10— The People,* translated from the Aztec by Charles E. Dibble and Arthur J. O. Anderson, Monographs of the School of American Research and the Museum of New Mexico, no. 14, pt. 11 (Santa Fe: School of American Research and the University of Utah, 1961), p. 31.

Photograph by Premda Wunderle

About the Author

Sarvananda Bluestone received his B.A. in history from Cornell University in 1961. From there he went to the University of Wisconsin, where he received his M.A. and Ph.D. degrees in American history. He taught at Roosevelt University in Chicago and the State University of New York College of Old Westbury.

After twenty years of college teaching, Bluestone and his six-year-old daughter, Hira, left for India to be near the ashram of Bhagwan Shree Rajneesh. They remained there for six months and then followed Rajneesh back to America. For four years they lived in a spiritual community in Oregon.

Since 1986, between various trips to India, Sarvananda Bluestone has been doing psychic readings for private clients at various Catskill hotels, and working on what was to become *Signs of the Times*.

Books of Related Interest

How to Read the Aura and Practice Psychometry, Telepathy, and Clairvoyance
By W. E. Butler

Pendulum Power
A Mystery You Can See, A Power You Can Feel
By Greg Nielsen and Joseph Polansky

Original Wisdom
Stories of an Ancient Way of Knowing
By Robert Wolff

Walking on the Wind
Cherokee Teachings for Harmony and Balance
By Michael Garrett

The Teachings of Don Carlos
Practical Applications of the Works of Carlos Castaneda
By Victor Sanchez

Sacred Geometry Oracle Deck
By Francene Hart

Inner Child Cards
A Fairy-Tale Tarot
By Isha Lerner and Mark Lerner

The Light and Shadow Tarot
By Michael Goepferd and Brian Williams

Inner Traditions • Bear & Company
P.O. Box 388
Rochester, VT 05767
1-800-246-8648
www.InnerTraditions.com

Or contact your local bookseller